Our Psychiatr

For Diana

Our Psychiatric Future
The Politics of Mental Health

Nikolas Rose

polity

First published in 2019 by Polity Press
Reprinted 2018, 2019

Polity Press
65 Bridge Street
Cambridge CB2 1UR, UK

Polity Press
101 Station Landing
Suite 300
Medford, MA 02155, USA

ISBN-13: 978-0-7456-8911-1
ISBN-13: 978-0-7456-8912-8(pb)

A catalogue record for this book is available from the British Library.

Library of Congress Cataloging-in-Publication Data

Names: Rose, Nikolas S., author.
Title: Our psychiatric future : the politics of mental health / Nikolas Rose.
Description: Medford, MA : Polity, [2018] | Includes bibliographical
    references and index.
Identifiers: LCCN 2018009173 (print) | LCCN 2018011035 (ebook) | ISBN
    9780745689159 (Epub) | ISBN 9780745689111 (hardback) | ISBN 9780745689128
    (pbk.)
Subjects: | MESH: Mental Health | Psychiatry | Health Policy
Classification: LCC RC454 (ebook) | LCC RC454 (print) | NLM WM 101 | DDC
    616.89--dc23
LC record available at https://lccn.loc.gov/2018009173

Typeset in 10.5 on 12 pt Plantin by
Servis Filmsetting Ltd, Stockport, Cheshire
Printed and bound in Great Britain by TJ International Ltd, Padstow, Cornwall

For further information on Polity, visit our website: politybooks.com

Contents

Acknowledgements

I have been thinking about the issues in this book since my time as an undergraduate in the 1960s. I was struck by the contrast between the image of psychiatry in my course on abnormal psychology and the experiences of my friends diagnosed with serious mental illness and undergoing treatment with antipsychotic drugs. Later I became involved with the critical psychiatry movement and with the work of 'concept houses' such as those run by the Richmond Fellowship, and I also taught an evening class with Peter Miller on the powers of psychiatry, which led to our edited volume *The Power of Psychiatry*, published by Polity in 1986. In the 1980s at Brunel University I convened a unique undergraduate programme which combined a degree in sociology and psychology with a qualification as a psychiatric nurse – teaching the remarkable students and visiting them on the wards in the Maudsley and Bethlem Hospitals brought me face to face with the challenges faced by dedicated psychiatric professionals, and gave me a clearer sense of the lives of those for whom they tried to care.

Over the intervening years, I have got to know many committed and thoughtful mental health professionals who are painfully aware of the challenges they face in trying to help individuals who are in distress, usually for reasons located not in their heads, but in the social conditions in which they find themselves. I have spent some time visiting mental institutions both in the UK and in a number of other countries. I have engaged with these issues via my work with the Nuffield Council on Bioethics, the Science Policy Committee of the Royal Society and similar organizations, and my research in the Social and Ethical Division of the Human Brain Project.[1] I have been fortunate to have friends with first-hand experience of the ministrations of the mental health system, and who have worked collectively to find new ways of thinking about and responding to mental distress. And I have lived for more than 40 years with a partner diagnosed with a severe and enduring psychiatric disorder. This book grows out of that relationship, that history and debates too numerous to mention. But while many people have helped me in developing my arguments, only I am culpable for them.

I have touched on the questions I discuss here in other books – notably in *The Politics of Life Itself* published in 2007, and in *Neuro: The New Brain Sciences and the Management of the Mind*, written with Joelle Abi-Rached and published in 2013 – and I have tried not to repeat myself; some of the things I address briefly here are given fuller treatments in those earlier books. Most of the chapters that follow arise from lectures that I have given since 2010. I would particularly like to thank Dr Franco Rotelli in Trieste for persuading me to take up the daunting challenge of giving the opening keynote lecture at an International Conference in 2010 celebrating the life and work of Franco Basaglia. That lecture – 'All in the Brain?' – morphed into a rather different one, entitled 'What Is Mental Illness Today? Five Hard Questions', which I first gave at the University of Nottingham in 2013; I thank Hugh Middleton for inviting me. That led, in a roundabout way, to Nick Manning joining me as a colleague at King's College London, which has resulted in many fruitful collaborations on the issues I discuss in this book; he and I share the view that sociology is a fundamental science when it comes to understanding mental ill health. Some years ago I worked closely with Ilina Singh on 'the promises and perils' of biomarkers, and I draw upon ideas developed in that collaboration. Des Fitzgerald and Ilina Singh worked with me on a related project – the Urban Brain Project – which helped me develop a number of the ideas that have found their way into various parts of this book. That project also led to a book with Des entitled *Vital City: Metropolitan Life, Mental Health and the Urban Brain*, to be published by Princeton University Press, some thoughts from which are included in my final chapter. I have also benefited from collaborations with Ayo Wahlberg which started many years ago in Copenhagen, continued in the BIOS Centre at the LSE, extended to our work in China, and now to his research back in Copenhagen – Ayo has generously given me permission to draw on sections of our joint paper, 'The Governmentalization of Living: Calculating Global Health', published in *Economy and Society* in 2015, in chapter 2 of this book. I have learned a lot from the generous historical scholarship on medicine, psychiatry and madness by Roy Porter: his voice is much missed in current debates. On general issues of 'the politics of life', I have benefited greatly, though he probably does not know this, from the work of Didier Fassin. Emily Martin's work remains an inspiration, to me as to many others, and her friendship is much valued. In many ways, this book grows out of the research on the genealogy of neuroscience that I conducted with Joelle Abi-Rached for *Neuro*, and I thank her for being the most excellent companion on that journey into the history of the present of neuroscience.

Among the other people who have invited me to lecture on these topics, and whose challenging questions have contributed – sometimes without them being aware – to these chapters are Sergio Carvalho, Tulio Giraldi, Ilpo Helen, Lochlann Jain, Uffe Juul Jensen, Pat O'Malley, Francisco Ortega, Andreas Roepstorff, George Szmukler, Mariana Valverde, Catherine Waldby, Simon Wessley and Elizabeth Wilson. I would also like to acknowledge the abiding influence on my thought of the students who took my courses on psychiatry and mental health at Brunel University, particularly Hilary Allen, Edana Minghella, Helen Griffin, Ben Thomas and Rob Tunmore. Thanks also to all those students and postdoctoral fellows who have debated these questions with me over the last three decades and more, many of whom are now in senior academic positions. I cannot mention them all, but especially would like to acknowledge Lisa Blackman, Des Fitzgerald, Angela Filipe, Ian Hodges, Linsey McGoey, Sam McLean, Léonie Mol, Tara Mahfoud, Sebastian Rojas Navarro, Carlos Novas, Scott Vrecko and Ayo Wahlberg.

Through working with my undergraduate, postgraduate and research students, and through my experience in many psychiatric hospitals, wards and clinics, I have come to realize that, whatever one may find in the thousands of texts on psychiatry and mental health, whatever styles of thought are dominant, and whatever technologies of intervention are available, there are many dedicated professionals working in our mental health system who, in spite of all the difficulties and challenges they face, and whatever their own conceptual orientation, are just superb – and often lifesaving – clinicians. I would like to pay special thanks here to Dr Nadia Davis.

Across that half century of encounters with psychiatry, I have learned most from people living under the description of severe and enduring mental disorder. Through these friendships, I have come to know more of mental health and the politics of psychiatry than I ever could have imagined. But I have also come to believe that the most fundamental transformation in the power of psychiatry will come not from the discovery of the genetic or neurobiological basis of mental illness, but because of the increasing recognition that the recipients of psychiatric ministrations, proclaimed to be for their benefit, are increasingly acquiring a voice, and some power, in contesting the ways that they are treated; to take this seriously requires a radical rethink of the profession of psychiatry and of the organization of, and power relations in, services for those in mental distress. I would particularly like to acknowledge Peter Campbell, Alison Faulkner and Louise Pembroke, whose work in this area has been pathbreaking.

Finally, this book would not have been written without my relationship with my partner of over 40 years, Diana Rose, who has taught me more than she will ever know about psychiatry, madness, commitment, life and love. I dedicate this book to her.

1

What Is Psychiatry?

This is a book about psychiatry, the part that it has come to play in the lives of so many of us across the world, and the challenging questions the pervasiveness of psychiatry raises about mental distress, about the promises and powers of psychiatrists, and about normality itself. Why focus on psychiatry and not mental health or mental illness? In fact, of course, the two are inextricable: the very idea of madness, mania, melancholy and more as *illnesses* is, in large part, a function of the history and reality of psychiatry, because it has shaped how we have come to know these conditions, how we speak of them and how we try to intervene upon them. To think of mental illness or even, to use the phrase becoming common, 'mental health issues' thus inescapably places us in relation with psychiatry. It is that relationship, our relationship to psychiatry, that is the focus of this book.[1]

But what is psychiatry? This seems a simple question – the dictionary tells us that, psychiatry is the branch of medicine concerned with the causes, diagnosis, treatment and prevention of mental illness.[2] Yet a moment's thought tells us that psychiatry, even in this simple sense, is a rather special 'branch of medicine' not least because it seems to have become a part of the lives of almost all of those who live in advanced liberal democracies and increasingly for some of those in the developing world.[3] So let us begin by exploring the 'territory' of psychiatry today.

Our psychiatric lives

This sense that our everyday lives are increasingly intertwined with psychiatry becomes even stronger if we accept the description of the scope of psychiatry which is now used by the World Health Organization (WHO) and many other organizations. For these bodies, notably when they compile their estimates of the prevalence of mental disorders, the territory of psychiatry does not merely include familiar conditions such as depression and schizophrenia; it also covers neurodegenerative disorders such as Alzheimer's disease, includes complaints such as anxiety and panic, extends to relatively recent diagnoses such as dyslexia as well as to conditions such as addiction, substance abuse and obesity, which some might not think of as mental disorders at all. Taken together, estimates put the prevalence of such a wide array of conditions at over 25 per cent of the adult population in the European Union in any one year, and 50 per cent over a lifetime – these are broadly the same for the United States.[4] Indeed, perhaps the most often quoted recent figure for Europe estimates that over a third of the European population each year is afflicted with a potentially diagnosable 'disorder of the brain', even though many of these people never consult a psychiatrist or receive treatment (Wittchen et al., 2011: 843). If psychiatry is the name we give to those diverse experts and practices which deal with these conditions, it is clear that it is no longer a matter of concern to a few unfortunate souls: over our lifetime, almost all of us are potentially suitable cases for treatment.

But right away we have hit controversy! *Should* we accept these estimates? Who made them and how? There seems to be a lot of slippage here – mental illness, mental disorder, brain disorder – don't we need much more precision? Can these conditions really affect one in four – or even one in three – of us each year? And what is implied by lumping all these conditions together – surely anxiety and Alzheimer's are rather different species of things? And in what sense are these 'brain disorders'? Apart from the banal fact that all mental activity has neural correlates, is it really the case that these diverse troubles share common mechanisms in the brain? Indeed, are some of these things 'disorders' at all? Surely obesity, which has increased greatly in many countries over the past 50 years, is a matter of lifestyle, not a disorder, let alone a disorder of the brain. Can't the same be said for all those mental health issues that almost everyone seems to suffer from at some time or another – mild depression and anxiety – or even more severe conditions such as post-traumatic stress disorder and self-harm, which are on the increase, especially among women? Are these not best understood as fundamentally *social* problems, exacerbated by the stresses and strains of everyday life in our 24/7 society with its constant barrage of social media and so forth?[5] And so on. Let us hold these thoughts for a moment, for we will revisit all of them in later chapters.

For now, we have established one important thing – that whatever psychiatry deals with, or wants to deal with, is no marginal matter.[6] If you or I are not directly among the number directly affected, it is very likely that a family member is – a spouse, a child, a relative. Indeed, when it comes to children, we are seeing a worldwide increase in the numbers diagnosed with problems of behaviour, or attention or ability that are deemed to be psychiatric, or at least thought likely to benefit from the attention of a psychiatrist or a related mental health professional. Numbers vary greatly from country to country, but a recent estimate in the UK is that one child or young person in every ten will suffer from a diagnosable mental health condition, with increasing numbers of young people being diagnosed with depression or self-harming, leading to the introduction of mental health pro-grammes in schools involving mindfulness and 'happiness lessons'.[7] And this does not include those who are diagnosed with attention deficit hyperactivity disorder, whose numbers in countries such as the United States have been the subject of much controversy. And given our demographic changes, in which so many of us are living longer, at the other end of life there are the dementias that are now no longer 'in the shadows', but are widely discussed, and that we now think are likely to afflict so many of us, our relatives and friends, as we age.[8]

It was once possible to think of psychiatry as a rather esoteric activity, conducted by doctors and nurses, who were almost as weird as those whom they treated, dealing largely with people locked away in mental asylums, and extending outside the walls of the mental hospital only to a few self-obsessed individuals receiving some kind of psychotherapy. That is the image portrayed in the movies from the 1940s to the 1970s, from *Spellbound* and *The Snake Pit* to *One Flew Over the Cuckoo's Nest* or *Morgan – A Suitable Case for Treatment*. But psychiatry now seems to be part of almost everyone's life, in many cases quite literally. That is to say, psychiatry is shaping the very experience of living as its languages and diagnoses pervade the ways we understand and respond to our problems and think of those of our children, our relatives and our own life course.

Everyone's little helpers

Another crucial dimension of this psychiatric reshaping of our life itself is the global reach of the most common psychiatric intervention

– psychopharmaceuticals. While figures vary from country to country, as a rough estimate about one person in ten in the countries that are part of the Organisation for Economic Co-operation and Development is taking a prescription pharmaceutical for depression, anxiety or some other mental health problem at any one time; for women, the figure is closer to one in six.[9] Once more, though, we immediately enter controversial territory. How can we account for the rise of the use of these drugs – not just the tranquillizers that were once such an object of cultural attention – 'mother's little helpers'[10] – but now the antidepressants, of which Prozac became the most famous.[11] In most of the countries where we have data, use of these antidepressant drugs doubled in the decade from 2000, with the greatest use in Iceland, Australia, Canada, Denmark and Sweden.[12] And these drugs, initially celebrated because of their specificity for depression, are now prescribed for a multitude of disorders, including panic disorders, anxiety disorders, shyness and social phobia. No country has seen a reduction in their use. Why has there been such a worldwide rise? Why are there such huge variations between countries? Surely not because the conditions themselves show such huge variations in prevalence. Have psychiatrists become so attached to the prescription of these drugs because their use seems to give them real treatments, and hence demonstrate the scientificity of their professional expertise, and ally them with the rest of medicine?[13] Do the drugs work, or are they just 'placebos'? Are we not just medicalizing normal problems of living, with psychiatrists in some countries more keen to do this than in others? And why do these drugs appeal to so many people? For while it is still the case that some people, not just those in psychiatric hospital but also some living in the community, are compelled or obliged to take such drugs, most do not do so under compulsion, but because they believe that they will, in some way, help. Once more, hold onto these thoughts, for we shall certainly come back to them in later chapters.

But for the moment, let me return to that simple dictionary definition answer to the question 'what is psychiatry?' The dictionary definition is deceptive for many reasons – indeed, the very question itself is misleading. Let me list four sets of reasons why, unfortunately, we need to make things more complicated.

Many psychiatries

First, of course, there is no one 'psychiatry' – psychiatry is heterogeneous with many different and sometimes incompatible conceptions of mental disorder, and many different treatment practices. While it is true, today, that biological psychiatry is dominant, at least in the field of Euro-American research, and that biological treatments, notably drugs, have the widest coverage of all psychiatric interventions, most practising psychiatrists in clinics and hospitals, even though they consider drugs essential to their practice, are not simply 'biological' in their ways of understanding, diagnosing and treating disorders.

We will spend some time in this book considering the argument made by some neurobiological researchers, and also part of the rationale for the heavily funded 'brain projects' that have been established in Europe, the United States, China, Japan and many other countries, that mental disorders should be considered as diseases of the brain.[14] But we also need to recognize that many psychiatrists, even if they accept the premise that the troubles they are dealing with have their roots in the brain, focus their diagnostic and therapeutic attention on matters that are normally thought of as mental rather than cerebral – that is to say, on disordered or repetitive thought patterns which may or may not have a biological basis, but which they hope can be ameliorated by cognitive therapies of various sorts. Indeed, many now recommend 'mindfulness', which has morphed rapidly from something associated with esoteric practices of Buddhists to a rather banal practice that aims to change the way we feel about stressful experiences,[15] and which has become an option in the toolbox of psychiatrists, psychologists, social workers – and indeed anyone who has access to the internet or a smartphone. Those responsible for setting out policy guidelines, such as the National Institute for Health and Care Excellence (NICE) in the UK, often advocate nonmedical activities for mild and first episode conditions, such as lifestyle changes, followed, if this is not effective, by psychosocial interventions – though in many countries, drugs remain a first, not a last, resort.

Of course, diagnostic and treatment guidelines for medical and psychiatric professionals – where they exist – vary from country to country and change over time, and not everyone follows such guidelines. Indeed – and this is something that should always be borne in mind – the diagnosis and treatment of mild mental health issues often never reach psychiatrists at all. Most experiences of mental distress are managed by families, friends and lay persons outside the mental health system; indeed, what professionals term 'primary care' is actually secondary care. Further, when such distress does come to the attention of a medical professional – a process much studied by sociologists (for a classic study, see Smith, 1978) – it is often managed in the general practitioner's clinic, where those reporting troubling moods or feelings are usually given prescriptions for psychoactive drugs, because these are the most readily available options, and because waiting lists for specialist consultations and psychological interventions are long even in the countries where they exist at all, except for those with the resources to pay. In some countries, even for those who are seriously distressed, and no doubt driven in part by the rising costs of hospital treatment and the pressure on bed use, 'social' interventions are favoured, whereby a person is treated in his or her own home and a multidisciplinary team monitors drug 'compliance' or 'adherence' – people who do not take their prescribed drugs tend to be seen as a serious problem in contemporary psychiatry.[16] In some cases – sadly, rare – a 'home treatment team' seeks to ameliorate some of the social pressures, such as finance, housing or domestic violence, that may be exacerbating their mental distress.[17] Indeed, outside the hospital and medically controlled clinic, a host of less medical practices thrive, from day centres to recovery houses, where biomedical approaches play a minimal role, and interventions are grounded on other conceptions of the nature of the problem at hand. If one moves one's focus of attention away from the 'Global North' to India, China, Southeast Asia, the rural areas of Latin America and the many African countries where medical professionals of any sort are very thin on the ground, things become even more complex, and for most people 'care' – or its opposite – happens outside any formal medical setting.[18] Thus, while I focus in this book on 'psychiatry' and will sometimes use that term to embrace all these different practices for addressing 'mental disorders', it is necessary to treat any statement that implies a singular psychiatry (including mine) with a great deal of caution.

Psychiatry defines the boundaries

Second, psychiatry does not just understand and treat, it also defines and delimits. That is to say, psychiatric categories and practices of diagnosis help set the boundaries (and often blur the boundaries) of who is or is not a suitable case for (what kind of) treatment. Much discussion of this question over recent years has focused on the *Diagnostic and Statistical Manual of Mental Disorders* (*DSM*) of the American Psychiatric Association (APA), which published its long awaited fifth edition in 2013. Each new edition of the *DSM* has included more categories of disorder, seemingly endlessly expanding the kinds of conditions that are amenable to psychiatric classification and intervention. In the United States, a *DSM* diagnosis has important practical consequences – for example, one has to have a *DSM* diagnosis in order to be reimbursed for the costs of treatment under medical insurance schemes. Further, until very recently, if they hoped to get their research funded and published in the scientific journals, psychiatric researchers were obliged to use *DSM* diagnoses in framing their grant applications, selecting the subjects of their research and presenting their findings.[19] So, to some extent, such manuals define the boundaries of the empire of mental disorder.

Thus, especially in the United States, many authors who are critical of what they see as the expansionist tendencies of psychiatry have focused on the proliferation of categories of disorder in the *DSM* and the way in which they frame diagnosis – a checklist approach in which individuals are diagnosed with a particular condition if they have exhibited a certain number of behaviours over a specified period of time.[20] Critics point to the implicit value judgements in the application of such criteria, the lack of focus on the actual level of impairment of the individual in particular situations, and to the way in which this lack of precision widens the net of those brought into 'the empire of psychiatry'. They argue that diagnostic imperialism is leading to the psychiatrization of normal variations in the human condition: of sadness (Horwitz and Wakefield, 2007), of shyness (Lane, 2007), of anxiety (Orr, 2006) and much more.[21]

It is certainly the case that diagnosis both extends and delimits the empire of psychiatry, but we need to go beyond the *DSM*, and indeed beyond diagnostic manuals altogether, to grasp this process. This is not least because, despite the critical attention that has been lavished on the *DSM*, its history and its consequences, things are a little more complicated in the wild world of everyday life than in the pages of the diagnostic textbooks. First, not every country uses the *DSM*. In Europe, a different classification manual is used – the International Classification of Diseases, which differs in many respects[22] – and, in many European countries with a national health system of one sort or another, while a formal psychiatric classification may be required, it plays little part in the decisions about how to treat an individual. Perhaps more fundamentally, although the formal diagnostic classification system may be important when an individual comes into contact with a medical or psychiatric service, the path to contact is shaped by the beliefs about normality and pathology held by many others – the individuals themselves, their families, teachers or social workers, neighbours and employers. Research shows that these beliefs vary very widely both within and between countries, not just as a result of widely differing mental health care systems and the availability of trained practitioners, but also on such factors as the age, ethnicity and social class of the 'pre-patient', the range of available alternatives from herbal medicines to faith healing, and the prevailing social and cultural beliefs about the nature of the condition and the efficacy of various forms of intervention (Goldberg and Huxley, 2003). Nonetheless, by means of its authority to confirm or deny these other beliefs, through the giving or withholding of a diagnosis or even an agreement that someone is in need of treatment, in helping specify what ails them, and in managing them within and outside medical institutions, psychiatry and psychiatric classification systems play a significant role in shaping our understanding of normality itself.

I was tempted to put this more strongly and write that psychiatry 'defines the boundaries of normality', but this would be too simple. It is true that psychiatry is sometimes defined as the study of psycho*pathology*, and the old argument – that medical thought works by establishing a division between the normal and the pathological – remains true (Canguilhem, 1978). But when it comes to the scope of psychiatry today, can we still hold to the idea that, in some fundamental way, to be diagnosed with a mental disorder is to be classified as 'pathological' – with all the cultural resonances of that term when linked to mental illness: compulsive, extreme, uncontrolled, irrational, dangerous and so forth? Perhaps this conception of psychopathology still applies for severe mental disorders like schizophrenia, where stigma and exclusion still flourish despite the best efforts of anti-stigma policies and programmes to persuade people that mental illness carries no special threat or taint and is just an illness like any other. And of course we know that the old idea of the psychopath still plays an important role in popular discourses even if the term and the diagnosis are contested within psychiatry. But whatever one might think of the diagnoses, few would consider mild depression, anxiety or panic disorders as 'pathological' even if, in formal terms, they are often placed within the textbooks of psychopathology.

So should we think in terms of a less pejorative framing, substituting the idea of abnormality for that of pathology, and hence arguing that psychiatry defines the border between the normal and the *ab*normal? This is tempting. But if one-third of the population is diagnosable at any one time, and half of us over a lifetime, in what sense is it 'abnormal' to receive a psychiatric diagnosis? Indeed, one might almost say that it is 'abnormal' to live one's life without coming into the remit of psychiatry: without talking to a medical or other professional about one's mental troubles or conflicts; without taking one or other of the multitude of psychiatric drugs – even if only a sedative – to help one sleep; without practising one of the para-professional forms of mental self-help like mindfulness, even if accessed for free via the internet.

We know that the idea of the norm, as it came into use in the late nineteenth century, linked together the ideas of statistical normality, social normality and medical normality: the norm was the average, the desirable, the healthy, the ideal and so forth. Perhaps, today, this strong version of normality no longer holds, or holds differently in different societies or in different sectors. Is it abnormal to feel hopeless in a world beset by famine, conflict and injustice? Is it abnormal to feel guilty for thinking unpleasant thoughts, or for actions undertaken or not undertaken? Is my behaviour in polishing the taps or lining up the spice jars merely eccentric, or is it beyond the limits of normality? Is it abnormal to hear voices, or to experience strong thoughts that seem to come from outside? Is it normal to believe in a divine power that shapes one's fate? Clearly, normality – of what it is to be normal, to think of oneself as normal, to be considered as normal by others – leads to a set of rather profound questions.

We should probably accept that normality, today, is best thought of as a term of ascription, as *performative* – that is to say, it is a term that is best understood in its uses.[23] So rather than thinking of it as having some substantive meaning, we should always ask who defines who as normal in relation to what criteria, in what practices, and with what consequences. We might be tempted to dispense with the term altogether, were it not for the fact that any decision by a medical professional, a teacher, a social worker, a family member or an individual themselves that some kind of treatment is required invokes, even if implicitly, the judgement that something – a bodily feeling, a way of thinking, of speaking, of feeling, of acting – is not 'normal' for a particular person: for a man or a woman, a child or an adult, a member of this or that generation, of this or that ethnic group, a person with these or those experiences and so forth.[24]

If anything, the issue of normality is becoming even more problematic in medical thought, for every week seems to bring us new diagnostic technologies – genetic technologies, scanning technologies and so forth – that claim to reveal abnormalities within the previously invisible interior of the body or the brain: these are technologies that claim to identify 'markers' showing that an individual is likely to develop a disease long before they themselves feel symptomatic. Such a person is suffering from a pre-disease; he or she is 'presymptomatically ill' (Rosenberg, 2006). For some researchers and policymakers, the identification of these pre-diseases represents a great advance for medicine; they are excited by the idea of identifying, treating and preventing diseases before they start to afflict the individual concerned. For others, the hunt to identify and treat pre-diseases is simply a widening of the empire of medicine and psychiatry, treating individuals who may never become ill at all, just because a test shows that they have a probability – but not a certainty – of developing a disorder in the future.[25] Perhaps, then, normality has to be understood as having a negative not a positive function, in the sense that, for psychiatry and indeed more generally, normality is *that which does not require expert intervention*.[26] In these terms, there are few of us in the Global North who are normal in this sense, as so many of us listen to experts who advise us to adjust our diets, take up exercise, take everything from vitamins to cholesterol-reducing pharmaceuticals, to keep us 'normal'. We will return to this question of normality throughout this book, for it raises a host of medical, social and ethical challenges.

What mental disorder *is*

Third, psychiatry and psychiatrists play a key role – though many others are involved too – in establishing what kind of a thing mental disorder *is*. Is it – as it was for some in the early twentieth century – a matter of instincts badly managed, of habits poorly trained? Is it a matter of the dynamic forces in the unconscious as it was – and still is – for psychoanalysis and the many related 'dynamic' psychotherapies? Is it an understandable and perhaps even normal reaction to difficult social circumstances, poverty, racism or traumatic events, as many social scientists have long argued? Is it a matter of dysfunctional patterns of cognition to be corrected by cognitive therapy? Is it an outcome of 'toxic stress' in childhood, to be countered by interventions directed at dysfunctional families? Or is a mental disorder, as is increasingly argued, a brain kind of thing, ultimately understandable in terms of neuronal processes?

Many psychiatrists and neuroscientists believe the issue is now settled – the key to understanding mental disorders is the recognition that, at root, they are brain disorders. I have already mentioned the 'big science' brain projects under way in Europe, the United States, China, Cuba, India and many other countries. The hope is not just that these will reveal "how [the brain's] roughly 86 billion neurons and its trillions of connections interact in real time . . . [and] revolutionize our understanding of how we think, feel, learn, remember", to quote Francis Collins in his National Institutes of Health (NIH) Director's Blog entitled 'Launching America's Next Moonshot';[27] it is also that they will transform "efforts to help the more than 1 billion people worldwide who suffer from autism, depression, schizophrenia, epilepsy, traumatic brain injury, Parkinson's disease, Alzheimer's disease, and other devastating brain disorders". One can find the same rhetoric in the funding of Europe's Human Brain Project – despite the fact that little of the research within that project focuses directly on mental disorders[28] – and in statements from the US National Institute for Mental Health (NIMH). Thus Thomas Insel, when he was Director of the NIMH, stated unequivocally that "[m]ental disorders are biological disorders involving brain circuits that implicate specific domains of cognition, emotion or behaviour", and his successor, Josh Gordon, asserts: "psychiatric disorders are disorders of the brain, and to make progress in treating them we really have to understand the brain . . . [if we can] get at questions of how neural circuits produce behaviour [this] may soon generate new treatments for psychiatric disorders" (quoted from Abbott, 2016) – although he does admit that we have no idea of which circuits are involved or how they might be modified.[29]

Of course, not all agree. For example, in the UK, the British Psychological Society (BPS) was speaking for many psychologists when it argued that we should turn our attention away from the brain towards the complex psychosocial experiences that lead to mental distress, and that these should underpin approaches to treatment.[30] And, as I have already stressed, psychiatry is a heterogeneous domain, and much clinical practice is agnostic about, and sometimes uninterested in, questions concerning the fundamental determinants or biological mechanisms of the conditions under treatment. Nonetheless, I think we should adopt a 'path-dependent' theory of truth when it comes to something like psychiatry. That is to say, there are many different paths that research can take, and hence many different 'truths' that research can bring into the domain of potential truths. I say 'the domain of potential truths' because, of course, the results and findings of research are constantly subject to contestation and they have to go through complex social processes before they become accepted facts (Fleck, 1979 [1935]; Latour, 1987). But if something is not researched at all, it cannot enter into the domain of potential truths. If it is on the path not taken, it cannot become even a candidate scientific fact. Most research in psychiatry depends upon funding, and so the paths of research are shaped by the interplay between the research priorities and predictions of funding agencies, and the interests, priorities and calculations of researchers themselves who are applying for funds. If the key funders make it a priority to seek the brain bases of psychiatric disorders, it is not surprising to find that a very significant proportion of research on psychiatric disorders focuses on these neurobiological processes. As a result, neurobiological processes and mechanisms are the most likely to come into the domain of potential truths as far as mental disorders are concerned.

The priorities, methods and findings of psychiatric research shape not just *what* we know, but *how* we should try to know what mental disorders are. There are various reasons for the molecular path that has been followed by much psychiatric research since the 1980s – that is to say, the focus on molecular mechanisms in the brain and the attempts to understand mental disorders in terms of anomalies or malfunctions in those molecular mechanisms (for more detail, see Rose and Abi-Rached, 2013). Of course, this 'molecularization' has been characteristic of biomedical thought more generally – the belief, that is to say, that life is not mystery but mechanism, and that pathological processes are best understood in terms of disorders or anomalies in fundamental biological processes of the human body, and that, if one can 'reverse engineer' the pathology to identify the molecular mechanisms that underpin it, one can and should target effective treatments on those molecular mechanisms (Rose, 2007b). While this molecular style of thought in biology dates to the 1930s (Kay, 1993), from the 1950s onwards it was undoubtedly boosted by the discovery, by Franklin, Watson and Crick, of the double helix structure of DNA, and the ways that DNA sequences code for the elements of proteins that make up the molecular structure of human organs including the brain.

As far as psychiatry is concerned, other factors also come into play. Notably, there was the belief that if psychiatric drugs developed since the 1950s work, it is because their constituent molecules lock onto molecules in the neurotransmitter system in the brain – notably, the locations on neurons that are responsible for transmission of nerve impulses across the synapses.[31] So if drugs such as LSD mimic psychiatric symptoms by interfering with the normal system of neurotransmitters, and if the early drugs for severe psychosis, such as chlorpromazine, turned out to modify neurotransmission, and if the first drugs developed to treat depression – such as iproniazid and imipramine – also worked on the neurotransmitter system, then it seemed pretty obvious that this is where research should focus. Of course, this had to be laboratory research, and, given that it was very difficult ethically to experiment on humans, researchers had to work with animals, which seemed to rule out any attention to a mental domain. Most researchers gave little thought to the mental lives of mice, rats or even macaques on which they experimented, assumed that they could produce models of mental disorders in such animals – anxiety, depression and so forth – and believed that the mechanisms they studied in such model animals were evolutionarily conserved and hence similar, if not identical, in humans.

This belief in the biological basis of mental disorder was coupled with the pervasive conviction, going back many centuries in lay understandings, formalized in theories of degeneracy in the late nineteenth century, in the eugenics of the first half of the twentieth century and in innumerable studies of lineages and of twins, that there was a strong hereditary element in mental disorders, and hence a genetic basis, so clearly one should study the genetics of these molecular mechanisms. Of course, much more was involved in the growing belief that mental disorders had a biological basis, to be searched for at the molecular level, but for present purposes the point is straightforward: whatever had its effect on mental disorder – whether genetics, family upbringing, adverse events, poverty and trauma – it must do so via its effect on the molecular mechanisms of the brain. And, as a corollary, if one wants to treat mental disorders, the most direct route is to act on those molecular mechanisms to correct their malfunctions, and the best way to do this is via drugs. Hence much of this research involves sometimes controversial partnerships of various sorts between researchers based in hospitals and universities and the commercial companies that produce drugs and other treatments for profit. The priorities that are identified for such research, the hypotheses that are thought worthy of examination, the research methods that are thought appropriate – such as animal experiments or clinical trials – in other words the investigatory 'set-ups' that are used in psychiatric research: these all shape what counts as truth and what will come to count as truth about the nature of mental disorders.

Psychiatry as a political science

Fourth, psychiatry is intensely political. Indeed, psychiatry, since its inception in modern form in the mid-nineteenth century, has been a political science (Rose, 1996c). The rise of the asylum gave psychiatry and psychiatrists a unique role – the capacity to compulsorily confine and treat individuals who had broken no law, but had transgressed norms of order, control, civility, cognition or desire – a capacity which it retains despite the 'death of the asylum', and even though this is now constrained by subsequent legislation and rights-based regulation.[32] The power of psychiatry to detain and compulsorily treat was central to the critique of psychiatry from the 1950s onwards, which I will discuss later in this book. But it would be a mistake to identify the politics of psychiatry with the problems of the asylum, important as that has been. Outside the asylum, in the second half of the nineteenth century, psychiatric practitioners were central to arguments about degeneracy and its sociopolitical implications. As arguments about the prolific breeding of degenerates morphed into eugenic strategies in the early years of the twentieth century, many psychiatrists accepted that there was a constitutional and heritable commonality between those who were mentally deranged and those who were feeble minded, alcoholics, prostitutes and a whole family of problematic types of person – we should not forget that the first of those who were 'euthanized' in Nazi Germany were the inhabitants of mental asylums (Proctor, 1988). But the political role of psychiatrists was by no means all 'negative' – seeking to confine or constrain. Eugenics also had its 'positive side' – encouraging the healthy to breed. And beyond eugenics, psychiatrists were key players in the mental hygiene movements in the first half of the twentieth century, making the link between poor mental hygiene and all manner of problems of maladjustment among children, factory workers, military personnel and others and seeking to maximize the mental health of the population (Rose, 1985a: chs 6–8).

As the movement for the closure of asylums spread across many countries in the 1980s, we saw an increase in the number of psychiatric and quasi-psychiatric institutions across the territory that became termed 'the community' (I discuss this in detail in Rose, 1986, from which the following paragraph is derived). Psychiatric medicine moved out from the asylums to psychiatric wards in general hospitals, special hospitals, medium secure units, day hospitals, outpatient clinics, child guidance clinics, prisons, children's homes, sheltered housing, drop-in centres, community mental health centres, domiciliary care by community psychiatric nurses and, of course, the general practitioner's surgery. And psychiatric practitioners, in alliance with psychologists and social workers, concerned themselves with infertility, pregnancy, birth and the post-partum period; infancy; childhood at home and at school; sexual normality, perversion, impotence and pleasure; family life, marriage and divorce, employment and unemployment, mid-life crises and failures to achieve; and old age, terminal illness and bereavement. Wherever problems arise – in our homes, on the streets, in factories, schools, hospitals, the army, courtroom or prison – experts with specialist knowledge of the nature, causes and remedies for mental distress are on hand to provide its diagnoses and propose remedial action. As I argued in 1986, it would not be too much of an exaggeration to say that, by that time, we were living in a 'psychiatric society' (for a related argument about the United States that informed my own approach, see Castel et al., 1979).

Critics of 'deinstitutionalization' argued that this process was leaving hundreds of severely disturbed individuals to fend for themselves on the streets, not only at risk to themselves, but, more importantly, a risk to others: the mad person figured "as the sign of a community that doesn't care, as a threat to a community that naturally cares for itself, as an instance of the uncaring nature of a fiscally straightened state, as an object of pity and of fear" (Rose, 1996c: 3). Psychiatrists' capacity to treat was, it seemed, less important than their capacity to assess and manage the risk that those with mental illness supposedly posed to others, despite the fact that, in reality, that risk was far lower than for many others (Szmukler and Rose, 2013). Both within the criminal justice system – where psychiatric reports play a key role in the decision as to the appropriate ways to deal with potential offenders – and outside it – where every individual in touch with mental health services is subject to risk assessment and risk management – the expertise of the psychiatrist is required (Rose, 2016). In the criminal justice system, psychiatric risk assessments may determine a verdict – murder or manslaughter on grounds of diminished responsibility – but much more frequently their risk assessments determine the sentence, especially in jurisdictions that have a separate sentencing hearing, and they also play a part in decisions over parole and early release. Outside the criminal justice system, psychiatric evaluations of risk shape decisions over whether an individual should be admitted to a psychiatric facility, the level of security that is required, whether he or she should be confined or treated against their will, as well as the timing and nature of discharge. Today, while the mongers of fear

have retreated to the shadows, a different political problematic has
emerged. Psychiatric estimates of the current and future prevalence
of mental disorders and brain disorders are linked to questions of
economic productivity in a knowledge economy, on the one hand,
and concerns about the economic burden of care for the afflicted, on
the other. This is what is termed, in a phrase I profoundly dislike, 'the
burden of brain disorders', which we will discuss in the next chapter.

The politics of psychiatry

Is psychiatry today, at its root, a political practice? This question
returns us to a controversy that has been rumbling since at least
the end of the Second World War. Is psychiatry, despite the pro-
fessed therapeutic vocation of its practitioners, fundamentally tied
to practices of social control? The radical Italian psychiatrist, Franco
Basaglia, put this most clearly: psychiatry, he argued, was riven by
the tension between control and care (for an excellent introduction
to Basaglia's work, see Scheper-Hughes and Lovell, 1987). Basaglia
was writing at a time when, in Italy and many other countries, psychiatric practice was inextricably linked to the involuntary confinement
of patients in the custodial mental hospital. In the Italian case in
the 1960s, when Basaglia carried out his most well-known work in
the transformation and eventual closure of the Gorizia psychiatric
hospital in northeast Italy, the similarities of the hospital to a prison
were clear. In Erving Goffman's terms, they were 'total institutions'
– his analysis, published in 1961 in *Asylums: Studies on the Social
Condition of Mental Patients and Other Inmates*, was based on a year
of observations in a psychiatric hospital in Washington, DC – that
stripped those confined within them of the material, symbolic and
practical elements of personal identity and subjected them to the
rules of the institution, transforming them in body and in soul from
persons to inmates (for an intriguing discussion, see Hacking, 2004).
The horrors of the asylums in the mid-twentieth century had been
revealed in earlier studies, such as Albert Deutsch's *The Shame of the
States* (1948) and portrayed in movies such as *The Snake Pit* (also
released in 1948), and while Goffman theorized its mode of action
on those within it, Basaglia sought, in a range of ways, to "restore a
subjectivity to the way in which patients were viewed . . . he would
take the side of the patient, as a person who suffers and is oppressed
[entailing] a refusal of accepted ways of organizing suffering, and an
involvement in transforming the patient's life" (Scheper-Hughes and

Lovell, 1987: 9). But Basaglia, like Michel Foucault, whose *Folie et déraison: Histoire de la folie à l'âge classique* was also published in 1961, asked questions about the social functions of the asylum and its carceral form, and hence about the sociopolitical role of the psychiatrists who were its custodians, and the knowledge that grounded their claims to expertise. To put the matter concisely, these critics argued that psychiatry was a highly normative discipline, and its role was one of social protection: to control those who deviated from or transgressed social norms, in particular refusing the twin obligations of production and consumption, simultaneously delegitimating their beliefs or actions as symptoms of illness, and normalizing them, or at least muting their resistance, by incarceration and/or treatment with powerful 'chemical coshes' – drugs used primarily for the purposes of control within institutions and management of conduct outside it.

Many psychiatrists were prepared to accept that their expertise *could* be used for purposes of political repression. This was the widely accepted view of the role of psychiatry in the Soviet Union as a means of, and a legitimation of, the incarceration of dissidents. Psychiatric diagnoses, notably Andrei Snezhnevsky's diagnosis of 'sluggish schizophrenia' (van Voren, 2009), were used not just to confine those who opposed the political regime in psychiatric hospitals, and not only to treat them with powerful psychiatric drugs against their will, but also to deny them legal rights when they were discharged, and effectively rob them of the chances of employment and much more. But outside the Soviet Union, did contemporary psychiatry have a similar function of constraining, controlling and medicalizing those whose views, beliefs, conduct and form of life were considered deviant and threatening to order and civility?

As will have been clear from my argument thus far, this would be to greatly simplify a very heterogeneous set of practices that go under the heading of psychiatry. Nonetheless, from its inception in the mid-nineteenth century, the asylum was utilized as part of an apparatus for the compulsory incarceration of troublesome individuals – those found troublesome by their families, their spouses, their communities or various authorities. Across the twentieth century, the power of psychiatry to detain individuals against their will, and often to subject them to harsh 'treatments', remained, and, even when unspoken, the shadow of compulsion fell over all voluntary decisions to accept hospitalization and treatment. There can be no doubt that we can see many instances, historically and more recently, when psychiatric language and powers have been utilized for frank control of norm-violaters. Think, for example, of the psychiatrization of homosexuality and the use by some psychiatrists of deeply unpleasant technologies of behaviour modification in an attempt to eliminate the deviant erotic desires of homosexuals (Bayer, 1981). Or consider the heavily heteronormative use of psychopharmaceuticals for women who either refused or found it difficult to conform to the forms of life allotted to them (Chesler, 1972; Metzl, 2003), or the 'protest psychosis' – the diagnosis of schizophrenia for young black Americans demanding their civil rights (Metzl, 2010). Or consider the racial stereotypes embodied in the overuse of the diagnosis of schizophrenia for young black men in the UK (Littlewood and Lipsedge, 1997). These examples could be proliferated.

More generally, risk assessment in the UK has become a routine part of the work of all psychiatrists, not just those working in specialist forensic services. "Psychiatrists are increasingly called upon to guard the entry and exit points to a new range of quasi-psychiatric institutions that seem to offer a solution to the problems thrown up by such public fears and political responses generated by the 'community psychiatry'" (Rose, 2002: 18).[33] Some of the most egregious examples of this have been modified. Thus the institutions set up to detain those deemed to have 'Dangerous and Severe Personality Disorder' – a term introduced in a UK government document in 1999 but which did not correspond to any known psychiatric diagnosis – have now been subsumed within ordinary psychiatric services, and the infamous 'indeterminate sentences for public protection', for those considered likely to remain dangerous when their sentences had been served, have been abolished.[34] However, several thousands of those sentenced in this way still remain in detention, and the number of persons detained under mental health legislation in the UK continues to rise. In the year 2015/16 the total number of detentions under the Mental Health Act 1983, as amended by the Mental Health Act 2007, increased by 9 per cent to 63,622, compared to 58,399 in 2014/15. As the official report noted, "This compares with an increase of 10 per cent between 2013/14 and 2014/15 and is the highest number since 2005/06 (43,361 detentions) a rise of just under a half over the period." Further, the use of Section 136, which enables individuals to be institutionalized in 'a place of safety' increased by 18 per cent over the previous year to 22,965. "At the end of March 2016, 25,577 people were subject to The Act of whom 20,151 were detained in hospitals" – 30 per cent of whom were detained in private hospitals.[35]

We cannot ignore the continuing presence of coercion within the psychiatric system: the statistics demonstrate quite clearly that the 'control' functions of psychiatry, its 'social protection' role in managing troublesome individuals, remains active and indeed may be increasing. Nonetheless, many problematic cases of the use of psychiatric power to compulsorily detain and treat do not relate to either norm-violation or the control of those who might pose a risk to others, but to more mundane, if no more acceptable, instances of institutional management and pacification of troublesome individuals. Even the use of lobotomies or leucotomies from the 1930s to the 1970s – psychosurgical operations which resulted in massive and damaging changes in personality for those subject to them – while to be deplored, cannot really be interpreted in terms of sociopolitical control of deviant, dangerous or politically problematic behaviour. These desperate remedies – like the shock therapies using malaria, insulin or electrically induced convulsions (ECT) – arose from a deadly combination of psychiatrists' genuine, if misguided, wish to find a physical basis for their practice, together with the vaunting ambitions and willing blindness to consequences of a few charismatic practitioners (Valenstein, 1986). But what of today?

Critical psychiatry today

When Peter Miller and I put together our collection on *The Power of Psychiatry* in the 1980s, we suggested that any comprehensive political analysis of psychiatry should not confine itself to a condemnation of the 'hard end' of coercion and compulsion, but should locate the carceral asylum and those desperate remedies within a wider set of psychiatric practices, spreading way beyond the asylum, whose function is not – or not only – the political or social control of deviance, but is to define, maintain or restore a particular notion of mental health (Miller and Rose, 1986). I think it is from this basis that we can begin to analyse the political role of psychiatry in the twenty-first century. But to take that position is to also to stand at a distance from some of the themes that underpin contemporary critical psychiatry. I have already touched on many of these in this chapter, but now let me turn to them directly.

We can start by returning to our dictionary definition: psychiatry is the branch of medicine concerned with the causes, diagnosis, treatment and prevention of mental illness. As will have become clear, if psychiatry is merely a 'branch of medicine', it is one that appears to many to have been, and to still be, a uniquely problematic one. No doubt there are many critics of obstetrics and gynaecology, of oncology and of many other 'branches of medicine' concerning the way that experts treat their patients, for the difficulty of accessing effective treatments, and the ways that pharmaceutical companies, and the medical device industry, make vast profits from human sickness and frailty. But few would argue that these 'branches of medicine' are fundamentally illegitimate, serve sociopolitical rather than therapeutic functions, offer pseudo-remedies for invented diseases, and should not exist. Yet ever since the birth of modern psychiatry in the mid-nineteenth century, it has been the topic of complaint, criticism, sometimes ridicule.

In the 1960s and 1970s, its very foundations came under attack from all sides. From right-wing libertarians such as Thomas Szasz, who thought the very idea of mental illness was a myth, that psychiatrists were peddling spurious diseases and ineffective treatments, and that those treated by psychiatry were not sick, but merely unable to cope with the demands of living (Szasz, 1962). From those on the left who regarded psychiatry as a political practice for the control of those who deviated from social norms, doing the state's business under the guise of medicine (Baruch and Treacher, 1978). From those who believed that psychiatry was actually in the control of the pharmaceutical industry, part of a vast machinery of 'disease mongering', inventing diseases for the sole, or main, purpose of increasing potential markets for financial exploitation by the drug companies (Moynihan and Cassels, 2005). From those who thought that, while major mental disorders were a reality, psychiatry had expanded beyond its legitimate borders, medicalizing the ordinary travails of human existences, such as inattentiveness in kids, shyness in adolescents, anxieties in parents, stress in business people, sadness in everyone (Conrad and Schneider, 1992). And, above all, from those who felt that, despite all its pretensions to be based on biomedical science, psychiatry's truth claims were invalid, lacking objective knowledge of the conditions it claimed to be able to diagnose, and its treatments today were as ineffective and harmful as the purging, bleeding, cold baths, spinning chairs, malaria shock, lobotomies and electro-convulsive therapies of the past (Ingleby, 1981).

Today, these criticisms often merge with a more general distaste for the politics of the present, characterized by its critics as 'neoliberalism' (Cohen and Timimi, 2008; Moncrieff, 2008b).[36] That is to say, many argue that psychiatry today, in diagnosing increasing numbers of individuals with psychiatric disorders, masks the origin of those disorders in the political practices associated with neoliberalism: the celebration of markets, competition, individualism, personal responsibility and self-improvement through individual entrepreneurship in the world of work. In locating the origins of so many disorders in neurobiological anomalies, they suggest that it ignores or neglects the damaging neurobiological consequences of austerity, the demeaning practices now forced on the benefit seeker, the job seeker, the asylum seeker, the disabled person subject to work capability assessments. In reindividualizing a disorder already individualized by our contemporary form of political economy, they contend that psychiatry, along with the other psy disciplines, merely repeats, in a revised form, the tension between care and control that has run through it since its inception in the mid-nineteenth century.

In the following chapters we will see that while many of these criticisms are overstated and overgeneralized, and some are frankly wrong, most have some grains of truth, and some accurately target flaws at the very heart of contemporary psychiatry. Yet, I will suggest, there are segments, forces, explanations and practices within the heterogeneous domain of this 'discipline of mental health' that offer hints of an alternative. As I conclude this book, I argue that we can identify some lines of escape, some hints that another psychiatry – no less evidence-based, no less rigorous, no less neurobiologically informed, indeed far more attuned to the reality of the ailment – is indeed possible.

Onwards . . .

It is necessary to resist the temptation to set out all the arguments of a book in its first chapter. I have tried to identify some of the multiple dimensions that map out the territory of contemporary psychiatry and to raise some of the problems that we will explore in this book. I will do this by addressing a number of 'hard questions' about mental disorder today – hard questions, because, in my view, there are no easy answers.

I start, in chapter 2, with the numbers. In the face of numerous estimates of the size and burden of mental disorders that seem to show that there are alarming numbers of people across the globe living with a diagnosable mental disorder, even if they do not seek, or cannot access, treatment, I ask whether we can trust these estimates: 'Is there really a global "epidemic" of mental disorder?'

In chapter 3, I consider the view of those who claim that there is indeed a high and growing level of mental distress, but argue that this is as much a political and economic issue as a psychiatric and therapeutic one. Those who argue this way link the rise in diagnoses of psychiatric disorders to a decline in the conditions of life for many of our fellow citizens, often attributed to political and economic strategies termed 'neoliberalism' and the linked phenomena of 'globalization' – with the movement of jobs from the Global North to the Global South – 'marketization' – the celebration of market individualism, competition and choice in all areas of life, not merely those of production and exchange – and the attacks on welfare states and their associated provisions of social security, in the name of autonomy, self-reliance and the like. In this chapter, then, I ask the hard question: 'Is it all the fault of neoliberal capitalism?'

In chapter 4, I return to the issue of what mental disorder 'is' and ask a version of the question made famous many years ago by David Rosenhan: 'If sanity and insanity exist, how shall we know them?' (1973: 250). Focusing specifically on the question of diagnosis, I ask: 'If mental disorder exists, how shall we know it?' and I evaluate the argument that changes in diagnostic practices, in particular those associated with the APA's *DSM*, have played a key role in the expansion of the territory of psychiatry over the last half century, transforming many of the ordinary vicissitudes of life – sadness, shyness, childhood irritability and so forth – into psychiatric categories and hence increasing the number of us who are 'suitable cases for treatment'. I also consider the linked argument that we can, and should, seek to find genetic or neural 'biomarkers' that would enable precise and objective diagnosis, enable early identification of those at risk of future mental pathology, and allow us to develop 'precision medicine' in psychiatry. It seems difficult to argue against the hope that biomarkers might enable those at risk of a mental disorder to be identified while they were still well, and therapeutic measures put in place to prevent, or at least ameliorate, the problem. Yet we shall see that the issue is not as simple as it seems.

In chapter 5, we consider the increasing emphasis on the role of neurobiology in understanding mental disorders, and the increasing focus on the brain in psychiatric research in Europe, North America and indeed across the world. Few, today, would resist the idea that brains are involved in mental distress, anxiety, despair, thought disruption, voice hearing and all the other symptoms now placed in the category of mental disorder. But of course, brains are involved in almost everything that humans think, feel and do! To speak of 'the brain' is to paint with a very broad brush the millions of neural circuits among the 100 billion or so nerve cells in the adult human brain and the 100 trillion synapses or connections among these cells, circuits evolved over millennia, developed from conception onwards, and changing at timescales ranging from the millisecond to the decade as a result of the transactions with body, milieu and physical, interpersonal, social and symbolic environment. And to accept that brains – in whatever sense we anatomize them – are involved in mental distress is neither to argue that disruptions in these circuits are the origin or cause of mental distress, nor that treatment should be directed towards them. I therefore ask: 'Are mental disorders "brain disorders"?'

In chapter 6, I ask a question that may seem paradoxical given that the rates of prescription of psychiatric drugs seem inexorably to be rising worldwide: 'Does psychopharmacology have a future?' For while drug use is on the rise, there are increasing doubts about the efficacy of these drugs, the founding hypotheses as to their modes of action are now discredited, and the large pharmaceutical companies are withdrawing from psychiatric drug development as they have had little success in bringing new and more effective drugs to market for any psychiatric condition, and are moving to invest in more profitable products.

In chapter 7, I examine the Movement for Global Mental Health (MGMH), and the claim that mental disorders are not merely a growing problem in wealthy industrialized nations, but also a major if largely unrecognized cause of undiagnosed illness and untreated suffering in low- and middle-income countries, where psychiatrists are few and far between, and the treatment of sufferers is often represented as one of neglect and isolation, often downright cruelty. Critics suggest that, knowingly or not, the MGMH is based upon a culturally specific Euro-American model of mental health problems, mistakenly believes that 'Western' definitions of illness and practices of intervention can be generalized to non-Western cultures and, for some, represents a new wave of psychiatric colonization. We examine this debate, and what it can tell us about the politics of mental health today, and ask 'Who needs global mental health?' For the issues raised – for example, those of the universality of diagnoses, of interpretation of clinical trials claiming to show the efficacy of particular treatments, of the ways in which social, economic, political and cultural factors shape the emergence, expression, experience and consequences of mental ill health – do not merely have relevance for the psychiatric future in low- and middle-income countries. They tell us a great deal about the ways in which we understand and govern those who are perceived to fail at the tasks of living what has come to be considered a normal life.

In chapter 8, I ask what the place of the patient is in the psychiatric system – that is, the user, the survivor, the consumer in the mental health system. I place this in the context of the powerful passage in Michel Foucault's preface to his book *Madness and Civilization* (1967), where he argues: "The constitution of madness as a mental illness thrusts into oblivion all those stammered imperfect words without fixed syntax in which the exchange between madness and reason was made. The language of psychiatry, which is a monologue of reason about madness, has been established only on the basis of that silence." Foucault was writing 60 years ago. Have things changed in our current world of empowerment, citizenship, recovery and the like? And if so, what are the challenges that confront us today?

This forms the prelude to chapter 9, where I discuss whether, in the light of the critical analysis in earlier chapters, another psychiatry is possible, and outline some of the key dimensions of an alternative: that is to say, I ask: 'Is another psychiatry possible?'

2
Is There Really an 'Epidemic' of Mental Disorder?

The total cost of disorders of the brain [in Europe] was estimated at €798 billion in 2010. Direct costs constitute the majority of costs (37% direct healthcare costs and 23% direct non-medical costs) whereas the remaining 40% were indirect costs associated with patients' production losses. . . . In terms of the health economic burden outlined in this report, disorders of the brain likely constitute the number one economic challenge for European health care, now and in the future.

Gustavsson et al., 2011: 720

It seems that Americans are in the midst of a raging epidemic of mental illness, at least as judged by the increase in the numbers treated for it. The tally of those who are so disabled by mental disorders that they qualify for Supplemental Security Income (SSI) or Social Security Disability Insurance (SSDI) increased nearly two and a half times between 1987 and 2007 – from one in 184 Americans to one in seventy-six. For children, the rise is even more startling – a thirty-five-fold increase in the same two decades. Mental illness is now the leading cause of disability in children, well ahead of physical disabilities like cerebral palsy or Down syndrome, for which the federal programs were created. . . . A large survey of randomly selected adults, sponsored by the National Institute of Mental Health (NIMH) and conducted between 2001 and 2003, found that an astonishing 46 percent met criteria established by the American Psychiatric Association (APA) for having had at least one mental illness within four broad categories at some time in their lives . . . What is going on here?

Angell, 2011: 20

Claims about the large numbers of adults and children suffering from mental disorder are becoming familiar.[1] Mental health and government websites in the UK and the United States regularly report that about one quarter of the adult population will experience at least one diagnosable mental health problem in any one year, and around 50 per cent over a lifetime; and that 20 per cent of children will have a mental health problem in any one year. International organizations tell us that approximately 450 million people worldwide have a mental health problem, and that mental disorders are rapidly becoming one of the world's leading causes of ill health.[2] We used to count the number of mentally disordered persons in terms of the populations of mental hospitals, yet even at their peak these numbered hundreds of thousands across Europe and the United States, not millions.[3] How have we come to such a view of the prevalence of these conditions in our own times? Is this an acknowledgement of the scale of disorder that has long existed across the world, but is only now fully recognized – after all, we would not be surprised by these figures if they referred to the prevalence of 'physical' – non-psychiatric – disorders? Or does this provide evidence of the rising numbers of those who are ailing from mental disorders in developed, developing and less-developed regions alike: a genuine epidemic[4] whose causes we need to identify and address?

Further, what are we to make of the fact that those who produce these and other similar estimates argue that the majority of those whom experts consider to be suffering with a mental disorder are not diagnosed and have neither been given, nor have sought, psychiatric help (Kohn et al., 2004; Rebello et al., 2014; WHO, 2017)? Does this so-called 'treatment gap' imply that we must demand a rapid increase in the numbers of psychiatrists and in the availability of mental health treatment, especially in those countries where such professionals and facilities are rudimentary? Or is this, as some critics have suggested, a gross overestimation, a sign of the 'psychiatrization' of more and more features of everyday existence, an inflation of figures by those who seek to benefit directly or indirectly from extravagant claims such as these?

Here is the first hard question that we must consider in this book, and the first dilemma with which we must struggle: is there really a global 'epidemic' of mental disorders? Is there really so much undiagnosed mental disorder demanding more research, programmes of disease awareness for professionals and lay persons alike, an increase in psychiatrists and practitioners of community mental health and so forth? Or are psychiatrists too ready to diagnose disorder for normal variations in mood or behaviour, and prone to overestimate the prevalence of disorder? If so, what are the forces that are leading psychiatrists to make these estimates? Let us begin by considering the phrase that is currently popular to describe these numbers: 'the burden of brain disorders'. For two things are implied by this phrase, in addition to the numbers themselves. The first is that these disorders are to be understood as 'burden' – a weight, a load, an encumbrance. And the second is that these disorders are matters of 'the brain'.

'The burden of brain disorders'

The idea that mental pathology was a burden – rather than an individual affliction, a family misfortune or a public danger – took shape in the late nineteenth century, with the widespread acceptance of the idea that disorders ranging from tuberculosis to insanity were symptoms of a heritable trait of degeneracy that hampered the overall power of a nation and its ability to succeed in international competition for territory and resources (Pick, 1989). This burden was partly a matter of expenditure, and partly a matter of fitness. On the one hand, supporting all those defectives, lunatics, alcoholics and others with a weakened and degenerate constitution imposed a financial cost on the healthy, who contributed through their taxes. On the other, a population whose fitness was weakened by an increasing number of degenerates would lose out in the imperialist struggle between nations. This made it imperative to identify those burdensome individuals and, if possible, to curtail their numbers, in the first instance by limiting their tendency to spawn so many genetically tainted offspring. A particular concern was with those termed 'feeble minded', who often passed among the normal population without clear visible signs of their inferiority, but who also reproduced their kind in large numbers, indeed larger than those of the civilized population who were limiting the size of their families. This eugenic style of thought, grounded intellectually in the work of Francis Galton (1904), took a lethal turn in Nazi Germany – and one that was carefully calculated in Reichsmarks. A famous illustration in *Volk und Rasse,* published in 1935, shows a healthy Aryan labourer carrying a beam on his shoulders with a caricatured mentally defective individual sitting at one end and a caricatured Jew at the other. The text reads: "You are sharing the load. A genetically ill individual costs approximately 50,000 Reichsmarks by the age of sixty" (Burleigh, 1994; Proctor, 1988).[5] However, eugenic ideas also underpinned policies of identification and segregation – and sometimes sterilization – of the feeble minded and other socially undesirable individuals in Britain, the United States, and in countries from Mexico to Japan; it continued in attenuated form in the Nordic countries until the mid-1970s and in China until the end of the twentieth century (Broberg and Roll-Hansen, 1996; Dikötter, 1998; Dowbiggin, 1997; Stepan, 1991).

Of course, now is not then. Today's use of the term 'burden' in calculating the costs of mental disorders or brain disorders to our economies does not partake of the same eugenic or political rationale, and the conclusions drawn from the estimates that experts produce are exactly the opposite – they are not used to demand exclusion and elimination of the unfit, but to press for treatment and inclusion to reduce the burden of mental disorder on themselves, their families and communities, and the direct and indirect costs to the economy. Nonetheless, many who are diagnosed with mental disorders find the language of burden insulting and demeaning – and many of those – including the present author – whose loved ones are so diagnosed do not consider that their relationship is one of burden. Perhaps we should look at this from a very different perspective. Could these conditions – however they are described – be the price that some of us pay for the demands that are made upon us by contemporary societies? That is to say, might many of those living under the description of mental disorders thrive in other cultural conditions, even though, for whatever reason, they lack the fortitude, the desire, or the resources required to live a life of freedom, choice, responsibility, and inclusion via wage labour? And might we think of our relationship with those who are diagnosed with mental health problems not in terms of burden, but in terms of care and solidarity? Such a relationship would entail the recognition that we ourselves might have been in that situation, and under those diagnoses, in the past and might very well be in the future. I shall return to these ethical and political questions later. For now, let me focus on the ways in which, today, the prevalence of these disorders has come to be construed as a governmental problem and framed in the language of burden.

Counting the costs

The European Brain Council took its report, 'Cost of Disorders of the Brain in Europe 2010', to the European Parliament on 4 October 2011.[6] The experts who contributed to that report estimated that around one-third of citizens of the European Union suffered from a diagnosable 'brain disorder' in any one year, most of whom were undiagnosed and untreated, and that the total cost of such disorders to Europe in 2010 was €798 billion (Gustavsson et al., 2011). One of the coauthors succinctly summarized the report's main argument for the Parliament: "People don't die from them, rather they live in a disabled state for most of their lives. That's why disorders of the brain are so costly" (Jes Olesen, cited in Andersen, 2011). How did mental disorders come to be framed in these economic terms and seen as "so costly"?

For many years it was routine for those working in psychiatry to complain about the relative lack of investment in research into mental disorder compared with other conditions such as cancer. But, as Ayo Wahlberg has argued (Wahlberg and Rose, 2015), partly a result of the shift among epidemiologists and health economists from calculating the cost of *dying* from disease to calculating the cost of *living with it*, problems of mental health and neurological disease have gained a newfound prominence in global efforts to set health priorities. Central to this shift in priorities has been the consolidation of psychiatric epidemiology as a subfield of epidemiology, and its shift of focus, in step with the rest of epidemiology, from the numbers themselves – the mapping of disease incidence and prevalence – to the calculation of 'disease burden'.

The Second World War marked something of a turning point in the way in which psychiatry conceived of its social vocation. Prior to the outbreak of war, to oversimplify, psychiatry was divided between the asylums – the institutions which enclosed and isolated both the inmates and the asylum superintendents – and the growing variety of provisions outside the asylums, whether these were psychiatric units in general hospitals, outpatient clinics or indeed private psychotherapy. During the war, in both the UK and the United States, psychiatrists were involved in the selection of personnel, in techniques of training, in strategies for the maximization of both military and civilian moral, as well as the treatment of 'problem cases'. In the British army, psychiatric discharges made up over 30 per cent of all discharges for medical reasons. It became clear, both to professionals and to the politicians, that psychiatry should no longer focus all its attention on the confinement of a small number of severely disordered persons. "To fulfil the task that society required, it needed to shift its attention to the detection and treatment of those large numbers of the population who were now known to be liable to neurotic breakdown, maladjustment, inefficiency, and unemployability on the grounds of poor mental health" (Rose, 1986: 62–3).

Given this changed perception of the extent of mental disorder in the non-institutionalized population, it is not surprising that, in the decades following the end of the Second World War, there were innumerable studies of the 'prevalence' of 'mental illness', 'mental distress', 'mental morbidity' and the like – in short, of what was to become psychiatric epidemiology. In a review of psychiatric epidemiology published in 1964, Michael Shepherd and Brian Cooper attribute this new postwar concern not to eugenics, but to "the unprecedented interest taken in the mental health of both the military and civil populations during the conflict" and to "the post-war renewal of interest in the psychosocial components of morbidity and the emergence as a separate discipline of social, or 'comprehensive medicine'" (Shepherd and Cooper, 1964: 279). What was surprising, however, given that eugenic thought was still active in the late 1940s and early 1950s, is the fact that eugenic arguments seem to have played no part in these studies.

The abiding concern from the 1950s to the 1970s, rather, was with the extent of the 'unserved' population. Morton Wagenfeld, in a paper published in 1983, reviewed the studies that had been carried out in the United States and their implications. There was "the 1954 survey of the entire non-institutionalized Baltimore population, in which it was determined that at any given point in the year, 10% of the total population (all ages) had a mental disorder classifiable by the ICDA [International Classification of Diseases, Adapted for Use in the United States]"; there was the Midtown Manhattan Study of 1954 which found that "23% of the adult population (age, 20–59 years) were affected by serious psychiatric impairments at any point in time"; and there was the 1967 study in New Haven, Connecticut, which "found a point prevalence mental disorder rate of about 16% in the adult population (age, 20+)" (Regier et al., 1978: 687). These studies were heavily criticized because of the vagueness of their object – they used different definitions and categories, raising the question "Just what was being measured?" (Wagenfeld, 1983: 171).

Nonetheless, by the early 1980s, it was widely believed that some 15 per cent of the adult non-institutionalized population suffered from mental disorder, much of which was unrecognized and 'unserved' by mental health services (Regier et al., 1978). Some were contending that the United States – and indeed the whole world – was facing a pandemic of mental disorder (Kramer, 1983).[7] The 1978 Report from President Carter's Commission on Mental Health was of the view that, in the words of the president, "one in seven Americans needed mental treatment of some kind at any particular moment".[8] The report estimated that while some 15 per cent of the general population needed access to mental health services, the majority did not succeed because of discrimination, fragmentation of services, and lack of official concern and of coordination between services for physical health and those for mental health. This was linked to a more general question about the specific population groups that had been 'unserved' by the community mental health policies since the Community Mental Health Centers Act of 1973 (Grob, 2005; US Government, 1978).

In the years that followed, epidemiologists radically increased their estimates of those afflicted by mental health problems. From the 1990s forward, surveys in the United States (Kessler et al., 1994; Kessler et al., 2005) and in Europe (Wittchen et al., 1994; Wittchen and Jacobi, 2005) were regularly estimating that 25 per cent of the adult population not receiving psychiatric attention could be diagnosed with a mental disorder in any one year, and 50 per cent in a lifetime. It is important to ask ourselves how these increased estimates were reached.

The method used by Kessler and his colleagues – which has remained basically unaltered since their first report in 1994 to the present – was based on an interview conducted in the National Comorbidity Survey (NCS) of the non-institutionalized civilian population of the United States, which was designed "to study the comorbidity of substance use disorders and nonsubstance psychiatric disorders" (Kessler et al., 1994: 8).[9] A randomly selected set of households are chosen and members interviewed using a research diagnostic interview schedule which is designed to be administered by nonclinical interviewers, and which evaluates subjects on categories based on the *DSM*. For instance, the baseline study administered in 1990–2 asked questions of the form "Have you ever had 2 weeks or longer when you lost the ability to enjoy having good things happen to you, like winning something or being praised or complimented?" or "Has there ever been 2 weeks or more when nearly every day you felt worthless?" – that is to say, questions that took the form of the *DSM* checklists of symptoms. The answers are used to decide whether that individual should be allocated to a diagnostic category.[10] The authors are clearly aware of criticisms about the validity of such a method based on self-reports and classified using a checklist methodology, but argue that, if anything, it *underestimates* rates of psychiatric disorders, for instance arguing that non-respondents have elevated rates of lifetime and current psychiatric disorder, and pointing out that they apply various corrective measures to adjust the data as well as checks on interviewer performance. However, it is clear that the summary statements – for example "Nearly 50%

of respondents reported at least one lifetime disorder, and close to 30% reported at least one 12-month disorder" (Kessler et al., 1994: 8) – are rather misleading, since the respondents did not report disorders at all, but merely responded positively when asked if they had had various kinds of experiences. And, while the surveys do ask, in certain cases, questions that require the interviewee to decide whether, for example, a fear of some activity or event was 'unreasonable' and they also ask whether the interviewee has consulted a medical professional, clearly the assessment of unmet need is not based on any clinical evaluation.

One of the researchers on the earliest of these studies was Hans-Ulrich Wittchen, who spent periods of time with Kessler and his colleagues at the NIMH each year between 1981 and 2000. It was Wittchen, based at the Max Planck Institute of Psychiatry in Munich, and later at the Technische Universität Dresden, who took the lead in the analogous studies in Europe. While the exact details of their methods are a little unclear, it appears that panels of experts were used to evaluate available evidence from existing epidemiological publications that used *DSM* or *ICD* (*International Classification of Diseases*) criteria. After the epidemiological data was compiled into tables, experts from various countries were asked to review the tables and state how much confidence they had in the prevalence estimates (Wittchen and Jacobi, 2005). The estimate that they arrived at based on these methods was quite close to that of Kessler et al., namely:

> that about 27% (equals 82.7 million . . .) of the adult EU population, 18–65 years of age, is or has been affected by at least one mental disorder in the past 12 months. Taking into account the considerable degree of comorbidity (about one third had more than one disorder), the most frequent disorders are anxiety disorders, depressive, somatoform and substance dependence disorders. When taking into account design, sampling and other methodological differences between studies, little evidence seems to exist for considerable cultural or country variation . . . Only 26% of all cases had any consultation with professional health care services, a finding suggesting a considerable degree of unmet need. (Wittchen and Jacobi, 2005: 357)

What differentiated the Wittchen studies most clearly from those of Kessler and his colleagues were two key moves: first, to make an explicit attempt to estimate 'burden' and, second, to group neurological and psychiatric disorders together as 'brain disorders'. Let me consider each of these moves in turn.

Burden today

It was in the early 1980s that studies of the prevalence of mental disorder ceased to be just a matter of counting the numbers of cases in different countries or cities and plotting their distribution against standard variables such as density or level of deprivation. Instead – or as well – there were attempts to estimate the costs of mental disorders – in particular of depression – to society. And this was to become the new meaning of 'burden'.

Alan Stoudemire and colleagues (1986) were among the first to frame a paper in these terms. "Despite the ubiquity of depression as a clinical entity," they write, "few systematic attempts have been made to approximate the economic burden that this form of mental illness places on American society" (1986: 387). In estimating burden, they suggested, one needs not only to take account of the direct treatment costs, such as doctor and hospital costs, pharmaceuticals and so forth, but also to include the indirect costs arising from time lost from productive work due to the illness "and the relative dollar value of that lost time" (1986: 387), which of course includes estimates of time lost in respect of those individuals with the condition who are not in receipt of treatment. The authors conclude:

> These economic figures, along with emerging epidemiologic data, demonstrate the magnitude of depression as a public health and socioeconomic problem of major proportions for our society. These data further emphasize that timely recognition and administration of currently available treatments for depression may result not only in decreased human suffering and reduced morbidity, but also potentially diminish the drain on our overall socioeconomic resources caused by this illness. The figures also provide a basis for calculating the potential cost savings to society by decreasing the morbidity and mortality of the illness by assuring rapid and effective treatment for affected individuals. (1986: 393)

The authors remark that "the full economic burden of depression would include not only the costs calculated here but also would take into account pain and suffering experienced by the individual involved and/or his family and friends" (1986: 388). But it would not be until the early 1990s that the costs of the nonfatal outcomes of depression and other mental disorders would come to be calculated in assessing this personal, familial and interpersonal impact.

In 2003, when Wang, Simon and Kessler reviewed the literature on the economic burden of depression and the cost-effectiveness of treatment, they assigned discussion of the "personal costs that depression exacts from afflicted individuals, families and communities" to "earlier research", and focused on economic calculations of burden, pointing out that "[i]n the past decade, research on the social consequences of depression has begun to focus on the economic costs" (Wang et al., 2003: 22). They attributed this change of focus to the growing recognition of the "sheer magnitude" of the economic burden, and to the social policy debate, especially in the United States, about the extent of health insurance coverage for mental disorders in the light of necessary decisions about the allocation of scarce resources. And indeed it is in cost–benefit terms that they cast their argument – concluding that the current inadequate and insufficient treatment practices compound the economic burden of depression, but that aggressive outreach and improved quality of treatments, which were currently resisted by primary care physicians, health care systems and purchasers of care, were, in fact, cost effective.

It was soon argued that this question of the burden of mental disorder was not merely a 'Western' problem or a problem of developed economies or societies: it was global. Actually, this transnational concern dates back to the first global burden of disease (GBD) study initiated by the World Bank in 1992. Reflecting on that study in 1993, its authors note:

> The results of the 1990 GBD study confirmed what many health workers had suspected for some time, namely, that noncommunicable diseases and injuries were a significant cause of health burden in all regions . . . Many diseases, for example, neuropsychiatric diseases and hearing loss, and injuries may cause considerable ill health but no or few direct deaths . . . Neuropsychiatric disorders and injuries in particular were major causes of lost years of healthy life as measured by DALYs [disability-adjusted life years], and were vastly underappreciated when measured by mortality alone. (World Bank, 1993)

Although questions of psychiatric disorders tended to languish in the background in earlier global estimates, depression features in the very first paragraph of the summary to an analysis of the data published in 1996: "The next two decades will see dramatic changes in the health needs of the world's populations. In the developing regions where four-fifths of the planet's people live, noncommunicable diseases such as depression and heart disease are fast replacing the traditional enemies, such as infectious diseases and malnutrition, as the leading causes of disability and premature death" (Murray et al., 1996: 1).

This new prominence was, at least in part, a consequence of the move from death to life, that is to say, from counting the consequences of disease in terms of the brute fact of death to counting consequences in terms of impaired lives. This study used a new measure of burden, the DALY, to make its estimates (Wahlberg and Rose, 2015). The DALY expresses in a single figure both years of life lost to premature death *and* years lived with a disability of specified severity and duration. One DALY is one lost year of healthy life. The study concluded that, in both developed and developing countries, depression in the middle years of life was the single most burdensome illness, accounting for at least twice the burden imposed by any other disease. It argued that traditional approaches to measuring the economic costs of disorders had seriously underestimated the burdens of mental illnesses, such as depression, alcohol dependence and schizophrenia, because they took account of deaths, but not of disabilities; and while psychiatric conditions are responsible for little more than 1 per cent of deaths, they account for almost 11 per cent of disease burden worldwide.

In 2001, the WHO published what was to become the foundational document of the new approach – *Mental Health: New Understanding, New Hope*:

> Today, some 450 million people suffer from a mental or behavioural disorder, yet only a small minority of them receive even the most basic treatment. In developing countries, most individuals with severe mental disorders are left to cope as best they can with their private burdens such as depression, dementia, schizophrenia, and substance dependence . . . Already, mental disorders represent four of the 10 leading causes of disability worldwide. This growing burden amounts to a huge cost in terms of human misery, disability and economic loss.
>
> Mental and behavioural disorders are estimated to account for 12% of the global burden of disease, yet the mental health budgets of the majority of countries constitute less than 1% of their total health expenditures. The relationship between disease burden and disease spending is clearly disproportionate. More than 40% of countries have no mental health policy and over 30% have no mental health programme. Over 90% of countries have no mental health policy that includes children and adolescents. (WHO, 2001: 3)

These figures, so stark and compelling, seem to speak for themselves of the need for political action. Indeed, the following words of the WHO report became iconic: "By the year 2020, if current trends for demographic and epidemiological transition continue, the burden of depression will increase to 5.7% of the total burden of disease, becoming the second leading cause of DALYs lost. Worldwide it will be second only to ischaemic heart disease for DALYs lost for both sexes. In the developed regions, depression will then be the highest ranking cause of burden of disease" (WHO, 2001: 30).

From 'mental disorders' to 'brain disorders'

In studies up to the time of the 2001 World Health Report, the object of calculation was variously referred to as mental disorders, behavioural disorders, neuropsychiatric disorders, or in terms of specific psychiatric categories such as depression. When the European Brain Council (EBC) was established in 2002, it decided that one of its first tasks should be to provide decision-makers with an accurate estimate of the cost, or 'burden', of neurological diseases and mental disorder – to bring together data on mental disorders and neurological disorders 'under one hat', as Jes Olsen, president of the EBC, put it in 2005. It therefore embarked on a study, funded by the Danish pharmaceutical company Lunbeck, that it called 'Cost of Brain Disorders in Europe'. This led to a whole series of publications, gathered together as a special issue of the *European Journal of Neurology*, edited by Andlin-Sobocki et al. (2005). The work was jointly commissioned by the European College of Neuropsychopharmacology (ECNP), and Hans-Ulrich Wittchen was central to the work of both organizations. The report of the ECNP, included in the special issue, was called the 'Size and Burden of Mental Disorders in Europe' (Wittchen and Jacobi, 2005). But the executive summary of the special issue marks clearly the move to a reframed object – 'brain disorders':

> Brain disorders (psychiatric, neurological and neurosurgical diseases together) figure amongst the leading causes of disease and disability. Yet, the knowledge of the epidemiological and economic impact of brain disorders has been relatively little researched in Europe. WHO data suggest, however, that brain disorders cause 35% of the burden of all diseases in Europe . . .
>
> There are an estimated 127 million Europeans currently living with a brain disorder out of a population of 466 million. The total annual cost of brain disorders in Europe was estimated to €386 billion in 2004. Direct medical expenditures alone totalled €135 billion, comprising inpatient stays (€78 billion), outpatient visits (€45 billion) and drug costs (€13 billion). Attributable indirect costs resulting from lost workdays and productivity loss because of permanent disability caused by

brain disorders and mortality were €179 billion, of which the mental disorders are the most prevalent. Direct non-medical costs (social services, informal care and other direct costs) totalled €72 billion.

Mental disorders amounted to €240 billion and hence constitute 62% of the total cost (excluding dementia), followed by neurological diseases (excluding dementia) totalling €84 billion (22%). Neurosurgical diseases made up a smaller fraction of the total cost of brain disorders in Europe, reaching a cost of €8 billion . . .

The huge cost and burden of brain disorders calls for increased efforts in research, health care and teaching. (Andlin-Sobocki et al., 2005: x–xi)

By 2011, on the basis of further analysis, Hans-Ulrich Wittchen and his colleagues upgraded these figures, estimating that "each year 38.2% of the EU population suffers from a mental disorder . . . this corresponds to 164.8 million persons affected", a total cost of "disorders of the brain in Europe" that they put at €798 billion in 2010. Their recommendations followed as night follows day:

Political action is required in light of the present high cost of disorders of the brain. Funding of brain research must be increased; care for patients with brain disorders as well as teaching at medical schools and other health related educations must be quantitatively and qualitatively improved, including psychological treatments. The current move of the pharmaceutical industry away from brain related indications must be halted and reversed. Continued research into the cost of the many disorders not included in the present study is warranted. It is essential that not only the EU but also the national governments forcefully support these initiatives. (Gustavsson et al., 2011: 720)

The quantification of the burden of 'living with disease' generated grids of epidemiological visibility through which these brain disorders gained a new-found prominence in developed countries, underpinning demands for increased political action and funding for research. But in addition, estimates of the burden in low- and middle-income countries, as in the regular WHO reports, formed a crucial rhetorical underpinning for those seeking to promote intervention on mental disorders in those regions:

Depression is the leading cause of disability as measured by Years Lived with Disability (YLDs) and the fourth leading contributor to the global burden of disease in 2000. By the year 2020, depression is projected to reach second place in the ranking of Disability Adjusted Life Years (DALYs) calculated for all ages, both sexes. Today, depression already is the second cause of DALYs in the age category 15–44 years for both sexes combined. (WHO, cited in Reddy, 2010: 1)

As a result, from a virtual absence in global health priority setting agendas, Prince et al. described a "recent rapid increase in the visibility of the [global mental health] field":

> About 14% of the global burden of disease has been attributed to neuropsychiatric disorders, mostly due to the chronically disabling nature of depression and other common mental disorders, alcohol-use and substance-use disorders, and psychoses. Such estimates have drawn attention to the importance of mental disorders for public health ... [Still] the burden of mental disorders is likely to have been underestimated because of inadequate appreciation of the connectedness between mental illness and other health conditions. (2007: 859)

These arguments led to the development of a powerful movement to address "the grand challenge in global mental health" (Collins et al., 2011) focused on schizophrenia, depression, epilepsy, dementia, alcohol dependence and other mental, neurological and substance-use disorders which are now thought to constitute 13 per cent of the total global burden of disease. As the Movement for Global Mental Health gained traction, some began to argue that mental health should be recognized as the most important challenge for global health.[11] Indeed, some went further. Vigo et al., for example, argued that, if the estimates were corrected in five problem areas – overlap between psychiatric and neurological disorders; the grouping of suicide and self-harm as a separate category; conflation of all chronic pain syndromes with musculoskeletal disorders; exclusion of personality disorders from disease burden calculations; and inadequate consideration of the contribution of severe mental illness to mortality from associated causes – "the global burden of mental illness accounts for 32.4% of years lived with disability (YLDs) and 13.0% of disability-adjusted life years (DALYs) ... Our estimates place mental illness a distant first in global burden of disease in terms of YLDs, and level with cardiovascular and circulatory diseases in terms of DALYs" (2016: 171).

So is there an 'epidemic'?

Let us be clear: numbers are political. Numbers are seldom, if ever, merely collected, train-spotter style. Numbers are assembled to be used in arguments – to make arguments, to try to settle arguments, sometimes in an attempt to depoliticize a disagreement by turning it into a technical question, more often to politicize something that has, in someone's eyes, not got the attention it deserves. Look how many suffer, look how many die: it is a scandal. Someone must be culpable for ignoring it, someone must be held responsible, or to assume responsibility, for doing something about it. When psychiatric researchers 'do the math' in such arguments – mental illness versus cancer, mental illness versus HIV . . . – it is not always an edifying spectacle as each group musters and organizes the evidence for the importance of 'its condition' to argue for more funding, more research, more attention. The ambition of the researchers does not depend on the precise figures – it is to force home to policymakers, research funders, pharmaceutical companies, educators and indeed the public that there is a genuine need for urgent action to pay attention to a very large amount of untreated illness that is not only causing individual misery and many related familial and social difficulties, but is also a heavy cost on economies, in both developed and less developed nations. We might adapt the term introduced by Howard Becker (1963) for this kind of labour: these advocates are 'moral entrepreneurs', not in the sense of crusading for public and political action to address a form of deviant conduct that outrages their own moral principles, but in the sense of seeking to highlight a wrong or an injustice to a group of persons that *should* create moral outrage, and demanding that those in authority direct their attention, their policies and their funds to try to rectify it.

But to say that numbers are political, and are mobilized in the service of moral objectives, is not to say that they are untrue.[12] As William Alonso and Paul Starr point out in the Introduction to their edited volume *The Politics of Numbers*, acts of quantification are 'politicized' not in the sense that they are corrupt, though they may be, but because "political judgments are implicit in the choice of what to measure, how to measure it, how often to measure it, and how to present and interpret the results" (1987: 3). Further, to quote Starr, while "the characteristics of people are myriad and subtly varied", statistical systems, such as the ones we have been discussing, reduce complexity, incorporating this myriad into a single domain and, very often, generating a single number that will appear in headlines, in speeches and in reports (1987: 40). In the process, they shape our images of our society through the reality they seem to disclose, and in this and many other cases, they frame and highlight certain domains as problems requiring attention, paradoxically simultaneously *depoliticizing* it, making it appear as simply a recognition of an objective reality, not the subjectivity of a political choice. And in a present in which statistics have become indispensable to government, they not only create a domain that requires government, but also create a means of judging success and failure.

So we should treat the numbers with care. And this is especially the case when, as with so many of the estimates of the prevalence of disorders that I have discussed here, the numbers do not include those who have sought medical attention for their mental distress, but only those whom experts believe could, would and should be included as suffering from a diagnosable disorder, if only they were picked up by medical personnel, if only they were diagnosed correctly. This leads us to a further hard question: how shall we distinguish a mental disorder from ordinary variations in human mood, emotion, cognitions and desires? How shall we 'diagnose' those who are suitable cases for treatment? If mental disorders exist, how shall we know them?

Before we turn to that question, we need to set the scene by asking another – one that is raised by many critics of our present social and political arrangements. Is there something in our current social, economic and political system that is leading so many of our fellow citizens to the forms of distress that are diagnosed as mental disorders? In other words, is 'neoliberal capitalism' at the root of the 'epidemic' that these numbers seem to reveal? This is our next hard question.

3

Is It All the Fault of Neoliberal Capitalism?

I want to argue that it is necessary to reframe the growing problem of stress (and distress) in capitalist societies. Instead of treating it as incumbent on individuals to resolve their own psychological distress, instead, that is, of accepting the vast privatization of stress that has taken place over the last thirty years, we need to ask: how has it become acceptable that so many people, and especially so many young people, are ill? The 'mental health plague' in capitalist societies would suggest that, instead of being the only social system that works, capitalism is inherently dysfunctional, and that the cost of it appearing to work is very high.

Fisher, 2009: 19

Neoliberalism is creating loneliness. That's what's wrenching society apart. What greater indictment of a system could there be than an epidemic of mental illness? Yet plagues of anxiety, stress, depression, social phobia, eating disorders, self-harm and loneliness now strike people down all over the world. The latest, catastrophic figures for children's mental health in England reflect a global crisis. There are plenty of secondary reasons for this distress, but it seems to me that the underlying cause is everywhere the same: human beings, the ultrasocial mammals, whose brains are wired to respond to other people, are being peeled apart ... Though our wellbeing is inextricably linked to the lives of others, everywhere we are told that we will prosper through competitive self-interest and extreme individualism ... Of all the fantasies human beings entertain, the idea that we can go it alone is the most absurd and perhaps the most dangerous. We stand together or we fall apart.

Monbiot, 2016

We have known, at least since the birth of social medicine in the nineteenth century, that there are social determinants of ill health

(Rosen, 1974). Through the pioneering work of Michael Marmot and many others, it is now beyond doubt that these social conditions – not just inadequate diet, polluted water and bad sanitation, but also poverty, unemployment, social isolation, insecurity, inequalities in status, power and control – affect mental health as much as physical health (Marmot and Bell, 2012). Indeed, Marmot begins his compelling book *The Health Gap* (2015) with an anecdote about his experience in psychiatry in the 1960s. A senior psychiatrist working in outpatients is confronted with a depressed woman who cries every day and feels life is not worth living. She explains that her alcoholic husband has started to beat her again, her daughter is pregnant, her son is in prison – and much more. The psychiatrist tells the woman to stop taking the pills she is currently on, prescribes some different medication, and sends her on her way. That is all. For Marmot, "It seemed startlingly obvious that her depression related to her life circumstances" and it was not enough for the psychiatrist to say – as he did – that there was little he personally could do about that; it was not only that we "should be paying attention to the causes of her depression", but there *is* something that can be done about those causes (2015: 2). Sadly, more than half a century on, this anecdote reflects a reality that is repeated hundreds if not thousands of times a day, in the Global North and increasingly in the Global South. No wonder, then, that Marmot ends the Introduction to his book with a call to action, quoting the Chilean poet Pablo Neruda: "Rise up . . . against the organisation of misery" (2015: 21).

So do the figures on the prevalence of mental distress, however it is categorized, reflect the personal consequences of the 'organization of misery' that characterizes the political management of so many societies in our contemporary world? We know from many empirical studies, especially those in low- and middle-income countries, that there are consistently strong associations between poverty – in particular, food insecurity, poor housing, financial stress and similar indicators of a precarious and demanding form of life – and 'common mental disorders' (Lund et al., 2010). The WHO's 2014 report, *Social Determinants of Mental Health*, written by a group that included Marmot,[1] makes these points forcefully. The report points to systematic reviews which consistently show that common mental disorders such as depression and anxiety "are distributed according to a gradient of economic disadvantage across society" (Campion et al., 2013), and that in low- and middle-income countries there was a consistent relation between common mental disorders and poverty (Lund et al., 2010).

As the report also recognizes, these studies raise important questions about how to define and measure poverty, and which dimensions are most significant (Lund, 2014; Burns, 2015). Education, food insecurity, housing, social class, socioeconomic status and financial stress all exhibit a relatively consistent and strong association with common mental disorders, while other simpler variables, such as income and employment, were more equivocal. Nonetheless, the fundamental finding – "that the poor and disadvantaged suffer disproportionally from common mental disorders and their adverse consequences" (WHO, 2014: 16) – is confirmed by many other studies dating back to the early years of this century, both in low resource settings (Patel et al., 2010; Patel and Kleinman, 2003; Fryers et al., 2003) and in countries in the Global North (Fryers et al., 2005).

Key to the analysis in the WHO report is the idea of 'stressful experience' (2014: 13). The authors of the report recognize that stressful experiences do not always lead to mental disorders, and such disorders can occur in the absence of such experiences. However, they point to research highlighting the relationships between mental disorders and "the level, frequency and duration of stressful experiences and the extent to which they are buffered by social supports in the community", and they suggest that those "lower on the social hierarchy" are more likely to be subject to such experiences, and have access to fewer buffers and supports (2014: 17–18). They particularly point to evidence on the importance of prenatal experiences and early life, the deleterious effects of stressors in early childhood on gene expression and neural mechanisms, and the consequences for poor physical and mental health of cumulative exposures to stressors over time, especially those arising from prolonged or frequent intense adversity (Shonkoff et al., 2012) – what has become known as 'toxic stress'.[2] The report suggests that such stress can be "buffered by social support provided by loving, responsive and stable relationships with a caring adult" (WHO, 2014: 18). It seems that the roots of mental disorder may begin even before birth, with adverse prenatal experiences if mothers-to-be are young, socially or economically disadvantaged, experiencing a hostile or violent environment or themselves suffering from mental health problems. And while schooling and home support throughout childhood can build 'emotional resilience', this too is less likely for children in families living in poverty and stressful circumstances: hence, the report authors argue that efforts to support poorer families, especially those where adults themselves are suffering poor mental health, will "help disrupt the intergenerational transfer of inequities" (WHO, 2014: 27).

It is easy to interpret these arguments as a reprise of earlier views on 'the cycle of deprivation' now rewritten in neural terms. The idea of the intergenerational transmission of social problems has a long history,[3] but it was reactivated in the UK in a 1972 speech by the then Secretary of State for Social Services, Sir Keith Joseph, in which he used this phrase and went on to ask: "Why is it that, in spite of long periods of full employment and relative prosperity and the improvement in community services since the Second World War, deprivation and problems of maladjustment so conspicuously persist?" This question was answered with reference to the personal, parental and cultural characteristics of the families whose children themselves went on to a life of deprivation marked by high levels of crime, and mental and social pathologies (Welshman, 2007). In the United States, the idea of a 'cycle of disadvantage' that began in early childhood and led to the reproduction of poverty, disadvantage, low school achievement and associated social problems took shape in the 1960s, as part of President Lyndon Johnson's so-called War on Poverty. A panel of experts developed a programme focused specifically on the needs of disadvantaged preschool children, which "became the blueprint for Project Head Start [launched in 1965] designed to help break the cycle of poverty by providing preschool children of low-income families with a comprehensive program to meet their emotional, social, health, nutritional, and psychological needs".[4]

In the 1970s, the view of many who researched and debated these issues was that these arguments about the transmission of poverty and deprivation across the generations led, in fact, to policies directed at poor families themselves rather than at the social conditions that thrust them into poverty (Wedge and Prosser, 1973; Rutter and Madge, 1976; Deacon, 2003). While the 2014 WHO report does lay emphasis on the importance of pregnancy, early childhood and family life to "give every child the best possible start", it clearly seeks to go beyond the idea of the family as the primary site of intervention: its first key message is: "Mental health and many common mental disorders are shaped to a great extent by the social, economic and physical environments in which people live." The report musters a compelling array of evidence to show that actions are required across the life course at the level of both communities and countries, including "environmental, structural and local interventions" which will "not only prevent mental disorders but also promote mental health in the population" (WHO, 2014: 8).

But if it has long been true that people are made sick by the conditions under which they have to make their lives, is there something about our present situation that is driving more and more of us, not just in the wealthy West, or the Global North, but also in less developed countries of the Global South, into states of anxiety, stress, depression, social phobia, eating disorders, self-harm, suicide . . .? What is it in our current 'organization of misery' that could be to blame? Could it be because of the rise of policies in so many regions of the world that seek to limit state expenditure, to transfer provisions of everything from health services to old age pensions to the private 'for profit' sector, to deregulate the economy, to celebrate the free market and competition, and – crucially – to promote the ethics of individualism, entrepreneurialism and relentless self-advancement? Is *neoliberalism* to blame?

Our unhappy present

It certainly seems to be the case that the diagnosis of the so-called 'common mental disorder' is on the rise; in the UK, surveys and reports show considerable increases in recent years. A study by Barr et al. (2015) of the prevalence of individuals aged 18–59 reporting mental health problems in the Quarterly Labour Force Survey[5] showed that there had been a significant increase since 2008, that the pervasive inequalities between those with low and high levels of education widened over this period and that the increases were greatest in those who were unemployed. On the basis of statistical analysis of the trends, Barr et al. ruled out the effects of decline in wages or unemployment itself, and concluded that the overall picture was one in which there was "a large increase in the proportion of the working age population facing the multiple disadvantages of being out of work, having a low level of education and reporting a mental health problem", which, they suggested, might well be linked to changes in welfare and austerity policies implemented since 2010 (2015: 329).

Increases in mental health problems in the UK were widely publicized in September 2016, when the *Guardian* ran an article entitled 'Mental illness soars among young women in England' reporting on an official study that has been carried out for the National Health Service (NHS) every seven years from 1993. This found that "12.6% of women aged 16–24 screen positive for PTSD, 19.7% self-harm and 28.2% have a mental health condition" – all of these having increased greatly for women, but at a lower rate for men, between 2007 and 2014.[6] We might blame some of this rise on the problematic status of psychiatric diagnosis that I discuss elsewhere in this book, and on the increased willingness of people to frame distress in this way. The authors noted that this was a problem when it comes to interpreting results of this sort. But even supposing that the actual increase in mental distress in women is half of that reported, these results suggest that something consequential has happened in the lives and circumstances of young women over the seven-year period in question. In this particular case, many commentators did not 'blame austerity' or neoliberalism, but pointed to sexual violence, childhood trauma and the pressures of social media, all of which might be thought to be greater for young women than for young men.

More generally, the NHS study also reported that since 1993 when the survey was first conducted, the proportion of the overall population with a common mental disorder (CMD) had risen from 6.9 per cent of 16–64-year-olds in 1993 to 7.9 per cent in 2000, then to 8.5 per cent in 2007 and to 9.3 per cent in 2014: overall, "one adult in six had a common mental disorder: about one woman in five and one man in eight. Since 2000, overall rates of CMD in England steadily increased in women and remained largely stable in men" (McManus et al., 2016: 8). Of course, one could identify many potential social causes of these increases: while most of those who speak of 'neoliberalism' date its emergence to the closing decades of the twentieth century, 2008 is often cited as the start of the 'financial crisis' that led to the UK governments and many others in Europe and the United States cutting welfare and other state services, and introducing 'an age of austerity'.[7] Thus, tellingly, the study also found that most mental disorders "were more common in people living alone, in poor physical health, and not employed. Claimants of Employment and Support Allowance (ESA), a benefit aimed at those unable to work due to poor health or disability, experienced particularly high rates of all the disorders assessed."[8] Indeed, one person in eight receiving ESA screened positive for bipolar disorder, a third for attention deficit hyperactivity disorder (ADHD), and almost half of people in this category had attempted suicide at some point.

Studies in other countries also seem to show that anxiety, depression and the use of psychiatric medication is on the increase, at least in some groups. As far as depression is concerned, as early as 1989, Klerman and Weissman reviewed a number of large epidemiological and family studies carried out in the United States, Sweden, Germany, Canada and New Zealand using similar diagnostic instruments, and found "an increase in the rates in the cohorts born after World War II; a decrease in the age of onset with an increase in the late teenaged and early adult years; an increase between 1960 and 1975 in the rates of depression for all ages; a persistent gender effect, with the risk of depression consistently two to three times higher among women than men across all adult ages . . . and the suggestion of a narrowing of the differential risk to men and women due to a greater increase in risk of depression among young men" (1989: 2220). While they do not wish to disregard genetic factors, Klerman and Weissman point, somewhat inconclusively, to a range of potential environmental and cultural factors that might be involved.

On the basis of a survey of adults in the United States conducted in 1988 and 2000, Twenge (2015) found that, despite some increases in reports of depressive symptoms, such as feeling everything was an effort, there were no significant differences in the numbers of adults reporting that they felt depressed. However, as we will see in more detail in chapter 6, the following decade saw a huge increase in the use of the so-called 'antidepressant' drugs across all the OECD (Organisation for Economic Co-operation and Development) countries, from Korea, through France, Germany and Spain, to Iceland, although with very large differences between them. The quantity of antidepressant prescribing varies widely between countries, for example, in 2010, when more than six times as many antidepressants per person were prescribed in Iceland than in Estonia. And while the United States is not included in the OECD analysis, the National Center for Health Statistics reported that 11 per cent of Americans aged 12 and over were taking antidepressant medication in 2008, and that antidepressant prescriptions were most frequent amongst persons aged between 18 and 44. Compared to the period from 1988 to 1994, the rate of antidepressant use in the United States among all ages had increased nearly 400 per cent by 2008 (Pratt et al., 2011).

As far as young people in the United States are concerned, Olfson and colleagues report that "[t]he percentage of youths receiving any outpatient mental health service increased from 9.2% in 1996–1998 to 13.3% in 2010–2012 . . . the absolute increase in annual service use was larger among youths with less severe or no impairment"; they also found that there were significant overall increases in the use of psychotherapy for youths, and in psychotropic medications, including stimulants (for the treatment of ADHD), antidepressants, and even antipsychotic drugs (2015: 2029).[9] Twenge and colleagues (2010) looked at 'real-time reports' of psychiatric symptoms in young people in the United States and found large generational increases in psychopathology among college students between 1938 and 2007 and among high school students between 1951 and 2002 on the MMPI-A (Minnesota Multiphasic Personality Inventory®-Adolescent). Five times as many of the current generation of young people scored above common cut-off points for psychopathology on these scales.

How should we account for these rising trends? Let us, for a moment, put to one side our doubts about diagnostic accuracy, and about the changes in the willingness of individuals to report symptoms or to code them in ways that make them candidates for a psychiatric diagnosis. If we take the example of the use of anti-depressants, we first run into the problem that there are very large variations between countries which do not seem to be related to variations in the numbers of persons with depressive symptoms, or the socioeconomic situation of the country in question. Instead, they may be related to variations in the health care services themselves, in the attitudes and prescribing practices of physicians, in the willing-ness of people to frame their symptoms as being in need of medical attention, or in social attitudes to mental health problems (Lewer et al., 2015). Perhaps we can also put this problem aside for now, given that everywhere we look, we see a rising trend, albeit at varying rates. Could that overall rise be related to sociopolitical or socioeconomic trends, such as the rise of austerity-type politics associated in some minds with 'neoliberalism'? Even if such an explanation is too general and oversimplistic, it seems clear that we cannot understand the rise in such conditions by starting our investigations with a search for something going on in 'the brain' and merely adding in 'the environ-ment' as a provoking or protective factor.

Unfortunately, this 'brain-first' view does shape a funding regime and a system of professional status that directs the efforts of the most able researchers towards neurobiology rather than to the exploration of the causal webs that start from the sociopolitical environment, and seeks to unravel the mechanisms by which they act on body and brain. This is not to argue for 'psychiatric exceptionalism' – quite the reverse. As with diabetes, hypertension, coronary disease or lung cancer, while these are indeed conditions of bodily tissues, it would be rash to claim that either causes or treatments can focus on those tissues alone. Even for severe mental disorders there is growing epidemiological evidence about the role of childhood adversity and trauma in the development of psychosis (Frissen et al., 2015; Varese et al., 2012; McGrath et al., 2017; Read et al., 2014). There are almost certainly biological and psychological mechanisms that trans-late such adversity and stress into severe distress and disorder. But rather than thinking of the consequences as 'brain disorders', which suggests that 'the brain' is primary, these conditions could equally well be called 'social adversity disorders'.

But if the role of adversity in the genesis of mental ill health is now well established, is 'social adversity' on the rise, and if so, why? As I have said, many critics blame 'neoliberalism'. They argue that the conditions that ail us are real, that mental illness is no myth: it is not as simple as it was in the 1960s, encapsulated in the slogan "do not adjust your mind, there is a fault with reality!" The contemporary epidemic of mental ill health, for today's critics, is a grim reality. But, they suggest, our understanding of this epidemic is framed in a way that misses the point because it locates the ailments within ourselves rather than in our societies. There are more radical and less radical versions of this argument. The most radical uses the rise of mental ill health to denounce the capitalist system in its neoliberal form and to argue for a radical reconstruction of our forms of life to accord more closely with the realities of who or what we humans are, as intrinsically social and cooperative beings; in the words of George Monbiot, in the same piece cited at the head of this chapter: "This does not require a policy response. It requires something much bigger: the reappraisal of an entire worldview."

There are also less radical versions of this argument, congenial to many social psychiatrists, that try to identify particular 'factors' or problems that correlate with raised rates of mental disorders. Many have framed those problems in terms of 'social capital' – a rather ill-defined term that, at the most general level, refers to the extent and strength of the social bonds of community and trust that bind individuals together; where 'social capital' is low, they suggest, common mental disorders are more prevalent. While, as we shall see, there are conceptual and empirical difficulties with social capital-based approaches, a related approach focuses more specifically on loneliness as a causal factor, and identifies some features of the neurobiology of loneliness that might be candidate mechanisms for its consequences for mental health (Cacioppo et al., 2014; Cacioppo and Patrick, 2008). Others blame childhood trauma, itself heavily linked to social disadvantage and hence distantly to socio-political questions, and – as in the Marmot report discussed above – many point the causal finger at childhood toxic stress (McEwen and McEwen, 2017; Shonkoff et al., 2012). In this chapter I will examine these arguments in some detail, focusing here largely on the debate in the Global North; in chapter 7, I will consider these arguments in a global context, in the course of my evaluation of the movement for 'global mental health'.

The factory of unhappiness

Critics sometimes suggest that it is easier to imagine the end of the world than it is to imagine the end of capitalism. Capitalism, in particular in its neoliberal version that stresses the key role of the market, competition and the ethic of individual striving for self-improvement and seeking only to maximize one's self-interest – or, in the words of Gary Becker, human capital – has been naturalized: it presents itself to us as an inevitable, unchangeable reality. We have witnessed the death of old-fashioned 'Fordist' capitalism, with its images of a job for life on the production line, the sociality of the factory or the office, the life course structured by the perpetual recurrence of childhood, adolescence, school, adulthood, marriage, employment, retirement, decline and death. In its place, we have seen the birth of a new world, described by Franco 'Bifo' Berardi as 'The Factory of Unhappiness' (2001).[10] This looks very much like the future imagined by Gilles Deleuze in his little essay 'Postscript on the Societies of Control' (1992). Work and life are now inseparable. The old distinctions – employed versus unemployed, work versus leisure, home versus office – fade away with casualization, zero hours contracts, the 'gig economy', 24/7/365 emails and so forth. Instability is the new normal, time itself seems to have lost its structure, as we are caught up in a cacophony of flows of information, in multiplicities of webs of communication, overlapping and competing demands with shorter and shorter timelines, demanding immediacy of attention. For Berardi, this transition from 'the social factory' to 'the factory of unhappiness' produces real and malign cognitive and emotional effects: the incessant flows of information that overwhelm the social brain, which, when coupled with the constant demands of attention and the wholesale marketization of desire, result in panic and depression.[11] In this experience, to which we give the name of autonomy, the soul is enslaved: every dimension of the human mind – language, creativity, affects – is trapped in the trick of self-enterprise, as it is mobilized to generate value; depression becomes a common experience, and one that is inevitably managed by psychiatric medication (Berardi, 2009).

This is also the world as portrayed by Christian Marazzi (2010), in which, as Mark Fisher summarizes, "post-Fordist workers are like the Old Testament Jews after they left the 'house of slavery': liberated from a bondage to which they have no wish to return but also abandoned, stranded in the desert, confused about the way forward. The psychological conflict raging within individuals cannot but have casualties" (2009: 35). For Marazzi, the bipolar lurches of capitalism, in which hyped-up bubbles of irrational exuberance give way to depressive come-downs, cannot but be reproduced in the wave of bipolar disorders of individuals.

For these cultural critics of capitalism, the diagnostic data is not subject to doubt, nor is the reality of the distress that it charts. Thus, for example, for Fisher "[i]t goes without saying that all mental illnesses are neurologically instantiated, but this says nothing about their causation. If it is true, for instance, that depression is constituted by low serotonin levels, what still needs to be explained is why particular individuals have low levels of serotonin. This requires a social and political explanation; and the task of repoliticizing mental illness is an urgent one." Until that time, "[c]onsidering mental illness an individual chemico-biological problem has enormous benefits for capitalism . . . it provides an enormously lucrative market in which multinational pharmaceutical companies can peddle their pharmaceuticals (we can cure you with our SSRIs [specific serotonin reuptake inhibitors])" (2009: 41).

In these societies shaped by neoliberalism, inequalities of income, of capital and of forms of life grow ever steeper. While the richest 1 per cent live as if on another planet, the majority may delude themselves with entrepreneurial fantasies of affluence, pleasure and escape through work, or through luck in the lottery, but actually experience a world of debt and precariousness, while at the same time being bombarded by solicitations to buy, choose or gamble, in order to improve themselves via consumption. We are overwhelmed by information overload. There is no privacy any more, advertising has infiltrated "its visual and auditory messages in every inch of our visual space and every second of our time. The diffusion of screens in public spaces (railway stations, airports, city streets and squares), is an integral part of this abusive occupation . . . Everywhere, attention is under siege . . . A cognitive space overloaded with nervous incentives to act: this is the alienation of our times" (Berardi, 2009: 108)

However hyperbolic, most of us who live in the Global North, and increasingly in rapidly capitalizing countries such as China, can recognize something in that picture that resonates with our own experiences. In a more mundane vein, other critics also argue that neoliberalism is responsible for our current mental malaise. Under neoliberalism, they argue, the social protection obligations of welfare states have been degraded, their agencies outsourced to private companies or not-for-profit organizations, social security and social benefits criticized for encouraging welfare dependency, restricted and made dependent on a complex bureaucracy of assessments and tests designed to encourage the ethic of work. Normality has been reconceptualized as a desire for individual success to be achieved through personal striving. Thus Phil Thomas, a former NHS consultant psychiatrist, long an ally of radical critics of psychiatry,[12] links current increases in mental ill health to an attack on benefit claimants under neoliberal economic policy intensified by the banking crisis of 2008. He argues that an increasingly authoritarian regime coerces those with mental health problems through techniques such as Work Capability Assessments to seek low-paid work or unsuitable jobs based on zero hours contracts, reframing individual unemployment as a psychological problem of faulty attitudes and benefit dependency, driving many to increasing despair and even suicide (Thomas, 2016). On the one hand, individuals seek mental health support in the form of pharmaceuticals or therapy to enhance their capacities to improve themselves or to cope with the seemingly personal inadequacies that inhibit their self-improvement. On the other, those forms of life and those beliefs that depart from these market logics of and for personhood are pathologized, individualized, responsibilized, medicalized and treated with psychiatric drugs. If this was not bad enough, it is the most marginalized – the poor, racial and ethnic minorities, immigrants and refugees – who experience both the oppressive social conditions and the worst forms of coercive pharmaceuticalized intervention that individualizes, biologizes and medicalizes their distress (Moncrieff, 2006; Esposito and Perez, 2014; Brown and Baker, 2012).

While these accounts of the mental health consequences of neoliberalism are often weakened by exaggeration and overgeneralization – especially in the blanket use of 'neoliberalism' as a term of description, explanation and critique (Venugopal, 2015) – I find myself in agreement with the core of the argument. The evidence supports the conclusion that much contemporary mental ill health in the Global North has its roots in increasingly unequal societies and in the rise of governmental strategies to reduce the size and scope of welfare provisions, to promote the idea that individuals thrive best when they are encouraged to improve themselves through work, and to maximize their quality of life through consumption. This is coupled with other developments, some recent, such as the competitive online childhood world created by social media, some longstanding, such as the increasing levels of loneliness in large urban conurbations – a condition that the social neuroscientist John Cacioppo has long studied, and that I discuss in a later section of this chapter (Cacioppo et al.,

2014). These developments are amplified by some of the forces that I discussed in the previous chapter – the increasing discussion of mental health problems in the media, the encouragement to 'speak out' about mental ill health and the promotion of a language in which to do so, and the education of professionals from general practitioners and social workers to university lecturers to 'recognize' the signs of mental health problems in those they deal with. Together, these sociopolitical and ethical dynamics are, on the one hand, increasing levels of distress experienced by many who are at the sharp end of welfare state retrenchment, and, on the other, increasing the willingness of individuals, and of professionals, to place that distress under the description of mental ill health, and to give it a psychiatric diagnosis.

Social capital

If the pathogenic effects of neoliberalism lie not only in its material consequences for the worse off, but also in its celebration of individualism and autonomy, is it the case that the reverse is actually good for one's mental health? This question has led many social psychiatrists to explore the possible links between mental health and 'social capital'.[13] Pierre Bourdieu introduced this term in the 1980s, arguing that it was not possible to account for the structure and functioning of the social world unless the centrality of capital is reintroduced, but that capital must not be restricted to the form recognized by economic theory.

> Social capital is the aggregate of the actual or potential resources which are linked to possession of a durable network of more or less institutionalized relationships of mutual acquaintance and recognition – or in other words, to membership in a group . . . – which provides each of its members with the backing of the collectivity-owned capital, a 'credential' which entitles them to credit, in the various senses of the word. These relationships may exist only in the practical state, in material and/or symbolic exchanges which help to maintain them. They may also be socially instituted and guaranteed by the application of a common name (the name of a family, a class, or a tribe or of a school, a party, etc.) and by a whole set of instituting acts designed simultaneously to form and inform those who undergo them.[14]

A similar idea was developed by James Coleman, initially in an article entitled 'Social Capital in the Creation of Human Capital'

(1988). For Coleman, social capital is a quality embodied in relations among a network of persons: it is composed of obligations to others, and expectations that things done for others will be in some sense repaid. Social capital thus inheres in levels of trustworthiness among participants in a network within a social system: the sharing of information that facilitates action, together with the existence of norms of conduct that one should forgo self-interest and act in the interests of the collectivity. These norms are reinforced by such things as social support, status and honour. In short, then, for Coleman, social capital is the simple idea that individuals benefit in a range of ways from their membership of a network of trust, material and symbolic exchange, and also from the expectations, beliefs and actuality of reciprocity amongst others.

Now, of course, being a sociological concept, this simple idea of social capital has been subject to criticism, refinement, subdivision and general complexification. Thus we find the distinction, sometimes attributed to Robert Putnam, between 'bonding' social capital, which exists within homogeneous groups – Putnam suggests criminal gangs are an example – and 'bridging' social capital, which brings together those from heterogeneous social groups, such as choirs and – as in the example used in the title of Putnam's well-known text (1995) – bowling clubs.[15] Others introduce different subdivisions. 'Linking' social capital refers to connections with officials and authorities of various forms. 'Structural' social capital arises from the location of networks within a social system or social structure, and allocates different powers and capacities to those within that network. 'Cognitive' social capital refers to the psychological dimensions of values, attitudes and beliefs that predispose individuals to reciprocity and trust, or arise from such relations. And so on. Unsurprisingly, many scholars now conclude that the term is so vague, with so many varied and incompatible definitions, that its analytical usefulness is limited.

That said, if we sidestep this scholarly confusion and critique, it might seem obvious that, in the face of so much contemporary emphasis on individual responsibility for one's fate – and indeed for one's health – we should instead stress the salutary consequences of the fundamental embeddedness of individuals in interpersonal and social networks, and the importance of relations of trust, reciprocity and social support. The idea of social capital as protective, as mitigating the consequences of distress and enhancing recovery from such distress, seems common sense. Surely, we are 'better together' – psychiatrically as well as politically. But when one starts to think about this more deeply, sadly things get complicated. Perhaps, as Kawachi and Berkman (2001) suggest, strong social ties are only beneficial for mental health when an individual is under stress. Or perhaps social ties may be beneficial, not in themselves, but when they support beneficial health-related behaviour such as exercise, or stopping smoking and other forms of self-care, and of course strong social ties to those with other values may encourage exactly the opposite. Or maybe it is not so much the real existence of strong social ties, but individuals' *beliefs* that there are such social ties and social supports that reduce the stress arising from some adverse event. Or perhaps social ties can work in paradoxical ways: for example, women's supposed propensity for intimate relations may lead to a kind of 'contagion of stress' so they will suffer more from other people's problems – and, reciprocally, widowhood or isolation in old age may have a worse effect on them.

Kawachi and Berkman also point to other contradictory effects of strong social networks. They cite Brown and Harris (1978), who, in their classic study of the mental health of women in communities in the Outer Hebrides, seemed to show that the higher the level of participation of women in traditional community life, the lower their rate of depression but the higher their rate of anxiety: high demands for conformity lead to anxiety among those who do not conform to the values of their community. And, of course, as Kawachi and Berkman point out, the kinds of personal networks identified by researchers on the role of social capital are always embedded in, shaped by and dependent on wider social and structural forces. So while we know there is a relationship between 'social capital' and mental health – if we think of it simply in terms of the strength of ties among individuals, both actual and perceived – it is clear that this is not always beneficial to the mental health of those so embraced.

When Astier Almedom of the Department of Biology at Tufts University reviewed the evidence on social capital and mental health in 2005, the situation was much the same. A host of authors had proposed the importance of social capital for mental health (McKenzie et al., 2002; Dannenberg et al., 2003; Henderson and Whiteford, 2003; Jackson, 2003; Kelleher, 2003; Saegert and Evans, 2003; Sartorius, 2003; Muntaner, 2004) as had others concerned with the wider issues of poverty, health and social exclusion (Wilkinson, 1996; Kawachi et al., 1999; Muntaner et al., 2000, 2001; Edwards et al., 2001; Krishna, 2002; Carlson and Chamberlain, 2003; Pearce and Davey Smith, 2003). However, it seemed the debate "has been marked by polarized political undertones and mixed philosophical undertones" (Almedom, 2005: 944) and the results of empirical research had been confused, not just by the various subdivisions I have described above – bonding, bridging, linking, cognitive – but by the use of different definitions and different measuring instruments, and a certain naivety in trying to measure 'social capital' "in isolation from the political and historical context of any given society" (Almedom, 2005: 946).

While all agree that humans thrive more in groups than in isolation, social ties may constrain as well as support, there may be trade-offs between strong stable ties and weak and flexible ties (Granovetter, 1973), and researchers may be using the term to refer to macro level and structural relations or to micro level and individualized psychological relations. All in all, by 2005, it seemed that the field had not overcome these conceptual and operational issues in relation to social capital, and the picture was even more confused because of the variety of dimensions of mental health that had been studied. After reviewing a dozen studies, and identifying challenges to social capital-based accounts from power relations, poverty, unemployment and wider sociopolitical factors, as well as from multiple methodological problems, Almedom's conclusion was exhortatory rather than conclusive – more and better interdisciplinary research was needed "to unravel mechanisms whereby social capital and mental health might be meaningfully associated" (2005: 943).

A basically similar conclusion was reached by another systematic review published in the same year. While there was strong evidence for an inverse relationship between individual cognitive social capital and common mental disorders – that is to say, those diagnosed with depression, anxiety and the like tended to have weaker feelings of reciprocity or trust in others as measured by questions and statements such as "Generally speaking, would you say that most people can be trusted?" or "You can't be too careful in dealing with people" – the direction of causality and the mechanisms of this relation were unclear, and overall the diversity of methods and definitions presented a confusing picture and certainly one that was not strong enough to inform the development of "specific social capital interventions to combat mental illness" (De Silva et al., 2005: 619).

Over the next ten years, the situation remained more or less the same. There were many papers on social capital and mental disorder in different countries, based on different age groups and in relation to different diagnostic categories. But the only finding that seemed relatively consistent was that individual cognitive capital – measured by asking those with mental disorders about their feelings of trust – was inversely related to the diagnosis of a common mental disorder, and even here the direction of causality and the mechanisms involved were unclear (Ehsan and De Silva, 2015). In general, while the debate on social capital and health was, in Moore and Kawachi's (2017) words, "rich and productive" because of its conceptual and methodological diversity, that very diversity of definitions, methods and approaches made it difficult to extract any general lessons. It is tempting to argue that the malign psychiatric consequences of neoliberalism derive from its attempts to introduce marketized individual competition into all areas of life, and that trust, reciprocity and solidarity are protective, but the evidence for a causal relation is equivocal.

Loneliness

Perhaps we should turn the question on its head. For what is the inverse of feelings of trust, of the psychological sense that one has important relationships and bonds with others? It is loneliness. So, rather than starting with the rhetorically and sociopolitically powerful idea of social capital, we should perhaps start with the more empirically specifiable question of loneliness.

That is the focus of longstanding research by the 'founder' of social neuroscience John Cacioppo.[16] Actually, it seems that loneliness is not exactly what one might think: it is not a quantitative matter of the number of friends one has, or the number of social encounters in a given period. Loneliness is 'subjective'; it is a feeling of isolation, a matter of how one understands one's situation in the world. John Cacioppo, researching 'social connection' since the early 1990s, "quickly surmised that it was an individual's perceptions of the social situation that mattered most", and hence has focused his work on "perceived social isolation – loneliness", not only because of its intrinsic importance, but "as a model system for studying the role of the social world in human biology and behavior" (Cacioppo and Patrick, 2008). He traces the need for social connection, and the power of social connection, to hominid evolution, and suggests that this special importance of 'other human beings' is embedded in human 'neural wiring' and indeed that "the need to send and receive, interpret and relay increasingly complex social cues . . . drove the expansion of, and greater interconnectedness within, the cortical mantle of the human brain . . . The social environment affects the neural and hormonal signals that govern our behavior, and our behavior, in turn, creates changes in the social environment that affect our neural processes" (Cacioppo and Patrick, 2008: 11).

A major review conducted by Cacioppo with his partner Stephanie Cacioppo (who researches the neurobiology of love) identified multiple studies that have shown higher rates of morbidity and mortality in lonely versus non-lonely adults, and argued that loneliness is a risk factor for, and a predictor of, cognitive decline, as well as changes in psychological states that can contribute to morbidity and mortality, including depressive symptomatology, anxiety and hostility (Cacioppo et al., 2014). Feeling isolated is related to changes in many neurobiological and hormonal processes, for example increased hypothalamic pituitary adrenocortical (HPA) activity, alterations in gene expression, increased inflammation, raised blood pressure, diminished immunity and higher rates of metabolic syndrome. Feeling isolated, they argue, primes individuals for alertness to social threats, leading to negative thinking and negative relations with others.

On the basis of some rather questionable brain imaging experiments with functional magnetic resonance imaging (fMRI), they argue that loneliness is linked to enhanced perception of negative social stimuli, different responses to positive and negative social scenes suggesting a focus on self-preservation, and even to changes in the size of brain regions thought to be related to social networks. Experimental studies in animals, which obviously cannot address *perceived* social isolation, nonetheless show that social isolation leads to changes in brain structure and processes in those brain regions most linked to the functional demands of social living for that species. Social isolation has a range of deleterious effects on the rate of neurogenesis – the production of new nerve cells – in animals, and some hypothesize that this could also be true in humans. Others suggest that reduced neurogenesis is a factor in a number of mental disorders, especially depressive disorders. Social isolation in animals impairs recovery after brain injury. All in all, then, nonvoluntary isolation and perceived loneliness are bad for one's mental health, not simply because of the kinds of behaviour changes that are hypothesized in lonely individuals with low social capital, but because of the effects on the brain itself; it is the brain that is the key organ for social connectedness, and hence the key organ that is disrupted when an individual perceives a sustained lack of desired social connectedness.

Cacioppo ends his book on loneliness by considering the implications of his argument for our current sociopolitical situation. Leading up to his final pleas for increasing connectedness, he issues a damning verdict on the policies of the present, suggesting that the valorization of independence, working patterns that break up communities and reduce the possibility of social gatherings, housing developments that raze neighbourhood communities in the name of urban renewal: all this increased atomization can only be bad for us. "Feelings of isolation engender depression and hostility and impair self regulation. Nonetheless, many political leaders cut funds for community-building in favor of building larger prisons for those whose lack of self-regulation makes them hostile and out of control. The data tell us that loneliness seriously accelerates age-related declines in health and well being, yet the idea of promoting connection is rarely discussed alongside the heated issues of the cost of pharmaceuticals and other medical interventions necessary to deal with an increasingly lonely, isolated and ageing population" (Cacioppo and Patrick, 2008: 250–1).

Loneliness is pathogenic. Cacioppo has certainly made his case, and he and others in the popular press often speak of an epidemic of chronic loneliness, with surveys showing the percentage of Americans saying they regularly or frequently felt lonely rising from between 11 and 20 per cent in the 1970s and 1980s to between 40 and 45 per cent in 2010.[17] In the UK, the proportion of adults who live alone is on the increase. In 2011 the Office of National Statistics estimated that there were 7.1 million single-person households in England and Wales, slightly up from the previous decade, though only around 13 per cent of the UK population lives alone, while in Germany, Finland, Sweden and Denmark the figure is around 20 per cent. A survey reported by the Mental Health Foundation in 2010 estimated that one in ten people in the UK often feels lonely.[18] And in the UK in 2017, there was much media coverage of a publication by the Jo Cox Foundation that argued that loneliness was 'a giant evil of our time' and a 'social epidemic' affecting almost 20 per cent of the population, and which tried to quantify its personal, social and economic cost.[19]

However, it would be more difficult to argue that the kinds of policies Cacioppo and others deprecate for damaging collectivities and connectedness are either recent or connected with the rise of neoliberal economic and social policies. On the one hand, the competitive individualism Cacioppo castigates has long been central to American culture, and the regeneration that disrupts communities has been analysed at least since Peter Willmott and Michael Young's famous 1957 study of *Family and Kinship in East London*, which charted the way postwar slum clearance destroyed the rich informal networks of social support. On the other hand, responses to recent horrific incidents in the United Kingdom, from terrorist outrages to lethal fires destroying high rise blocks of social housing, have given the lie to a view of our present as consisting in isolated, self-centred individuals. On the contrary, these have demonstrated the continued existence of networks of mutual care and support among even the poorest and most marginalized. No doubt, loneliness is pathogenic, but its roots are longer and deeper than 'neoliberalism', and the informal networks and rituals of social interaction persist.

Stress

How about 'stress'? The Marmot report that I discussed at the start of this chapter suggested that 'stressful experiences' form the intermediary between the social determinants they identify and poor mental health. So is 'stress' the bridging mechanism that links these rising rates of disorders such as depression, anxiety and PTSD to today's changing character of socioeconomic and sociopolitical relations? There is a long history of research on stress and mental illness.[20] One of the key figures has been Sheldon Cohen, whose Laboratory for the Study of Stress, Immunity and Disease at Carnegie Mellon University focuses on "the possibility that our psychological states and traits may influence our immune systems in a manner that might alter out bodies' abilities to fight off infectious disease".[21] Cohen and Denise Janicki-Deverts begin their review of the changing distribution of psychological stress in the United States by pointing to the widespread belief that potentially stressful life events increase the risk of disease "when one perceives that the demands these events impose tax or exceed a person's adaptive capacity" and that "the perception of stress may influence the pathogenesis of physical disease by causing negative affective states (e.g., feelings of anxiety and depression), which then exert direct effects on physiological processes or behavioral patterns that influence disease risk" (2012: 1320). They report, on the basis of national surveys in 1983, 2006, and 2009, that overall stress levels did not change over those 25 years; however, the surveys did show that there were "greater stress-related health risks among women, younger adults, those of lower socioeconomic status, and [middle-aged, college educated white men in full time employment] potentially subject to substantial losses of income and wealth" (2012: 1320).

Note that 'stress' here – as with loneliness earlier – does not refer to some objective set of conditions – the fact of being unemployed, an employer who demands long hours of difficult labour, living in overcrowded and insanitary accommodation; stress, like loneliness, is a perception, a subjective state. And this takes us to the heart of a century-long debate about the nature, meaning and consequences of stress, for health in general, and mental health in particular. From Walter Cannon's (1914) initial formulations of the hormonal cascades generated in mammals in situations of threat, through Hans Selye's (1936, 1956) formulation of the stress response and the pathological consequences that follow if the adrenal cascades are sustained because of unrelieved insults and pressures on the body, through a host of research in the United States in the 1960s and 1970s, stress has been a favoured, yet controversial, name for the process by which social adversity is transformed into physical and mental ill health (this history is detailed in Jackson, 2013). And yet the very advantages of the capacious language of stress turned out to be its disadvantages. From the nineteenth century onwards, stress was widely invoked, both in everyday speech and in medical texts, to draw attention to what were thought to be the damaging health consequences of social changes and industrial developments: noise, speed, the smells of coal fires and refuse, the insecurity of work in mine and mill, and the crowds and throngs of the big cities. It seemed obvious that such stress could damage health, especially among the vulnerable, and even more so when combined with vicious conduct such as indulgence in alcohol, rich food or other vices of the flesh. Hence the mechanisms discovered by Cannon and those who came after him seemed ideal candidates for the relays between the outside and the inside, between the experiences to which people were increasingly exposed and their interior bodily and mental states. But the very versatility and intelligibility of the language of stress actually undermined its explanatory utility.

The original arguments by Selye and those who thought like him were that stress was a hormonal response to specific objective 'insults' on the body. On the basis of animal experiments, he argued that, whether such insults came from extreme heat or cold, the administration of toxic chemicals, or from excessive overcrowding, the response was the same – sustained overstimulation of the adrenal glands led to a cascade of other hormonal reactions which generated physical diseases and behavioural abnormalities. But was the same true of people? Apparently not. For human beings, stress was, it seemed, not objective, but a subjective response to particular objective circumstances. One person's stress, to be avoided, was another's excitement, to be actively sought out. The experience of crowds, noise and revelry might be wonderfully exciting for those who participate in a carnival or festival, incredibly distressing if experienced by a young woman on her own in a big city. Throngs are stressful, but so is isolation. Work is stressful, but so is unemployment. In short, everything could be stressful for some people at some times. Stress was, it seemed, not so much an objective factor, that could be measured in terms of density or decibels, but a subjective and variable form of experience, depending on one's culture, one's biography, one's disposition and one's personality. After dozens of sociological and anthropological investigations of stress, by the late 1970s, Amos Rapoport was probably speaking for most researchers on urban and environmental stress in humans, when he argued, in a special issue of *Urban Ecology* on 'quality of life' in 1978, that a subjective perception of particular urban features and cues modulated the stress relationship and that this depended on culture, context, norms, symbolism, the individual's own sense of control and much more (Rapoport, 1978).

It was in the light of such confusion that, John Mason remarked, in 1975, "Perhaps the single most remarkable historical fact concerning the term 'stress' is its persistent, widespread usage in biology and medicine in spite of almost chaotic disagreement over its definition" (1975: 6). However, research on the role of stress in mental ill health is once more at the forefront of what one might term 'social neurobiology'. Current research has argued that stress affects the immune system in a measurable fashion, and that variations in immune responses can be linked through plausible neurobiological pathways both to physical disorders and to mental ill health through modulating the HPA axis, formed by the connections between the three adrenal glands of the hypothalamus, the pituitary gland and the adrenal glands. Chronic stress – or what is often now termed 'toxic stress' – generates continued activation of the immune system, producing cytokines that act on other cells leading to behaviour changes, changes in the size of the amygdala, the medial-frontal cortex and other brain regions, and is associated with depression-like symptoms (Dantzer et al., 2008; Pariante and Lightman, 2008; van der Kooij et al., 2014; Sandi and Haller, 2015).[22]

Bruce McEwen has been one of the most tenacious researchers seeking to update the concept of stress in the context of contemporary developments in neuroscience and immunology (see McEwen and Lasley, 2002). As McEwen puts it in a paper entitled 'Brain on Stress: How the Social Environment Gets Under the Skin', the brain is "the central organ of stress and adaptation"; "Stress is a state of the mind, involving both brain and body as well as their interactions" (McEwen, 2012: 17180) and both the social and the physical environment get "under the skin" through the neuroendocrine, autonomic and immune systems, both in the course of early development and experience, which can help build resilience or can induce its opposite, and later in relation to health damaging and health promoting experiences across the life course. The brain both shapes what is perceived as stressful, and determines the consequences of that stress. Culturally shaped perceptions that one is in a stressful, pressured or threatening situation act on the structural plasticity of the hippocampus and other brain regions, notably the amygdala, the prefrontal cortex and the nucleus accumbens. "The growing recognition of the adaptive plasticity and stress vulnerability of the brain itself, which began with research on the hippocampus, now includes other brain regions such as the amygdala and prefrontal cortex and fear-related memories, working memory, and self-regulatory behaviors. The interactions between these brain regions during the biological embedding of experiences over the life course determines whether events in the social and physical environment will lead to successful adaptation or to maladaptation and impaired mental and physical health, with implications for understanding health disparities and the impact of early life adversity and for intervention and prevention strategies" (McEwen, 2013: 673).

McEwen argues that one key mechanism is epigenetic; that is to say, that stress produces these neurobiological changes by acting on gene expression. This normally produces adaptive change, but causes damage when stress is excessive or chronic, and, in McEwen's view, such 'toxic' stress has "implications for understanding health disparities and the impact of early life adversity and for intervention and prevention strategies" (2013: 673). There is a growing literature, focused in the United States, arguing that 'toxic stress' in infancy and childhood lies at the root of later problems in physical and mental health, and that this must be the focus of public health interventions (Shonkoff et al., 2012; Shern et al., 2016). McEwen, writing with his brother, the sociologist Craig McEwen, has recently used arguments about the effects of toxic stress in childhood, its epigenetic and psychological consequences, and its effects on corporeal and cerebral development, to try to explain why children of poor parents are more likely to be poor as adults than other children (McEwen and McEwen, 2017). However, especially given the level of structural inequality, discrimination, social exclusion and the like in the United States, many may feel that we do not need to resort to neurobiological explanations, even those that indict social inequality as the cause. There are more than adequate sociological accounts of the reproduction of poverty across the generations, and neurobiological explanations of poor school performance of children from poor families, however worthy and antireductionist, rather miss the point.

But rather than focusing on childhood in pathological families, as in the debates on the 'cycle of disadvantage' that I mentioned earlier in this chapter, could one refocus on toxic stress in the here and now, whether generated by the experience of austerity, unemployment, marginalization, work capability assessments and the like, or generated by the ultracompetitive world of social media, or intensified by the sense of isolation and the lack of genuine trustworthy relations with peers? Do stress and its consequences constitute the mechanism underlying rising trends in common mental disorders? What would a biopolitics look like that organized its analysis and interventions around the problem of stress and mental health? I shall return to this issue in my final chapter.

So is it all the fault of neoliberal capitalism?

I have already expressed my reservations about the blanket use of the term 'neoliberalism' as both description, explanation and critique. All the elements – critiques of the extended welfare state, concerns about dependency, policies of welfare austerity, ideologies and practices of responsibilization, individualization and the like – have a longer history and are part of many different rationalities of government (Rose, 1996a, 1996b, 2000). Further, proponents argue that the widespread adoption of policies that reduce the role of state, privatization, marketization, competition and so forth, coupled with globalization, have actually reduced global poverty, and hence, by extension, have reduced, not exacerbated, adversity.[23] But even the World Bank, the leading advocate of such policies, recognizes that the situation is more complicated (see also, for example, Kiely, 2007; Rudra and Tobin, 2017). Reporting in 2016, the World Bank argued that although nearly 1.1 billion people have moved out of extreme poverty since 1990, progress has been uneven. The reduction in poverty was mainly driven by China, Indonesia and India, but half the extreme poor still live in sub-Saharan Africa and the vast majority of the global poor, over half of whom are under the age of 18, live in rural areas, have limited access to education and are mostly employed in the agricultural sector: "It is becoming even more difficult to reach those remaining in extreme poverty, who often live in fragile contexts and remote areas. Access to good schools, healthcare, electricity, safe water and other critical services remains elusive for many people, often determined by socioeconomic status, gender, ethnicity, and geography. Moreover, for those who have been able to move out of poverty, progress is often temporary: economic shocks, food insecurity and climate change threaten to rob them of their hard-won gains and force them back into poverty."[24]

But while adversity remains widespread, we need to be sceptical about some of the diagnostic assumptions that underpin the global and national estimates of the prevalence of mental disorder made by psychiatrists. We need to be aware of the ways in which an individual's own perceptions and reports of their mental distress are shaped by the increasing availability and acceptability of the language of mental disorder. In addition, there are also many dimensions of adversity that have little to do with current economic or political policies. That being said, however, I think there are good arguments, supported by evidence, to suggest that poverty, injustice, precarious employment, marginalization, discrimination and the experience of severe adversity are bad for health, including mental health. The evidence supports the conclusion that as these dimensions of inequality increase, as they have under many political regimes over the last three or four decades, they are indeed throwing more and more of our fellow citizens into lives of misery, and generating the forms of mental distress – depression, anxiety, panic and 'post-traumatic' disorders – that are becoming more and more common. Such a conclusion, as I have pointed out, is supported by the WHO's 2014 report, *Social Determinants of Mental Health*. Thus, even if we do not recognize the characterization of our present as a 'factory of unhappiness', there is no doubt that the stresses created for those experiencing increasing adversity are likely to be exacerbated by the contemporary celebration of autonomy – an ethic that can only be a fiction for those who have no possibility of 'realizing their potential' by acts of choice in a social and economic marketplace.

While we may not fully agree with Bifo (Franco Berardi) in his portrayal of the pathogenic overload of cognitive space by attention-grabbing images and sounds, and despite the undoubted benefits of the internet in terms of communication and access to information, the communication overwhelms to which we are all subject, and the corrosive nature of much social media, which especially afflict the lives of young people, are undoubtedly bad for mental health. While the language of social capital is, in my view, too vague to capture the dimensions of our reality that can exacerbate or alleviate mental distress, I think it is also clear that isolation, the breakdown of trust and, increasingly, the loneliness of our current forms of life – where we are so often alone among throngs – all play their part. And, as I have suggested, some versions of the contemporary neurobiology of stress are beginning to trace out the complex biosocial dynamics by which these experiences of our present 'get under the skin'.

There is little if anything in contemporary mental health systems that even begins to recognize, let alone to address, these biopolitical determinants of mental disorder. To demand a radical change in the point of view of research into mental distress, and in the way we address mental distress in our societies, is not to demand the impossible. As Michael Marmot says, it is not only that we should be paying attention to the social causes of mental distress, it is also that many of those causes are made by humans and can be unmade by humans. There *is* indeed something that can be done about them: another psychiatry, one that plays a leading role in a different biopolitics, is possible.

4

If Mental Disorders Exist, How Shall We Know Them?

My liege, and madam / . . . since brevity is the soul of wit, / And tedious-ness the limbs and outward flourishes, / I will be brief: your noble son is mad: / Mad call I it; for, to define true madness. / What is't but to be nothing else but mad? / But let that go . . .

> William Shakespeare, Polonius to Gertrude, *Hamlet*,
> Act 2, Scene 2

[T]he doctor is not necessarily acting outside his proper scope if he attends to people who are not ill. Extension of the doctor's province has gone very far in psychiatry . . . He is nowadays often, and quite prop-erly, asked to investigate and treat disturbances of behaviour in children which can hardly be included within any warranted conception of illness . . . He may likewise investigate or treat criminals, drug addicts, prostitutes and sexual perverts. It may be that there is no form of social deviation in an individual which psychiatrists will not claim to treat or prevent – the pretensions of some psychiatrists are extreme. That time has not come, fortunately.

> Lewis (1967 [1953])

We have never been more aware of the arbitrary and constructed quality of psychiatric diagnoses, yet we have never been more dependent on them than now, in an era characterized by the increasingly bureaucratic management of health care and an increasingly pervasive reductionism in the explanation of normal, as well as pathological behaviour.

> Rosenberg (2006)

My title for this chapter is, of course, a version of the question made infamous by David Rosenhan in his paper 'On Being Sane in Insane Places': "[I]f sanity and insanity exist, how shall we know them?" (1973: 250).[1] Rosenhan's paper emerged in the midst of a controversy over the validity of psychiatric diagnosis that went back many decades. I have already touched on many of the problems of psychiatric diagnosis in earlier chapters; in this chapter I will address then directly.

Shakespeare's Polonius bears witness to the fact that debates over what it truly is to be mad go back centuries. But for present purposes we can date the start of the perplexities – in Anglo-American psychiatry at least – to the aftermath of the Second World War. Experience with the recruitment and discharge of military personnel in the Second World War seemed to show mental disturbances in very large numbers of people who had no previous encounters with psychiatry. Reflecting on that experience after the war, the US psychiatrist Karl Menninger came to the conclusion that "some people have some degree of mental illness at some time, and many of them have a degree of mental illness most of the time" (1965: 33).[2] Karl's brother William, who was appointed Director of the Neuropsychiatric Consultants Division of the Surgeon General at the outset of the war, took a similar view. He urged his fellow professionals to make every effort to spread psychiatric information to 'the average person' so that they can apply it to their own situation. He was aware that this would probably increase the number of patients who seek help from a psychiatrist, just as a campaign about cancer increases the number of patients who go to doctors about these problems. But, he believed, that was a small price to pay for the recognition that mental disorder was not a problem confined to the very few, but part of the experience of most, if not all, people (Menninger, 1947).

But if it really is the case that almost everyone is, in some way or other, and at some time or other, a suitable case for treatment, what is the role of diagnosis? The first definition of diagnosis in the *Oxford English Dictionary* is: "Determination of the nature of a diseased condition; identification of a disease by careful investigation of its symptoms and history; also, the opinion (formally stated) resulting from such investigation." On the one hand, diagnosis is to *differentiate* those who are diseased from those who are not. On the other, within the empire of disease, it is to identify *which* disease is present. A disease, in this view, is to be understood as a specific condition, and the role of diagnosis is to tell the doctor – and presumably the patient and anyone else who needs to know – precisely what that condition is. By the 1970s, where psychiatry was concerned, both dimensions of this diagnostic activity were subjects of controversy, perhaps even of crisis.[3]

On the one hand, more and more people were being diagnosed with psychiatric conditions and being referred for treatment. David Rosenhan's 'experiment' (1973) did indeed seem to show that psychiatrists were not very good at diagnosing sanity. He and seven other 'pseudopatients' were admitted to a number of different psychiatric hospitals in the United States, merely on the basis of claiming that they had heard voices, without falsifying anything else about their personal or psychiatric history, almost all with a diagnosis of schizophrenia, and, despite showing or reporting no other abnormal behaviours, were all eventually discharged with the diagnosis of 'schizophrenia in remission'. Critics argued that this confirmed the views of those like Thomas Scheff: diagnoses of mental disorder were not 'objective' assessments of an individual's mental state but were socially and contextually determined (Scheff, 1966). However, the response of most psychiatric experts was to say that these pseudopatients were unfortunate in encountering badly trained psychiatrists, and that, in most cases, it was actually quite difficult to get admitted to a psychiatric hospital. Nonetheless, Rosenhan's experiment added to the sense that psychiatrists were far too ready to make diagnoses on the basis of trivial evidence, and that, once a person was diagnosed as suffering from a psychiatric condition that diagnosis stuck with them for life, even if classified as 'in remission'.[4] Further, it seemed that even when a person thought to be mentally ill saw a specialist at the clinic, psychiatrists were rather bad at making reliable diagnoses – that is to say, they did not consistently agree on precisely what it was that a given patient was suffering from. Indeed, some studies showed that the probability of two psychiatrists agreeing on a diagnosis for a particular patient was often hardly better than chance (Beck, 1962).

It was not only the critics who were disturbed by this issue. Psychiatrists themselves were troubled by the lack of reliability in diagnosis, and government and health insurers were concerned that there seemed to be no way of defining the limits of who was a suitable case for treatment; or, in the case of the insurance companies, who was a suitable case for reimbursement. No wonder that, at the start of the book he published in the midst of the debate, *The Role of Diagnosis in Psychiatry* (1975), Robert Kendell quoted a remark made in 1893 by Daniel Hack Tuke: "the wit of man has rarely been more exercised than in the attempt to classify the morbid mental phenomena covered by the term insanity". Hack Tuke, whose great-grandfather founded the York Retreat for the care of the insane in 1796, went on to add that the results of such attempts at classification had been disappointing.

Kendell's view was that the situation in which psychiatry found itself almost a century later was much the same.

This was the context in which Anthony Clare, then a researcher at the Institute of Psychiatry and an honorary senior registrar at the Bethlem and Maudsley Hospitals, London, published *Psychiatry in Dissent: Controversial Issues in Thought and Practice* (1976).[5] Clare took a clinician's pragmatic view of diagnosis, arguing that "every diagnosis in general medicine and psychiatry is a hypothesis to be tested and refined. The practising psychiatrist is a clinician, that is to say someone who, in Feinstein's memorable phrase 'depends not on a knowledge of causes, mechanisms or names for diseases, but on a knowledge of patients'" (1976: xv; he is quoting Feinstein, 1967). The clinician, for Clare, is not obsessed with reducing a patient to a diagnostic label, but is an observer and organizer of clinical data, and indeed the astute clinician is perfectly aware that normality and madness – to use his terms – are not distinct and dichotomous states of mind, but "ends of a continuum . . . on which most of us find ourselves positioned in that grey and shady area between the two opposing poles" (1976: 32). Nonetheless, Clare believed that there were clear characteristics, such as disturbed streams of thought, thought possession or compulsion, and delusional thought, that are characteristic of mental illness. He believed that these could be identified in clinical practice, because the clinician is aware – or should be aware – that diagnosis is not an academic exercise but a hypothesis formed on the basis of careful observation and analysis during interactions with the patient, which is to be tested, refined or amended in the course of clinical practice.[6]

Later in this chapter we will consider the controversy around the development of the fifth edition of the APA's *Diagnostic and Statistical Manual of Mental Disorders*, published in 2013. Many practising clinicians, especially in Europe, espouse views similar to those of Clare and regarded the controversy over *DSM* with a kind of detached amusement.[7] Why all the fuss? A diagnostic manual in psychiatry is just a provisional map of the territory, a map of the kinds of troubles that psychiatrists work with in their practices.[8] It is a kind of 'rough guide' that will help the practitioner get oriented, maybe to read on the plane like those other 'rough guides' so beloved of tourists, but best put to one side when one is actually on the ground, that is to say, in the clinic. This very British position is attractive. It probably represents the views of most practising clinicians in the UK. It would probably be wise if it were to be widely adopted by everyone involved in mental health – policymakers, planners, epidemiologists, the WHO, pharmaceutical companies, the European College of Neuropharmacology, hospital record keepers, insurance companies, employers, researchers, patient groups and patients themselves. But, of course, it is rather disingenuous. Because diagnostic manuals are not merely passive descriptions – far from it.

Diagnostic manuals do things. They do more than describe a territory: they shape and configure it. They don't just 'sort things out'; they also link things together (Bowker and Star, 1999). While several different pathways intertwine in the history of psychiatric classification, the first diagnostic manuals of the modern type were created in the nineteenth-century asylums (Esquirol, 1838; Bucknill and Tuke, 1874). These asylums gathered together a heterogeneous group of individuals: voice hearers, those with delusions of grandeur or extreme religious beliefs, alcoholics, unmarried mothers, dementing elderly people, prostitutes, vagrants and many more. These people had little in common except for their violation of the web of norms that underpinned conceptions of civility and order in industrializing and urbanizing societies in the nineteenth century. In placing descriptions of all these figures within the same covers, in organizing their diverse ailments into a single system, the early diagnostic manuals implied that, despite their many differences, they were all suffering from the same kind of thing – mental disorders. Further, all these troubled individuals came under the care of a single authority figure – the doctor – implying that a medically trained person was the appropriate authority, both in terms of knowledge and in terms of power, to diagnose, treat and manage each of them.

Contemporary manuals, like the *DSM*, also mark out, shape and configure a territory for psychiatry to occupy. Today, this is not the asylum, but the territory of everyday life, or, as it is sometimes misleadingly termed, 'the community'. Like their predecessors, in placing all the heterogeneous figures that contemporary psychiatrists see – or believe they should see – within the same covers, within the same framework, they imply that they are all ailing from the same kind of thing, and that this is the kind of thing that a particular sort of person – a medically trained psychiatrist – can diagnose, treat and manage. And this, of course, was precisely the problem that psychiatrists found themselves with in the 1970s – indeed one that was already visible to Aubrey Lewis in the 1950s when he gave his lecture 'Health as a Social Concept' (1967 [1953]).

As we saw in the quote from his lecture at the head of this chapter, Lewis recognized that the psychiatrist was "often, and quite properly, asked to investigate and treat disturbances of behaviour in children which can hardly be included within any warranted conception of illness", and indeed worried that, given the pretensions of some psychiatrists, there might come a time at which "there is no form of social deviation in an individual which psychiatrists will not claim to treat or prevent – the pretensions of some psychiatrists are extreme". In 1953, his view was that that time had (fortunately) not yet arrived. But by the mid-1970s, it seemed to be approaching. Could one draw a boundary around the proper scope of psychiatry? This was surely one key role of diagnosis, and indeed it was one of the key objectives of the Task Force on Nomenclature and Statistics of the APA, which was beginning its work when Anthony Clare published *Psychiatry in Dissent*. In the half century that has elapsed since that publication, three solutions have been proposed to the 'problem' of psychiatric diagnosis. Each tried to deal with the failures of its predecessor, and each in its turn has failed. As we shall see, the solution adopted in *DSM-III* was grounded in the attempt to provide precise descriptive criteria to define the phenotype. When this solution seemed to be generating its own problems, a second solution was proposed, which sought objectivity and reliability, not in the phenotype, the observable symptoms, but in biological indicators of various sorts. This underpinned the search for biomarkers in physiological anomalies, in genetic sequences, in brain images. When, by around 2010, it became clear that, despite a huge research programme, this attempt to ground *DSM* classifications in objective biological markers had failed, a third solution to the problem of psychiatric diagnosis was proposed: we should give up on our existing classifications and find new ones by looking directly to the brain. Later in this chapter I will consider each of these in turn. In conclusion, I will consider a fourth solution, one that harks back to an earlier approach, pre-*DSM-III*, associated with the name of Adolph Meyer. This lightened the weight placed on diagnosis in favour of 'formulation'. But first, let us ask why diagnose at all, or, to put it another way, what do diagnoses do?

Diagnosis as a social phenomenon

It is easy to think that the main purpose of making a diagnosis is to identify the nature of the condition so that, if possible, one can identify and treat its causes or at least mitigate its harmful consequences. We also know that medical diagnoses have long had the function of organizing professional communication, education and research so that medics who use a particular diagnostic term can be assured that they are talking about the same thing, students can be educated about different diagnostic categories and taught the correct professional language to use, and researchers can carry out their various studies, confident that they know which disorder they are researching. But today, diagnosis – that is to say, the allocation of a name to a condition – has acquired many other functions for professionals and policymakers. We can start with listing ten:

1 A diagnosis is a condition of eligibility of an individual for treatment – if you have no diagnosis of pathology, there is no case for treating you.
2 In insurance-based regimes, a diagnosis is a condition of financial coverage of the cost of treatment.
3 For those who are employed, a diagnosis is a condition of legitimate absence from work.
4 For those who are unemployed, a diagnosis may be a condition for access to welfare payments.
5 For hospitals and medical establishments, a diagnosis is an organizing feature of patients' records and statistical overviews of their work, and these statistics often shape the allocation of funding from those who commission services for different conditions.
6 For lawyers, a diagnosis can be a condition for involuntary detention and treatment.
7 In the school system, a diagnosis may be the basis of allocation to special educational provision.
8 For epidemiologists, diagnostic categories are the very basis of their estimates of incidence and prevalence, and for their correlations of diagnoses with one another and with other social factors.
9 For planners of services, those estimates and the predictions based on them are the essential raw materials for their work.
10 For funders of research a diagnosis may delineate a problem that is really worthy of investigation, and for charitable organizations, it becomes 'their' diagnosis around which they organize.

It is relevant, then, to ask 'diagnosis for what?' and 'what kind of diagnosis is relevant for each purpose?'. For many of these professional and organizational purposes, an estimate of levels of impairment and capabilities is more relevant than a categorical label. Of course, as in the 'social model' of disabilities, levels of impairment and capabilities are inherently dependent on the social norms, expectations and conditions at particular times and places – but that is the reality within which patients and others have to live their lives. For other purposes, diagnosis in the clinical sense may also be irrelevant. For example, in the criminal justice system, a judgement of capacity, or of fitness to plead, is more relevant than diagnosis in assessing competence to stand trial, and an assessment of responsibility is more relevant than a diagnosis in determining culpability. Where epidemiological estimates are to be used for assessing the need for certain services or the direct and indirect costs of mental health problems, specific diagnoses are not much of a guide to service use or capacities for employment, and are likely to be misleading. As we saw in our discussion of Anthony Clare's approach, it is only since the 1970s that some have dreamed of a single system that could fulfil all these roles, as well as those of clinical judgement, professional communication and research. And, in the conclusion to this chapter, I will suggest that it is time to give up that dream.

Nonetheless, diagnosis, especially categorical diagnosis – the allocation of a particular name to a specific experience of illness – has crucial social and cultural characteristics that make it difficult to abandon altogether.[9] Diagnosis is deeply embedded in our contemporary notion of medical care. We have an expectation that a visit to the doctor will result in a diagnosis that, among other consequences, legitimates the ailment. Each category, and each array of categories, provides a language for speaking of our distress, making it thinkable in a way that also provides some kind of account of its nature, origins and likely implications. When a diagnosis is given, it reframes symptoms into a pattern that appears recognizable to both doctor and patient. For the doctor, this enables the patient's history to be organized into a narrative, which provides a shape for the past and an orientation to the future – it is performative. For the patient, who may be experiencing symptoms that are often diffuse and transient, who may be struggling with behaviours that can be seen as merely personal inadequacies, diagnosis reframes these troubles into an illness. The diagnosis enables a story to be created about it – what has led to it, what it is, how it will be treated, what the outcome might be, how it can be spoken about with family, friends, employers and others. No wonder patients and their families sometimes become attached to their diagnostic labels, and protest if for some reason they are eliminated altogether from the official psychiatric lexicon.[10] Sometimes even the most apparently devastating diagnoses – for instance, of early stage Alzheimer's disease – can thus provide a certain kind of relief. In non-psychiatric cases, a diagnosis of a medical condition usually – though not always – leads to a reduction in personal responsibility, the mutation of implied culpability into sympathy and compassion, and a reduction in stigma, although we know that this is not the case in psychiatry. It may open a pathway to effective treatment – although sadly, once again, this is not always the case with psychiatry.

Of course, sometimes those diagnosed do not find their diagnosis a relief, and do not wish to align their own understanding of their condition with that provided by medical authority. Psychiatry is not alone in generating such disputed diagnoses, but the contests in the area of mental disorder are often the fiercest. Some refuse to accept that there is anything wrong with their mind, their conduct or beliefs that require psychiatric treatment, a refusal that some psychiatrists consider itself to be a psychiatric symptom: 'lack of insight'.[11] For others, a psychiatric diagnosis seems a denial of their own account of the causes of their troubles – for instance, implying that their physical symptoms of 'Gulf War Syndrome' or 'Multiple Chemical Sensitivity' are 'all in the mind'. And psychiatric diagnoses may generate stigma, not just 'in the community' but also among professionals, in wards, clinics, day hospitals, where different diagnoses carry different moral values and elicit different responses from doctors, nurses and others (Sartorius, 2002). The diagnosis shapes the way in which care staff interpret speech, conduct and distress. Problematic conduct may be a matter for blame where the patient is diagnosed with personality disorder, for sympathy where the diagnosis is bipolar disorder. In short, diagnosis is often a transformative moment for the person diagnosed; it is the moment when they embark on a 'moral career' as a mental patient, with the changes of self-perception and treatment by others that this entails (Goffman, 1959). Of course, that moral career need not be all negative. Diagnoses can sometimes become a basis for social mobilization, with support groups, pressure groups and charities forming around their diagnostic categories, pressing for better services and research for 'their' condition, sharing experiences with other 'patients like me'.[12] Thus, even if each diagnosis is merely a hypothesis for the clinician, it is also a psychological, social, cultural, economic, political reality for doctors, patients, families, bureaucrats and many others.

Clare, as we have seen, believed there was a continuum between 'normality' and 'madness'. But psychiatric diagnoses since the 1980s have taken a categorical form – each diagnosis purports to define a specific condition, with internal coherence and clear separation from other conditions, and with a distinct aetiology, pathology and prognosis. Over the last three decades, such categorical diagnosis has had a crucial role in the generation and organization of psychiatric knowledge. The whole apparatus of psychiatric research has become predicated on diagnostic categories – allocation of research funding, methodology of clinical trials, selection of individuals for inclusion in such trials, choice of treatments, development of hypotheses, interpretation of results, publication in high impact refereed journals and much more. Categorical diagnosis has also been an organizing feature of genetic research, from lineage studies to the more recent investment of enormous amounts of time and energy into genome-wide association studies – for how else would one identify 'cases' and 'controls' if one could not choose the former because they had been ascribed to a particular category by their diagnosis. Attempts to simulate diagnostic categories have also been a driving force behind the creation of animal models, so ubiquitous in psychiatric research that seeks biological bases for mental disorders: you manipulate genetic and other parameters in order to 'model' the key observable features of a diagnostic category such as schizophrenia in your mouse (Crawley, 2007). And, of course, at least since the 1950s, categorical diagnosis has been the basis of pharmaceutical development, and the creation of psychiatric drugs – each targeted and marketed to a particular diagnosis. How did categorical diagnoses of this sort become not just the preferred solution to the crisis of diagnosis, but also the organizing principle of psychiatric knowledge?

Solution one: Define the phenotype

Systematic classifications of patients diagnosed with mental illness go back at least to the nineteenth-century reforms of the lunatic asylums. As Sander Gilman shows us in his exemplary study *Seeing the Insane* (1982), diagnoses initially took a visual form. Thus, each of the 27 diagnostic categories in Esquirol's 'Atlas' of 1838 is illustrated with a line drawing of a patient with that diagnosis, accompanied by a written description of salient features and a case history, thus not just directing the gaze of the clinician, but actually teaching the clinician how to see and how to interpret. External appearance continues to be central to diagnosis throughout the nineteenth century, whether in the carefully posed photographs that illustrate Bucknill and Tuke's *Manual of Psychological Medicine* (1874) or in the artfully staged films created by Charcot and his colleagues at the Salpêtrière in Paris (Didi-Huberman and Charcot, 2003).[13] But while there were fierce debates over classifications throughout the nineteenth century, not just concerning the classifications themselves, but also about the very possibility of rigorous systematization of mental diseases, "nosologies tended to be general and fluid, and judgments about individual patients represented pragmatic choices that had few practical consequences" (Grob, 1991b: 422).

But statistics were another matter. Across the nineteenth century, congresses and associations of alienists, of medical superintendents of asylums and similar organizations advocated the collection and analysis of statistics of those confined in asylums, generally using rather simple classifications – mania, melancholia, monomania, dementia, general paralysis of the insane, epilepsy, toxic insanity, congenital mental deficiency and – in Britain at least – moral insanity (Grob, 1991b). Enumeration of the insane was linked to a wider belief in the role that statistics could and must play in the practice of governing, revealing the state of a nation and its rates of disease, death, crime and depravity. To govern a population, one now had to *know* it (Rose, 1991: 676). Attempts to enumerate the insane in the United States began with the census of 1840, and continued in each subsequent census, inflected in every case by the political anxieties of the time.[14] According to Grob, it was pressure from the US Bureau of the Census for a usable and agreed classification system for their data that finally led the American Medico-Psychological Association to appoint a Committee on Nomenclature of Diseases. Its *Statistical Manual for the Use of Institutions for the Insane*, published in 1918, "divided mental disorders into 22 principal groups [that] rested for the most part on the belief that mental disorders had a biological foundation" (Grob, 1991b: 426).[15] This classification persisted in the United States through ten editions of this *Manual*, with minor variations, until the Second World War. But while the numbers were often referred to in political debates, the system of classification itself was of little concern to psychiatrists themselves and had minimal consequences for patients.

As I have already noted, the experience of the Second World War refocused the attention of psychiatrists away from the closed institutions, and towards those who had never been institutionalized but nonetheless were thought to be suffering from various forms of undiagnosed mental troubles. While the experience of shell shock in the First World War had provided an entry point for psychiatrists into the military (Rose, 1985a), their experience in the military during the Second World War seemed to reveal, for the first time, the numbers of individuals who appeared quite normal but who were found, on psychiatric examination at the time of recruitment or when invalided out of the battlefield, to be suffering from a mental disorder.[16]

For William Menninger it seemed that these minor mental troubles, arising in otherwise seemingly normal individuals with perhaps a propensity to develop a mental disorder, could be treated outside any institutional setting if they were caught early enough. Menninger shared Adolf Meyer's psychobiological approach to the nature of psychiatric disorder: disorders were individual reactions to particular adverse situations, themselves dependent on the ways in which the biological and physiological constitution of each individual had been shaped by their life history. This underpinned a new approach to diagnosis that was embodied in the first edition of the *DSM*, published in 1952 (APA, 1952).

Menninger, in his wartime role, led the committee that developed this new classification system. It first appeared in 1943 as a War Department Technical Bulletin known as Medical 203, and was eventually adopted by all Armed Forces (Houts, 2000). At the end of the war, this approach migrated, along with the military psychiatrists, to the mental hospitals and clinics where they now worked. This classification system also influenced the approach taken by the WHO, which published the sixth edition of their *International Classification of Disease* in 1949. For the first time, the *ICD-6* contained a section on mental disorders, with categories for psychoses, psychoneuroses, and disorders of character, behaviour and intelligence. However, in the view of Menninger and those who thought like him, the *ICD* classification still failed to recognize that many conditions were actually reactions to circumstances; they believed that this recognition was vital if the diagnostic system was to be appropriate for clinical use. Thus the APA's Committee on Nomenclature and Statistics began to prepare a revised version of psychiatric nosology specifically adapted for clinical use.

The classification system that it developed embodied Meyer's psychobiological style of thought. On the one hand, there was a group of mental disorders that seemed to arise from an impairment of brain function.[17] On the other, there were those that arose from an individual's inability to 'adjust': psychotic disorders such as depressive reactions, paranoid reactions and schizophrenia, and psychoneurotic disorders, including reactions such as anxiety, phobia, depression, antisocial behaviour, alcoholism and sexual deviation. These psychiatric conditions, whether psychotic or psychoneurotic, were not disease entities, but were reactions of an individual with a particular biological and physiological make-up to the stresses generated by his or her experiences. Symptoms were symbolic, meaningful expressions of these reactions, and in order to treat, the psychiatrist needed to *interpret*. This Meyerian style of thought was not only embodied in *DSM-I*, it was intrinsic to the curriculum for training US psychiatrists in the 1950s.

The reaction against this idea of mental disorders as 'reactions' began with the revision of *DSM-I* to *DSM-II*, which was eventually published in 1968 (APA, 1968). Officially this new edition was intended to facilitate the exchange of ideas between US psychiatrists who used *DSM* and those in the rest of the world who used the new mental disorder section of the most recent version of *ICD*, *ICD-8*. But more was at stake. Indeed, as Robert Spitzer – who was to go on to head the task force for *DSM-III* – put it in an article written with Paul Wilson of the APA: "One of the most striking differences between *DSM-I* and *DSM-II* and perhaps the one that will generate the strongest feelings, is the elimination of the term *reaction* from many diagnostic labels" (Spitzer and Wilson, 1968: 1620). Spitzer and Wilson argued that the new classification system was *not* a "return to a Kraepelinian way of thinking, which views mental disorders as fixed disease entities", but simply an attempt to avoid terms that carry implications about the causes of a disorder, especially where there is controversy. But this was disingenuous, for *DSM-II* was to foreshadow the major epistemological and ontological shift that would lead to the publication of *DSM-III* in 1980.

Central to this shift was the work of a group in the Department of Psychiatry of the University of Washington, brought together by John Feighner (I have drawn here on the historical account provided by Kendler et al., 2010). This group was united by their opposition to what they took to be the dominant position among American psychiatrists, which they characterized, not entirely accurately, as based on Freudian psychoanalysis.[18] They were not only opposed to the questionable interpretations that such psychiatrists made of their patients' symptoms, but also to their hostility to any attempt at rigorous evaluation of their approach. Indeed, Feighner and colleagues believed that these Freudian psychiatrists were so misguided as to consider diagnosis not only of little clinical use, but sometimes actually harmful to patients. For the Washington group "[t]his was a disastrous state of affairs in a discipline trying to become a science" (George Murphy, quoted in Kendler et al., 2010: 134).

The Washington group adopted an approach based on five phases: clinical description, laboratory studies, delimitation from other disorders, follow-up study, and family studies. An unspoken commitment to categorical diagnosis – that is to say that there were indeed disease entities in mental disorders that revealed themselves in symptoms and must be captured by diagnosis – underpinned this approach. The premise was that there are distinct psychiatric disorders with distinctive symptom sets, and that these are, in principle, clearly separable from one another. The first step was to define the symptoms. Hence, they reviewed the literature on a number of major diagnoses, identified the common characteristics of each and turned these into a 'checklist', so that, for a diagnosis to be made, a certain number of these symptoms had to be present. But which symptoms and how many symptoms?

The Feighner group were dismissive of the approach in *DSM-II* "in which diagnostic classification is based upon the best clinical judgement and experience of a committee and its consultants" (Feighner et al., 1972: 57). But their own approach was no less based on deliberations of a group of experts. Take depression, for instance: constipation was dropped as a criterion for depression and self-reproach or guilt was added, because, on balance, the group felt it produced more realistic criteria. And as for the number, Feighner and his colleagues "relied a lot on an article by Cassidy", who had specified ten criteria and decided on a threshold of six out of ten for a diagnosis: when asked why six, he purportedly replied "It sounded about right" (Kendler et al., 2010: 136). But, of course, ultimately they believed that the diagnosis would be confirmed by "laboratory studies" – chemical, physiological, radiological and anatomical, which they considered to be "generally more reliable, precise and reproducible than are clinical descriptions"; however, as they remarked sadly: "Unfortunately, consistent and reliable laboratory findings have not yet been demonstrated in the more common psychiatric disorders" (Robins and Guze, 1970: 107–8). Nonetheless, the expectation of those who adopted this Feighner diagnostic methodology and embodied it in *DSM-III* was that each clinical syndrome "would ultimately be validated by its separation from other disorders, common clinical course, genetic aggregation in families, and further differentiation by future laboratory tests" (Feighner et al., 1972: 57).

From that time forward, an ideal image of a psychiatric diagnosis took shape. A diagnosis would identify a specific underlying biological substrate for each unique condition, which, if not the sole cause of that condition, was an 'obligatory passage point' for its emergence – that is to say, genetic, developmental, biographical, environmental, psychological or other forces generated that condition by means of their actions upon that biological substrate. Of course, this image is driven by an analogy with the rest of medicine. Charles Rosenberg points out that this idea of an underlying lesion, of reading through the symptoms to their hidden cause, emerges to dominance in general medicine in the late nineteenth century, with the acceptance of the germ theory of infectious disease and the growing significance of postmortem pathology, which often identified the precise lesion underlying diverse symptoms (Rosenberg, 2002). It was strengthened by the growing use of histological, physiological, biochemical and genetic investigations into pathology – all seemed to confirm that the truth of a disease was to be found in the tissues. Hence, it seemed to go without saying that the naming of a disease should, in principle, be a designation of that biological substrate. From the 1970s onwards, psychiatric nosology thought of this as its ideal logic, notwithstanding the fact that its searches for those underlying lesions were almost entirely in vain.

Despite its self-proclaimed 'agnosticism' about explanations of the symptoms that it classified, these premises underpinned the third edition of the *Diagnostic and Statistical Manual, DSM-III*, published in 1980 (APA, 1980).[19] It had 265 categorical diagnoses, each defined as a set of apparently observable behaviours, seeming not requiring interpretation and hence, so it was hoped, equally evident to psychiatrists from different schools of thought. It construed each of these diagnostic categories as a distinct disorder, believing that each would, eventually, be underpinned with a unique aetiology, and amenable to a specific treatment.

As I have already suggested, one hope of those who developed this approach to diagnosis was that it would draw a clear line between those who were genuinely in need of psychiatric attention and those who might be troubled in various ways, and might even benefit from advice or counselling from a therapist, but did not fulfil the criteria for a psychiatric diagnosis, hence were not suffering from a mental disorder and were not appropriate for psychiatric intervention. But the reverse turned out to be the case. Conditions ranging from bothersome conduct in children to difficulties in getting an erection could find a diagnostic category in *DSM-III*. This became even clearer in the next revision – *DSM-IV* – published in 1994, which identified 350 distinct disorders, from acute stress disorder to voyeurism. The authors stressed that the categories were heterogeneous and tried to limit the utility of the diagnoses to clinical situations. But the expansion of diagnostic categories seemed to validate the claim by Menninger that most people have some degree of mental illness at some time. And now, that claim was linked to the idea of neurobiological specificity: that each diagnosis could be linked to a definable aetiology or prognosis, a specific neurobiological anomaly.

However, the problems of *DSM-IV* were manifold and obvious even to those who were proponents of this approach to diagnosis. While there seemed to be an improvement in reliability of diagnoses, this was not the same as validity, and it had not proved possible to discover either the genetic markers or the laboratory-based tests to underpin diagnoses that Feighner and his colleagues had hoped for. Psychopharmaceuticals developed with claims to be specific to particular *DSM* diagnoses soon turned out to be far less specific, and far less effective than initially claimed. In addition, the expansion of categories led to further criticisms that *DSM* was leading to an increasing medicalization of normality; categorical diagnosis based on symptoms was rendered problematic by the problem of comorbidity in which very many patients required more than a single diagnosis; suggesting that perhaps symptoms did not cohere neatly around particular categories, the apparently objective criteria for diagnosis were leading to controversial diagnostic epidemics of autism and ADHD. In the face of these criticisms, leading psychiatrists argued for a further revision that would redress these problems; their hope was that 'objectivity' in diagnosis could be provided by biomarkers.

Solution two: Find the biomarker

"Biomarkers Trump Behaviour in Mental Illness Diagnosis." This was the title of a 2007 article in *Nature Medicine* by Amanda Leigh Haag. She argued that psychiatric diagnosis had hardly changed over the past century, but that a radical shift was about to occur, with diagnosis "relying more on changes in physiology than in behaviour. Scientists are increasingly turning to biomarkers, such as genes or proteins, to distinguish between symptomatically indistinct illnesses." Biomarkers would also allow early treatment, better prognosis, ultimately enabling scientists to intervene even before the full-blown disease strikes.

Steven Hyman, Director of the US National Institute for Mental Health from 1996 to 2001, was a key proponent of the revision of the *DSM* to include biomarkers. Writing for a popular audience in *Scientific American* in 2003 he put it thus: "By combining neuroimaging with genetic studies, physicians may eventually be able to move psychiatric diagnoses out of the realm of symptom checklists and into the domain of objective medical tests. Genetic testing of patients could reveal who is at high risk for developing a disorder such as schizophrenia or depression. Doctors could then use neuroimaging on the high-risk patients to determine whether the disorder has actually set in. I do not want to sound too optimistic – the task is daunting. But the current pace of technological development augurs well for progress" (2003: 103).

But this optimism was misplaced. For more than 25 years, *DSM* categories had been mandatory for research into the neurobiological basis of mental disorders. To get a grant from a major research funder such as the National Institute for Mental Health in the US, one's study had to be framed in terms of *DSM* categories, one's sample had to be recruited in terms of *DSM* diagnoses, and one's results had to be directed towards the potential neurobiological validation of the symptom check lists in the *DSM*. If one was working with animal models, those animals had to be selected or bred so that they behaved in ways that simulated the symptoms listed in a *DSM* disease category (Crawley, 2007). *DSM* categories were the basis of clinical trials, genetic research using the most advanced techniques, brain imaging and much more. Surely this massive research effort – involving hundreds of studies, thousands of researchers, millions of dollars, conducted in a style of thought that was embedded in the training, textbooks and manuals of the discipline, embodying the hopes and expectations of pharmaceutical companies, policymakers and organizations set up around specific diagnoses such as schizophrenia or manic depression – would have produced at least some confirmatory findings. One might have expected this, even if the confirmations arose from researchers' expectations, publication bias and all the other processes for producing facts that are the stock in trade of science and technology studies. But despite the hopes of the committees of experts established for each diagnostic category in the long process that would lead to the fifth edition of *DSM*, the answer was no. It proved impossible to identify clear neurobiological bases for any of the symptom clusters for any *DSM* category: the new edition would not be able to include a single clinically validated biomarker for any of its diagnoses.

The most perceptive researchers began to realize this well before *DSM-5* was due to be published. Just five years after his optimistic piece in *Scientific American*, Hyman wrote: "Efforts to identify risk-conferring alleles . . . have been largely unrewarding . . . The underlying genetics of common neuropsychiatric disorders has proved highly complex . . . there is much evidence that similar neuropsychiatric symptoms can result from different combinations of genetic risk factors [and] that the same genetic variant may be associated with multiple DSM-IV diagnoses . . . The identification of common risk-conferring variants has . . . proved extremely challenging in most cases, because of their relatively small contribution to the disease phenotype . . . because of the diverse genetic, environmental and random factors that lead to these common disease." He concluded: "[W]hat we think of as a single 'disease' is not in a strict sense a homogeneous entity for which there is a 'Platonic' ideal phenotype. Common diseases are more likely to represent families of diseases that share major pathophysiological and symptomatic features, but can differ in important characteristics such as age of onset, severity of symptoms, rate of progression, and response to treatment" (2008: 891). Hence, he believed, we needed to start to think of dimensions without sharp boundaries between distinct disease entities. And, perhaps most damaging for the hopes that were vested in neurobiology to resolve the diagnostic problems of psychiatry, he questioned the view that it might ever be possible to draw clear boundaries between ill and well.

It is true that, in 2009, Darrel Regier and colleagues, who were overseeing the *DSM* revision process, still expressed their hope that "[m]ental disorder syndromes will eventually be redefined to reflect more useful diagnostic categories ('to carve nature at its joints') as well as dimensional discontinuities between disorders and clear thresholds between pathology and normality." However, optimism had given way to pessimism – hope had to be deferred: "our immediate task is to set a framework for an evolution of our diagnostic system that can advance our clinical practice and facilitate ongoing testing of the diagnostic criteria that are intended to be scientific hypotheses, rather than inerrant Biblical scripture" (2009: 649). Many had hoped that *DSM-5* would at least make a start towards a move away from categorical diagnosis, recognizing the dimensional nature of many disorders, their 'fuzzy' borders, and going some way towards a system that diagnosed in terms of degrees of impairment of functioning rather than allocation to static categories.[20] But when it was published, in May 2013, it became clear that none of this had happened. The symptom-based checklists for the allocation of categorical diagnostic codes were, if anything, more complex than before. Comorbidities were acknowledged, but nothing more. Dimensions were absent, merely gestured to by the fact that some diagnoses allowed for a classification of severity – mild, moderate or severe. In all these respects, despite the involvement of dozens of experts and the investment of hundreds of person hours, the politest verdict one can make is that the *DSM* remained embedded in the health care bureaucracy of the United States – for which it served the purposes outlined earlier in this chapter – but it made few, if any, clinical, scientific or intellectual advances over its predecessors.

By 2010 it was becoming clear that, to say the least, categorical diagnosis of the type advocated by the Feighner group was no longer an essential underpinning for a scientific understanding of mental disorders, but, rather, the reverse. Three years before the publication of *DSM-5*, Hyman – by then Provost of Harvard University, soon to become Director of the Stanley Center for Psychiatric Research[21] – was even more explicit in his rejection of the whole approach embodied in categorical diagnoses, now adopting the notion of 'reification' to describe the approach advocated by the Washington group and underpinning *DSM*s from the 1970s onwards. Concurring with generations of sociological critics of psychiatric diagnosis, Hyman asserted that psychiatric disorders are not 'natural kinds': "The wholesale adoption by the *DSM-III* . . . of phenomenologically based operationalized criteria in the service of interrater reliability, and of a wholly categorical approach to disorder, unwittingly exacerbated the difficulty of capturing etiologically diverse and phenotypically heterogeneous syndromes" (2010: 170). It was necessary to recognize the dimensionality between health and illness, the biological and genetic heterogeneity of pathways to similar symptomatology, the overlaps at the biological and genetic level between major psychiatric disease categories, and the fact that family studies in schizophrenia, bipolar disorder and similar severe conditions show that symptom clusters do not cohere across generations and span across very different diagnoses. What then needed to be done? What was required was a fresh, bottom-up analysis, that would recluster disorders according to neurobiological and neurogenetic data. The key to unlock the mysteries of diagnosis, it seems, lies not in symptomatology, but in the brain.

Solution three: Straight to the brain

The NIMH, under Hyman's successor Thomas Insel, began to set out its alternative approach well before the ink was dry on *DSM-5.0*. Faced with the reality that *DSM* did not, and would not, map on to neurobiology, the choice was clear – abandon *DSM* as a guide to psychiatric research, or abandon the belief that one could discover clinically relevant neurobiological bases for specific psychiatric conditions. In June 2011, NIMH set out its alternative approach – the Research Domain Criteria (RDoC). Like Hyman, Insel and his colleagues acknowledged the failure to find neurobiological markers for

DSM categories. But this did not mean that one should give up the hope for specificity in the diagnosis of mental disorders, for, "could specificity in fact exist, but not for the currently recognized clinical categories? ... If we assume that the clinical syndromes based on subjective symptoms are unique and unitary disorders, we undercut the power of biology to identify illnesses linked to pathophysiology and we limit the development of more specific treatments."[22]

The solution now, it seemed, was to allow "the power of biology", and not the experience of the patient, the symptoms of the disorder, or the judgement of a clinician, to delineate diseases – it was the body, not the patient, that was sick. This process would be, to say the least "agnostic about current disorder categories. The intent is to generate classifications stemming from basic behavioral neuroscience. Rather than starting with an illness definition and seeking its neurobiological underpinnings, RDoC begins with current understandings of behavior-brain relationships and links them to clinical phenomena." At the end of April 2013, Thomas Insel took the next painful, but logical step. He announced: "NIMH will be reorienting its research away from *DSM* categories" on the grounds that "[m]ental disorders are biological disorders involving brain circuits that implicate specific domains of cognition, emotion or behavior" – and it was in terms of these that diagnosis should proceed and towards these that treatment should be targeted.[23] *DSM* may be a useful clinical guide and bureaucratic tool. But when it came to characterizing the aetiology of mental disorders, one must trust in the brain, not in *DSM*.

In his essay entitled 'The Tyranny of Diagnosis: Specific Entities and Individual Sickness' (2002), Charles Rosenberg points to the fact that, as we entered the twenty-first century, it seems as if we could be objective about disease only when we could pin down the specific character of an underlying pathology – he refers to this as "the specificity revolution". As the phrase suggests, it was not always so. Indeed, he is drawing here upon an earlier great historian of medicine, Owsei Temkin. According to Rosenberg, Temkin distinguished two ways of understanding disease – ontological and physiological. Ontological: individual diseases exist independently of their manifestations in particular men and women. Physiological: disease is a fundamentally individual phenomenon, the consequence of uniquely configured factors in particular men and women interacting with their environmental circumstances. Physiological here is a strange term: this is the approach that Rosenberg calls "individual sickness".

Temkin wisely warns against celebrating either the ontological or the individual conception. But today, medical research has veered strongly to the former – the ontological notion of disease. Despite its turn away from *DSM*, NIMH's RDoC conception of diseases is ontological, based on the wager that mental ill health arises from disorders that are diseases like any other, and that different diseases have distinct brain-based pathophysiologies. Even though they hypothesize that the underlying pathophysiology is complex, involving anomalies on a number of distinct neurobiological circuits, RDoC is based on the belief that mental disorders must, in the end, be understood as disorders of the brain. But the fundamental question is this: will an appeal to the brain, or to the genetic sequences that shape the structure and function of the neuronal architecture, or to the new visibility apparently conferred by neuroimaging, finally enable clinicians to delineate the boundaries of normality, and to differentiate within disorder – to decide who is, and who is not, a suitable case for which kind of treatment? Could neuroscience ever provide psychiatry with the objectivity that it seeks?

As we will see in chapter 5, evidence suggests that, if one compares large numbers of 'cases' of those with disorders against 'controls' who have not been diagnosed with a disorder, one may indeed find small variations in basic neurobiology – cell membranes, ion channels and so forth – that are slightly more common in cases than in controls. However, not only are the effect sizes very small; none of these variations is either necessary or sufficient to distinguish the groups – there is considerable overlap between cases and controls. Researchers hope to aggregate many of these small variations to find an algorithm that can cluster the data in a way that can inform clinical decisions. But do these statistically generated algorithms map causal biological pathways? We don't know. Can one move from probabilities in populations to interventions on individual cases? With great difficulty. Should one base individual treatment decisions on brain signatures rather than clinical presentations? That would be unwise, for surely an anomalous 'brain signature' without symptoms cannot justify intervention?

What does this mean for the dream of precision medicine in psychiatry?[24] Precision medicine seeks to use biomarkers, not only to ensure accurate diagnosis of individuals when they are being assessed by a doctor, and not only to guide treatment decisions, but also, it was hoped, to underpin early, and even presymptomatic, diagnosis and preventive intervention. Thomas Insel and others argued that the complexity and indeterminacy that I have outlined above would persist as long as psychiatric research sought to find precision through research based on classifications of symptomatology, as developed in *DSM*. We needed to move away from *DSM* symptom-based classifications which lumped together diseases that were very different neurobiologically, and artificially divided those with similar neurobiological bases. However, by 2014, Insel seemed to recognize the need to go beyond brain-based biomarkers. He still believed that RDoC would open the way for "a precision medicine approach to mental disorders" but recognized that this would take "a decade of intense scientific work – from molecular factors to social determinants – to understand normal and abnormal behavior, based on a deep understanding of mechanism", and that for this to happen psychiatry must not just "embrace contemporary biology" but also "cognitive science, and social science to augment the reliable assessment of signs and symptoms". RDoC would now build "on clinical description and subjective experience to create a matrix of information for individual patients, leading ultimately to precision medicine for psychiatry" (Insel, 2014).

Now few would argue that it would be useful to be better able to characterize the nature of an individual's ailment before developing a plan for treatment. And I would certainly agree that we need to reject neurobiological reductionism when it comes to understanding aetiology, and to build not only on 'subjective experience', but also on 'social determinants'. But to adopt this position requires a rather fundamental mutation in styles of thought when it comes to explanations of mental disorders, and one that recognizes that the very idea of the psychiatric biomarker organizes thought, research and first line intervention in the wrong way.

Perhaps it was partly because of a recognition of this that, in 2015, Insel left NIMH to join Google Life Sciences, for Google specializes in analysis of different kinds of data – not brain data, but the real life 'psychosocial' behaviour of individuals in the online universe. Barely 18 months later, Insel left that company, now called Verily, for a start-up called Mindstrong.[25] As he put it in 2017, when he made that jump (as quoted in Rogers, 2017): "I spent 13 years at NIMH really pushing on the neuroscience and genetics of mental disorders, and when I look back on that I realize that while I think I succeeded at getting lots of really cool papers published by cool scientists at fairly large costs – I think $20 billion – I don't think we moved the needle in reducing suicide, reducing hospitalizations, improving recovery for the tens of millions of people who have mental illness. I hold myself accountable for that." That is quite an admission. Surprisingly, Insel does not actually apologize for the $20 billion spent on cool papers that completely failed to fulfil their promises of translating into better mental health care and improved recovery. But the implications are clear. After 13 years of arguing that the key to understanding problems of mental health lies in research in neuroscience and genetics, if the aim was to improve services for those with mental illness, the result has been failure.

Solution four: Beyond diagnosis

Let me return to Insel's claim that "[m]ental disorders are biological disorders involving brain circuits that implicate specific domains of cognition, emotion or behaviour",[26] a view that still seems to be held by Insel's successor as Director of NIMH, Josh Gordon, as we shall see in the next chapter. It may seem pernickety, but how we evaluate this claim depends on how we understand the words like 'are', 'involving' and 'implicate'. Few, I think, would dispute that, in principle, neurobiological processes are involved in variations in cognition, emotion, volition and other human faculties. But what is their status? Are anomalies in these processes 'fundamental causes' of mental distress and disorder? Or are they simply elements in a much more complex and intertwined network of contributing factors and exposures?[27]

To address this question, let us return to the style of thought of the first *DSM*, which, as I have said, drew on the approach of the once very influential and now disregarded figure of Adolf Meyer (Lamb, 2014). As we saw, Meyer regarded mental disorders as 'reactions' of the individual to specific life circumstances. And in order to understand such reactions, what was required was not so much a 'diagnosis' as a 'formulation'. As the *Oxford Textbook of Psychiatry* put it in 1996, a "formulation is a concise statement of the case . . . it is a discussion of alternative ideas about diagnosis, aetiology, treatment and prognosis and of the arguments for and against each alternative. A good formulation is based on the facts of the case and not on speculation. It may contain verifiable hypotheses about matters that are uncertain at the time of writing. A formulation is concerned not only with the disease concepts, but also with understanding how the patient's lifelong experiences have influenced his personality and his ways of reacting to adversity" (Gelder, 1996: 48–9).

This was very much the approach set out by Adolf Meyer in the 1920s. For Meyer: "If the physician wishes to understand the mental patient he must not treat him as an experimental animal in a physiological laboratory, but must do justice to the fullness of human nature and the complexity of the social environment."[28] To do this, the physician must start from "the complaint": "With my students and co-workers I cultivate much more conscientiously than ever 'the complaint' as offered by the patient and the lay observers and family and the family physician ... the facts one determines ... in the taking of the history of the present illness, its setting and antecedents, the early history and the family history and the personality make-up and assets. This ... tends to keep before us the therapeutic problem of the patient and nurses and the physician in charge, the short-term and long-term problems of management, and the assets as well as the actual difficulties, the course, and the probabilities of outcome and the formulation for the family and the patient and the best technical statement" (Meyer, 1928: 370)

Meyer's approach starts from a meticulous investigation, documentation and psychobiological formulation of the individual patient's case history to identify the causal pathways in the reaction of the individual to his or her circumstances in the light of his or her particular assets. This grounds causality in the temporal chain of transactions of the living organism in its milieu. It also grounds causality, not in a set of 'objective contingencies', but in the patient's story – his or her narrative, the way in which that situation is rendered into thought in language and meaning. The disordered reaction is intelligible – and treatable – only in this light.

I am not suggesting we become Meyerians: there is much to be critical of when it comes to Meyer, his writings and his career, not least his ambivalent attitude towards some very dubious psychiatric practices (Double, 2007). But his approach puts the brain back into its place in the life history of the organism, as does the approach of the neurologist and psychiatrist Kurt Goldstein, for whom disease was a condition of the whole living organism in its milieu. As Goldstein put it: "only such methods will really carry us further which consider the single phenomenon in its significance for the whole organism. Only investigations with that emphasis will give us an understanding of the actual meaning of a phenomenon in respect to its functional significance ... for the organism in question" (1939: 215).

From this perspective, to understand the nature and aetiology of the complaint, one must begin with the person in his or her situation and seek to trace the constellation of factors across the life course that have shaped the ailment as a reality that is both biological and social. Indeed, a disorder is *both* biological and social. It is also mental, in the sense of being shaped by mental life, not just by experience as a brute fact – for example, poverty, isolation, exclusion, threat, hatred – but how these are made intelligible and meaningful by the individual, using the linguistic, symbolic and cultural resources available to them. Patterns in forms of life, ways of making sense of the world, localities in city or countryside, webs of interactions with family and community: these are not external to the disorder, influencing the expression of an essential neurobiological anomaly. They are constitutive of the complaint and its inscription in body and brain. It is in a form of living with its possibilities and its limits that the disease inheres. Only by understanding that will research on the brain translate into clinical practice.

This may sound like woolly hand-waving when compared with the rigour of the laboratory, the gene sequencer or the brain scanner. Indeed, this is what many think about Meyer's psychobiology and Engel's (1977) biopsychosocial model. But some recent developments in neuroscience, which I discuss further in my final chapter, enable us to put the brain back in its body, in its organism and in its milieu. While much research in biological psychiatry is reductionist, in other areas of neurobiology a different image has taken shape, in which the brain is perhaps the most open and malleable organ of all, and both structural organization and functional differentiation of brain circuits are shaped, from the moment of conception if not before, by immersion in both the internal milieu of the organism, and the external environment – physical, interactional, social – in which that organism develops. I am thinking of work on epigenetics, neuroplasticity, the microbiome, the exposome and the integration of these and other elements into novel pathways such as the immune pathways related to stress. In other words, you have an open, dynamic, plastic brain in which – to use the phrase that is now becoming a cliché – experience (and adversity) can 'get under the skin'. In my final chapter I return to these ways of thinking, which try to trace out complex circuits that link brain, body and social world, and argue that these can go some way to help us understand the psychopathological consequences of the experience of chronic adversity or trauma and generate very different conceptions of therapy.

From diagnosis to formulation

Some psychiatrists would argue that formulation rather than, or alongside, diagnosis actually captures the approach of most clinical psychiatrists, who formulate, for themselves and for the patients, a complex story of the origins of the distress currently being experienced, even when their response is simply to prescribe medication in the hope that it will enable the distressed individual to cope with those stresses. Others suggest that formulations cannot really address all the other ways that diagnoses, especially categorical diagnoses, work in our societies. I have already suggested that, for many purposes, categorical diagnoses are not necessary. For instance, in assessing the need for the provision of various kinds of mental health services, estimates of capabilities and impairments are much more appropriate than diagnostic labels, which do not give any sense of what or how much an individual can or cannot do given whatever levels of social support are available.

But how about the need for doctors and patients to be able to name, narrate and communicate their troubles? A formulation – for instance, that I am suffering an acute anxiety reaction to the accumulated stresses of my life at present – does in fact enable a story to be told, which has the benefits of intelligibility as well as enabling the causal chains to be teased out in a narrative. Some diagnostic categories, for example post-traumatic stress disorder, do already embody something like such a formulation within them. Of course, it would require authorities to do more listening, rather than merely writing down a diagnostic category, but that would be all to the good.

What about research? Could that be undertaken without diagnostic categories? Well, we have already seen that the existing categories have not proved particularly helpful, to say the least. I suggest that research also needs to question the belief that a disease is a specific entity defined by a unique pathophysiology. Research on the causes of mental disorders and mental distress should also begin with the person in his or her situation, and seek to trace the constellation of factors across the life course that have shaped the ailment as a reality that is both biological and social – indeed, that requires us to question such a misleading distinction. As I argued in chapter 3, in my discussion of stress, the HPA axis, epigenetics and neuroplasticity, we are beginning to formulate a language with which to speak about the mechanisms involved, and while the pathways may be dauntingly complex, this is no excuse for continuing to pursue strategies of research that have already proved to be unproductive. Undoubtedly, 'biopsychosocial' patterns will emerge; indeed, the social sciences have been tracing these for over a century. These patterns within the milieu are not merely external to the disorder, influencing its mode of expression – they are constitutive of the disorder and its inscription in body and brain. And it is in the milieu, in a form of living with its possibilities and its limits, that the disease inheres. And only by understanding that will research translate into clinical practice.

Inside and outside the clinic, then, our approach to mental distress, from mild to severe, should start in the experience of the ailing individual, the extent of their troubles, the pattern of impairment of some of their capacities in particular familial, social, cultural and, indeed, economic situations, their compensatory strengths and resiliencies.[29] What would a diagnostic system look like if it focused neither on disease entities nor on neurobiological markers, but on patterns of capabilities, impairment and resilience and which would thus help identify the kinds of support that might alleviate or mitigate them?[30] That, it seems to me, is a challenge to psychiatrists, psychiatric epidemiologists and neurobiological researchers. It is also, of course, a challenge to social scientists, who must resume their truncated dialogue with biological psychiatry and address the task of analysing how experience gets under the skin.

5
Are Mental Disorders 'Brain Disorders'?

Mental disorders are *characterized* by abnormalities in cognition, emotion or mood, or the highest integrative aspects of behavior, such as social interactions or planning of future activities. These mental functions are all *mediated by* the brain. It is, in fact, a core tenet of modern science that behavior and our subjective mental lives *reflect* the overall workings of the brain. Thus, symptoms related to behavior or mental lives *clearly reflect* variations or abnormalities in brain function.

US Department of Health and Human Services (1999: 39;
emphasis added)

[P]sychiatric disorders are disorders of the brain, and to make progress in treating them we really have to understand the brain ... [If we can] get at questions of how neural circuits produce behaviour [this] may soon generate new treatments for psychiatric disorders [because each individual's] neural circuitry [is] the 'wiring' in their brains that accounts for their particular personalities ... Neural circuits could be delivering treatments in 10 or 15 years. We don't yet know exactly which circuits we would want to modify to treat psychiatric disorders in humans. But now is the time to start thinking about which tools we are going to need to make this translational step possible, and invest in them.

Joshua Gordon, Director of NIMH, cited in Abbott (2016)

Are mental disorders 'brain disorders'? Few would deny that neural processes are involved in distress, and in disorders of thought, emotion or will – as they are in everything that humans do, feel and desire. But what, if anything, does that imply for the ways we understand and treat such conditions? I've already touched on some of the issues, and on the ways that disorders are being reframed in cerebral terms. But how, in what way and with what consequences? This is the question that we will address directly in this chapter

The philosophical debates about the relations between mind and brain seem interminable. Some point to trepanning as the earliest evidence of a recognition that what goes on within the skull shapes what goes on within the mind. A few scholars now explore the ways this issue was posed in the Arab world. All go back to the Greeks for the kinds of discussions that still preoccupy contemporary philosophy. In modern times, all refer us to Descartes's distinction between mind and body – crudely, that bodies (and hence brains as other organs) are spatially extended substances that cannot feel or think, while minds do not have spatial extension, and are thinking and feeling substances. Are we, today, still 'Cartesians' – dualists positing a fundamental distinction between these two realms? Or do we live in a post-Cartesian, a postdualist world?[1] Has neuroscience finally resolved this question, demonstrating that 'mind is what brain does'? Or has neuroscience misunderstood the question, attributing capacities to brains that can only properly be attributed to persons? And so forth. Is it possible to address our question without getting embroiled in these debates? Is it possible to abstain from these debates, as one might abstain from a heavy meal because experience shows it will end in indigestion? Let me try. For our question is not exactly that of the relation between mind, brain and body; it is better put as follows: what role do disordered brain processes play in the ways we should understand and treat mental disorders?

Many excellent histories show us that there is nothing new in the belief that madness, lunacy, insanity, mental disorder, mental illness – each of these frames the question to be explored in different ways – is a matter of 'the brain'. But we must always remember that the brain for the Greeks is not what it was for nineteenth-century German neurologists, nor what it is for today's 'neuropsychiatrists'. Nonetheless, given this long history, what is specific about neuropsychiatry today and the claim that mental disorders are brain disorders?

Before we examine what is meant by this claim, it is important to note that it throws two historically important lines of demarcation into question.

The first is an ancient distinction between 'functional' and 'organic' disorders. Now the notion of an organic disorder seems clear enough – it is a mental disorder believed to have its basis[2] in physical lesions or physiological anomalies in the brain. The notion of a functional disorder is less clear: it does not usually mean a disorder of specific functions, but, rather, either a disorder whose causes are construed as largely psychological – thus, for example, neuroses were often considered to be functional disorders which did not entail any organic pathology – or else simply as disorders whose causes are as yet unknown. In his Preface to the first edition of his book *Biological Psychiatry* (1987), Michael Trimble argues that "psychological theories of pathogenesis have been overtaken by a wealth of neurochemical and neuropathological hypotheses and findings, especially with regard to the major psychoses" and that "effective treatment with biological remedies" – by which he means "the neurochemical era, ushered in by the psychopharmacological discoveries of the 1950s" – have given us a new image of the brain and "a more complete understanding of the underlying functional and structural changes of the brain that accompany psychiatric illness". Hence, we can return 'functional' to its original usage of a physiological, rather than a psychological, disturbance; indeed, "with our present knowledge, the distinction between 'organic' and 'functional' melts away, stripped of its Cartesian dualism" (Trimble, 1987).

By the 2010 edition (Trimble and George, 2010), the Introduction and Preface now consist of a six-page run through of "the idea of seeking naturalistic origins of psychiatric disorder" – "naturalistic" here seemingly meaning cerebral – starting with Hippocrates on epilepsy and hopping rapidly over the theological and demonological views of the next 1,300 years to Europe in the seventeenth century. From then on we cover the revival of the idea that the brain was the seat of many mental diseases, notably in the work of Thomas Willis, the localization theories of the nineteenth century, the developmental and hierarchical view of brain functions put forward by Hughlings Jackson, and the arguments by William Griesinger in *Mental Pathology and Therapeutics* that the brain is the diseased organ in mental disease and that we must "in every case of mental disease, recognize a morbid action of that organ" (Griesinger, 1867: 1). We march through the German neuroanatomists Theodore Meynert and Carl Wernicke, Antoine Laurent Jessé Bayle's work showing that some forms of dementia were the late effects of syphilis – later confirmed by the discovery of the spirochaetes in the brains of patients with general paralysis of the insane – to Jean-Martin Charcot, here praised as a neurologist with no reference to his carefully stage-managed presentations of his patients, and to theorists such as Marshall Hall, who thought of neurasthenia as a disorder, not of the will or of character, but of the nerves of the spinal cord.

Noting in passing that "the first half of the twentieth century saw an apparent eclipse of progress in biological psychiatry", in which psychological theorizing had the "disastrous effect of accelerating the divisions between neurology and psychiatry", Trimble notes the role that encephalitis played, via the work of Constantin von Economo, who drew wider considerations for psychiatry from the fact that some of those who suffered from encephalitis lethargica had symptoms similar to psychopathologies such as obsessive compulsive and psychotic disorders and showed specific brain lesions on postmortem examination. Other episodes included linking epilepsy to abnormal electrical activity in certain brain regions, identification of brain regions linked to the experience of emotions, and the apparent success of biological treatments such as Moniz's lobotomies, Jean Delay and Paul Deniker's use of chlorpromazine, John Cade's introduction of lithium and the founding of the Society for Biological Psychiatry and its journal in 1954. Signing off their Preface from the delightful sounding location of Happy Acres Road in Cedar Mountains, North Carolina, Trimble, and his writing companion Mark George, are optimistic that biological psychiatry will play its part in "the most important scientific issue facing humanity": understanding "how the brain organizes thought and consciousness".

Trimble's 'recurrent history' rewrites the past in order to ratify the present of biological psychiatry.[3] Such a history consigns to the margins all that does not fit this schema – whether it be the failure of German neuroanatomy to find any neural correlates of any mental disorder, the naive celebration of Moniz's lobotomies in the first meetings of psychiatrists after the Second World War, or the tardive dyskinesia consequent on the chronic overuse of chlorpromazine by the successors of Delay and Deniker. But for our purposes, his account is useful, not only because it exemplifies a now quite common version of history, nor just because it so clearly tries to overcome the organic/functional demarcation, but also because it hints at another consequence of biological psychiatry's approach to the brain – the blurring of the professional demarcation between neurology and psychiatry. To explore this further, consider a paper written jointly by a professor of psychological medicine, a consultant neuropsychiatrist and a professor of cognitive and behavioural neurology published in the *British Medical Journal* a couple of years after Trimble's book, called 'Time to End the Distinction between Mental and Neurological Illnesses' (White et al., 2012).

White et al.'s proposal is simple and forthright: the demarcation between psychiatry and neurology is counterproductive, reflecting an outdated distinction between mind and brain, therefore "psychiatric disorders should be reclassified as disorders of the (central) nervous system" to foster the proper integration of psychiatry into the mainstream of medicine (2012: 1). White et al. argue that this reframing has become possible because of three lines of research: structural and functional brain imaging, neuropharmacology, and genetics. Along the first, "structural brain abnormalities are present in schizophrenia, bipolar affective disorder, recurrent depressive disorder, posttraumatic stress disorder, and obsessive compulsive disorder", and functional brain imaging shows neural representation of emotions, altered activation in the limbic system in depression and bipolar disorder, altered brain activity associated with hallucinations and even in conversion disorders (2012: 1; references omitted). Along the second, recent research "has begun to delineate the genetic architecture of these disorders, implicating allelic variants, copy number variants, gene-gene and gene-environment interactions and epigenetic features" (2012: 1; references omitted). Along the third, they make a claim that few would dispute: that psychotropic drugs alter brain function and structure, and argue that the "efficacy of antidepressants is correlated with brain activation in those parts of the brain that mediate mood" and point to the effects of these pharmaceuticals on neurogenesis. They also argue that nonpharmacological treatments such as cognitive behaviour therapy (CBT) "modulate brain activity" – an example of a common, but banal, argument, as almost everything modulates brain activity! They do not want to rule out a role for psychological and social factors, but, nonetheless, their point is straightforward: "most disorders of the central nervous system produce both 'neurological' – motor and sensor – and 'psychological' – cognitive, affective and behavioural – effects" (2012: 1). Thus, they believe, the division of neurology and psychiatry is both conceptually and clinically unwarranted.

For present purposes, I won't pursue the 'classificatory' implications that White and colleagues draw from their argument, as I discuss diagnosis and classification elsewhere. But they provide a useful synopsis of the three lines of argument that appear to warrant those, such as Josh Gordon stating so unequivocally that psychiatric disorders are disorders of the brain (see the quote at the head of this chapter). In fact, a lot hangs on that little word 'are' and its implications. But before turning to what might seem like a pedantic point, let us pause a while on each of the three dimensions: first drugs, then genetics, and finally what might seem the most compelling argument – that we can 'see' psychiatric disorders in the tissues and circuits of the brain itself.

Proven by psychopharmaceuticals?

Does the fact that psychopharmaceuticals have effects on the brain indicate that the disorders for which they are prescribed are brain disorders? It is, of course, not surprising that the pharmaceuticals used in psychiatry since the 1950s act in the brain. The story of the accidental discovery of the psychoactive effects of certain drugs is well known – first the neuroleptics (Ban, 2007; Caldwell, 1970; Carlsson, 2001), then the 'antidepressants' (López-Muñoz and Alamo, 2009), and later the 'tranquillizers' (Smith, 1991). Taken together with developments in measuring instruments, the increasing commitment of the pharmaceutical companies to psychiatric drug development and research that anatomized the synapse and its components (Rapport, 2005), the specialism of psychopharmacology was born in the late 1950s (Healy, 1996).

As to their mode of action, opinion gradually converged on the hypothesis that this was through their effect on neurotransmitters. Until the late 1950s it was thought that transmission across nerves was electrical, but in the famous war of 'soups and sparks' the argument that transmission was effected by chemicals that became known as neurotransmitters triumphed (Valenstein, 2005). The view took hold among both most neuropsychiatrists and most psychopharmacologists that mental disorders arose from disorders in these mechanisms of neurotransmission – in the synthesis, release, metabolism or re-uptake of neurotransmitters in the synaptic cleft that enable communication between neurons (Schildkraut, 1965). Initially, when only a limited number of chemicals responsible for neurotransmission had been identified, each mental disorder was linked to an anomaly in a single neurotransmitter system – for example, schizophrenia to an excess of dopamine, depression to a deficit of serotonin – and the mode of action of drugs that seemed to ameliorate the symptoms of a disorder was hypothesized to be via their effects on that neurotransmission pathway. This was based on laboratory studies of extracted preparations, on animal experiments, and on some analyses of cerebro-spinal fluids; these anomalies had never directly been identified in any human being diagnosed with these disorders. Increasingly, drugs were developed, branded and marketed in terms of the specificity of their actions on the anomalies of neurotransmission thought to underpin the different disorders, with an argument that, if the pharmaceuticals were more specific, they would not only be more effective, but some of the horrible unwanted effects of earlier drugs would be mitigated.

Unfortunately, problems with the first generation of psychiatric drugs soon became apparent. Chlorpromazine – under its trade names Largactil (because it had a large range of action) and Thorazine – became very widely used in controlling asylum populations in Europe and the US respectively. But it soon became clear that it produced a whole range of unwanted symptoms, initially including drowsiness, problems with movement and weight gain. This was not surprising because neurotransmission occurs in areas of the brain responsible for modulating activities in other regions of the body, as well as being directly involved outside the central nervous system, in nerve junctions and in junctions between nerves and other tissue throughout the body. Dopamine has a major role in muscle control, the regulation of hormone release, blood vessel dilation, kidney function and gastrointestinal activity. Serotonin was first discovered in the gut, and about 90 per cent of serotonin in the human body is actually found in the gastrointestinal tract – a fact that has led to a focus on 'the brain in the gut' (Wilson, 2004) – and is also involved in the modulation of muscle tone. Other neurotransmitters – and there are now known to be dozens of such substances operative in synapses in different vital systems – are also seldom confined to brain tissue. So it is obvious that drugs that modify the action of these substances are going to have wide-ranging – and usually unwelcome – effects across the human body.

To add to these problems, early reports of the efficacy of these drugs later turned out to be overenthusiastic. In the case of the phenothiazines such as chlorpromazine, physicians often responded to this reduction in efficacy by increasing doses (as well as actually welcoming some of the side-effects such as drowsiness, because they increased the docility of their patients). Gradually, the malign effects of long-term usage of the drugs at high dosages became impossible to deny. While psychiatrists initially believed that the so-called 'extra pyramidal effects' – muscle spasms, restlessness, slowness of movements, tremor, jerky motions and problems with swallowing linked to mouth and throat movements – were actually signs that the drugs were working, and some persisted in denying that they were drug induced, by the 1960s, a growing body of opinion argued that long-term use of drugs that acted on dopamine was to blame, and a combination of legal cases and professional investigations in the 1970s supported that conclusion (Gelman, 1999). This led to a search for smarter drugs that did not produce these symptoms, and

a switch towards newer compounds as well as claims about the existence of so-called 'atypical antipsychotics' (Healy, 2001).[4] However,
the unavoidable fact is that all the drugs currently used in psychiatry
act on neurotransmission throughout the body, in gut, in muscle and
elsewhere, often leading to weight gain, drowsiness, motor problems
and much more.

Some might say – and indeed do say – that these unwanted effects
(let us not call them 'side-effects' for they are as much direct effects
as are those on mental states) are a price worth paying for drugs that
are effective in controlling distressing symptoms. And, to return to
the claims that I outlined earlier, can we conclude, on the basis of
evidence of the efficacy of the drugs through their action on brain
tissue, that psychiatric disorders are brain disorders?

First, it is important to point out that, while anomalies in neurotransmission in living patients diagnosed with psychiatric disorders
were hypothesized, these have never actually been demonstrated in
the synaptic clefts of living patients diagnosed with a disorder. A
series of claims about levels of metabolites in blood, urine or cerebro-
spinal fluid of those with psychiatric diagnoses have proved either
not to be replicable, to be artefacts, or to be false. Since the early
2000s, advances in molecular neuroimaging have been used to try
to identify anomalies in real time (Alpert et al., 2003), with some
claiming to have identified differences in neurochemical activity in
particular brain activity during the performance of specific tasks
(Badgaiyan, 2013). However, the evidence is limited and ambiguous,
not least because such molecular imaging has not been carried out
with drug-naive patients, and so it is not possible to know whether
any anomalies *predate* diagnosis and treatment, or whether they are
the *effects* of diagnosis and treatment with psychoactive drugs. To
put it bluntly, there is no evidence that neurotransmitter function is
abnormal in patients diagnosed with mental disorders prior to their
treatment with psychiatric drugs.

Second, and perhaps more worrying for those who wish to use evidence about the efficacy of drugs to support a claim that psychiatric
disorders are brain disorders, is the sad fact that the drugs are not
particularly effective. I will discuss this in detail in the next chapter,
but for now, let me merely quote Steven Hyman, former Director
of the US NIMH and now at the Broad Institute and Harvard,
in a piece published at the same time as Trimble and others were
making their claims. Over the half century since the initial discovery
of the psychiatric properties of certain drugs, Hyman argues, what is
important is what has *not* happened:

Many antidepressant drugs have been developed since the 1950s, but none has improved on the efficacy of imipramine or the first MAOIs [monoamine oxidase inhibitors], leaving many patients with modest benefits or none at all. Antipsychotic drugs achieved a peak in efficacy – never equaled and still not understood – with the discovery of clozapine in the mid-1960s. Although valproic acid and other drugs developed as anticonvulsants were shown in the early 1980s to be mood stabilizers, lithium remains a mainstay of treatment for bipolar disorder, despite its serious toxicities. There are still no broadly useful pharmacological treatments for the core symptoms of autism – social deficits, language delay, narrowed interests, and repetitive behaviors – or for the disabling negative (deficit) and cognitive symptoms of schizophrenia. The molecular targets of all of today's approved psychiatric drugs are the same as the targets of their pre-1960 prototypes ... and their mechanisms of action are not understood beyond a few initial molecular events. Indeed, the critical molecular target (or targets) for lithium have not been established with certainty. (Hyman, 2012: 1; references omitted)

In other words, none of the new smart drugs has improved on the efficacy of those discovered by chance, and in no case has the actual mode of action been identified or demonstrated in living patients. As we shall see in chapter 6, even modest claims for efficacy have often been greatly overstated. It would, therefore, be a brave or rash person to conclude that evidence about the efficacy of psychiatric drugs and our understanding of their specific mode of action in the brain demonstrates that psychiatric disorders are brain disorders.

Discovered in the genes?

Have researchers begun to delineate the genetic architecture of psychiatric disorders, not only identifying anomalous gene sequences associated with such disorders, but also beginning to work out the effects of these anomalies on neural architecture and functioning? I will focus here not on the common or minor mental troubles, those once termed 'the neuroses', for even the most hardened biological psychiatrist would agree that these have a complex aetiology that is entangled with 'life events'. Instead, let us consider the condition termed schizophrenia, and the widespread belief that, if any mental disorder is a 'brain disorder' with a clear genetic basis, it is schizophrenia.

There is a long history to the belief that schizophrenia 'runs in families', that is to say that the tendency to develop schizophrenia is inherited. But ever since Emil Kraepelin's diagnostic category of dementia praecox was renamed schizophrenia by Eugen Bleuler, in a lecture at the German Psychiatric Association in Berlin on 24 April 1908 (Kyziridis, 2005), clinicians have recognized that it is not a homogeneous entity (for a good overview, see Jablensky, 2010).

> [Bleuler] acknowledged that the clinical subgroups of paranoid schizophrenia, catatonia, hebephrenia, and simple schizophrenia were not 'natural' nosological entities and argued that 'schizophrenia must be a much broader concept than the overt psychosis of the same name'. Along with the 'latent' schizophrenias, which presented attenuated forms of the basic symptoms, manifesting as aberrant personality traits, he also listed within the 'broader concept' atypical depressive or manic states, Wernicke's motility psychoses, reactive psychoses, and other nonorganic, nonaffective psychotic disorders as belonging to the group of schizophrenias, on grounds that 'this is important for the studies of heredity'. (Jablensky, 2010: 273–4)

Jablensky charts the multiple endeavours at subtyping schizophrenia, culminating in Kurt Schneider's claim that "nine groups of psychotic manifestations" designated as "first rank symptoms" (FRS), had a "decisive weight" in the diagnosis of schizophrenia: audible thoughts; voices arguing about, or discussing, the patient; voices commenting on the patient's actions; experiences of influences on the body; thought withdrawal and other interference with thought; thought broadcast (diffusion of thought); delusional perception; and other experiences involving "made" impulses and feelings experienced as caused by an outside agency (Schneider, 1950). This was the view that was incorporated into the third edition of the *DSM*, the tenth edition of the *ICD* and various other diagnostic texts. Despite many other attempts at subtyping, the genetic explanation most strongly associated with the work of geneticist Franz Josef Kallmann (1938, 1946) – that is to say that the predisposition to develop schizophrenia was constitutional and determined by a genetic factor – was still widely believed.[5] This belief that schizophrenia comprised a single family of disorders underpinned by a single gene of major effect was the premise of the classic paper by Robins and Guze, 'Establishment of Diagnostic Validity in Psychiatric Illness: Its Application to Schizophrenia' (1970). This provided symptom-based criteria for differentiating schizophrenias with good or bad outcomes, and also argued that family studies – that is to say, studies of the inheritance patterns of the condition – were significant contributors to diagnostic accuracy. This was part of the work that led Robins,

Guze and their colleagues to formulate the Feighner criteria with the assumption that each diagnostic category would eventually be underpinned with a biological substrate – an approach that would underpin the checklist-based methods adopted in *DSM-III*.[6]

Despite the recognition by some researchers that, at the very least, schizophrenia was a polygenic condition (e.g. Slater, 1958, Gottesman and Shields, 1972), the overarching term 'schizophrenia' was taken to be a clinically valid diagnosis of a condition that, with the exception of some rare sporadic cases, had a strong genetic complement comprising one or a small number of genes.[7] Indeed, in the very first article published in the first issue of *Behavior Genetics* in 1970, Elston and Campbell asserted: "A reanalysis of extensive data collected by Kallman (1938, 1946), shows that a major gene hypothesis satisfactorily accounts for the genetic component in schizophrenia; the results are consistent with the biochemical evidence to date. It is therefore unnecessary to postulate a polygenic theory for schizophrenia" (1970: 3).

The debate continued over the next two decades, notably via a series of studies of dizygotic and monozygotic twins, and of adoption studies of monozygotic twins who had been brought up separately. In 2001, under the headline 'First Gene for Schizophrenia Discovered', an excited article by Kristin Leutwyler in *Scientific American* announced the publication of a paper in the journal *Molecular Psychiatry* reporting a study conducted by a large team of geneticists and psychiatrists of a single German family lineage in which seven members had been diagnosed with catatonic schizophrenia.[8] The authors of the study concluded, on the basis of gene sequencing, that the common feature among those individuals in this family lineage who were affected was a single 'mis-sense' mutation in a candidate gene on Chromosome 22, 22q13.33, which resulted in changes to the conformation of the WKL1 protein that affected the operation of an ion channel exclusively in brain tissue (Meyer et al., 2001). Meyer et al. suggested that this showed the importance of genetic mechanisms in the aetiology of schizophrenia, and provided a better understanding of their pathogenesis; they concluded that their results "provided evidence that haploinsufficiency of WKL1 causes a periodic subtype of catatonic schizophrenia" and that "[t]he identification of a schizophrenia-related gene will furnish a powerful tool to the understanding of the etiopathogenesis of catatonic schizophrenia and related disorders. Development of causal treatments of these devastating and cost-intensive disorders may now be a realistic prospect and an attainable goal" (2001: 305).[9]

Unfortunately for the authors' hopes, but in a manner that is very familiar, other teams rapidly published papers which found no such association in other samples. For example, no evidence to support this hypothesis was found in a US study of 43 cases diagnosed with schizophrenia with a clear evidence of family history, including some from German lineages (Devaney et al., 2002); a study in the UK "screened exon 11 of the WKL1 gene in 174 cases of schizophrenia, including 22 cases of catatonic schizophrenia, but could not detect the previously reported mis-sense mutation" – while they did find other mutations and polymorphisms affecting protein structure in this region of the gene, the frequency of these did not significantly differ between cases diagnosed with schizophrenia and their 'normal' controls, (Devaney et al., 2002). A similar negative result emerged in a study that screened for this WKL1 mutation in 117 Israeli Jewish patients with schizophrenia and 176 matched controls (Kaganovich et al., 2004).

However, the lack of convincing identification of the gene or genes involved convinced genetic researchers such as Peter McGufffin, Michael Owen and Anne Farmer in the UK that while there was "an important genetic contribution to the aetiology of schizophrenia, with estimates of the proportion of variance in the liability of the disorder accounted for by genes of between 63% and 85%", conventional genetic studies that assumed the existence of one or a small number of genes of major effect probably failed because this was a false assumption; while there clearly was a strong genetic element, this was likely to arise from the interaction of a number of genes of small effect (McGuffin et al., 1995: 681). From the mid-2000s, on the basis of this belief, many psychiatric geneticists chose to proceed in the way that was becoming standard among geneticists exploring common complex disorders – Genome Wide Association Studies (GWAS). In a GWAS, researchers select a group of subjects on the basis of a particular diagnosis, and a group of 'controls' who do not have that diagnosis. All those in each group give a sample of DNA, which is then sequenced in an 'array' that focuses on what are known as 'single nucleotide polymorphisms', millions of places on the genome where individuals are known to differ on a single nucleotide – for example, where an adenine (A) is substituted by a thymine (T). The arrays of single nucleotide polymorphisms (SNPs) from cases are then compared with those from the controls, to see if there are significant differences in the frequency in which particular SNPs occur in the two groups, and if so, where in the genome they occur. Some refer to GWAS as 'hypothesis free', but of course this is an oversimplification, as they are based on the hypothesis that SNP variations are crucial for the disease or condition in question.

While GWAS research yielded promising results for some non-psychiatric disorders, their results for psychiatric disorders were disappointing. Some psychiatric geneticists were consistently optimistic about the results; thus Sullivan, Daley and O'Donovan, in a 2012 review in *Nature Genetics*, claimed that this research method, supplemented by other genetic investigations, had yielded new hypotheses about the genetic architecture of nine psychiatric disorders: Alzheimer's disease, ADHD, alcohol dependence, anorexia nervosa, autism spectrum disorder, bipolar disorder, major depressive disorder, nicotine dependence and schizophrenia – with implications for future research strategies. As far as schizophrenia is concerned, they pointed to 14 loci where significant differences in allele frequency had been found between cases and controls. However, although claiming statistical significance, the odds ratios in each case were small,[10] and there was overlap between cases and controls. That is to say, no variant was either necessary or sufficient to account for the development of a condition diagnosed as schizophrenia.

Nonetheless, by 2014, this group, and other researchers in the Schizophrenia Working Group of the Psychiatric Genomics Consortium, were reporting that, on the basis of "a multi-stage schizophrenia genome-wide association study of up to 36,989 cases and 113,075 controls", they had identified "128 independent associations spanning 108 conservatively defined loci that meet genome-wide significance, 83 of which have not been previously reported". They suggested that "enriched" associations were found "among genes expressed in brain providing biological plausibility for the findings" – pointing in particular to genes related to the neurotransmission of glutamate, and also to genes expressed in tissue related to immunity, "providing support for the hypothesized link between the immune system and schizophrenia" (Schizophrenia Working Group of the Psychiatric Genomics Consortium, 2014).

However, there are many problems with the claims made for studies of this sort.[11] First, at least 25 per cent of the loci identified do not, as far as is known, code for protein, so their role is unknown. Second, even those that do have known functions in relation to biologically active proteins seem to relate to very basic neural functioning, for example small variations in calcium channels, which, if significant at all, are no doubt involved in all manner of differences between individuals. Third, it is by now well established among geneticists that a significant proportion of the genetic risk for schizophrenia comes not from common variants identified by GWAS, but from rare variants, that is to say where a particular set of variants may be present in a few, or even a single family lineage. Indeed, as Jacob Gratten put it in 2016, on the basis of a very large DNA sequencing study of schizophrenia featuring more than 11,000 cases and controls from Sweden (see Genovese et al., 2016), "rare variants are common in schizophrenia" (Gratten, 2016). Researchers now believe that some rare variants that contribute to the risk of developing a disorder diagnosed as schizophrenia may be *de novo* – that is to say, newly arising – in the individuals or families involved, and these include copy number variations, or CNVs, where a particular sequence of nucleotides is repeated many times. Fourth, even taken together, the GWAS-identified loci account for a relatively small proportion of the 'heritability' that has long been thought to be a characteristic of schizophrenia, and for each locus there is considerable overlap between cases and controls. And fifth, of course, these studies all rely on the diagnostic category of schizophrenia, which, as we have already seen, is widely believed, at the very least, to encapsulate an array of different phenotypical and genotypical conditions. Indeed, to complicate still further the interpretation of these findings, research-ers themselves point out that "schizophrenia shares risk alleles with other neuropsychiatric phenotypes, such as bipolar disorder, major depressive disorder, autism spectrum disorder, intellectual disability and attention-deficit hyperactivity disorder" (Rees et al., 2015: 8).

So what, in fact, have we discovered? Simply, that there are many hundreds of small variations in basic neural processes, each of which, in various combinations, may lead to a slight increase or decrease in the risk of being diagnosed with any one of a whole variety of mental disorders. We have found evidence of many variations among individuals in basic neuronal processes, some but not all of which, unsurprisingly, are linked to variations in inherited DNA. But have we discovered anything about the genetic basis of a brain disorder termed schizophrenia? I do not think so.[12] Indeed, as Sir Robin Murray, doyen of the Institute of Psychiatry of King's College London, concluded in his reminiscence, 'Mistakes I Have Made in My Research Career': "I expect to see the end of the concept of schiz-ophrenia soon. Already the evidence that it is a discrete entity rather than just the severe end of psychosis has been fatally undermined . . . Presumably this process will accelerate, and the term schizophrenia will be confined to history, like 'dropsy'" (2016: 256).

No doubt, few schizophrenia researchers would agree completely with Murray.[13] Yet many *would* agree that we need to discard the classical notion of schizophrenia as a discrete category with subtypes, as well as the belief that it is a condition that leads to inevitable mental decline. For Murray, the way we conceptualize psychosis needs to be rethought; he suggests that there is a single dimension of this disorder, manifested at different levels of severity and in different symptom clusters. Yet research to find the genetic and neurobiological basis of schizophrenia seems to continue as if nothing had changed in the fundamental premise that it makes sense to research a disease entity called schizophrenia, that it has a genetic basis, and that it is possible to identify specific neurobiological anomalies in those living under the description of schizophrenia which may have both diagnostic and clinical relevance. When it comes to psychiatric genetics, one might be forgiven for recalling the famous lines in Tomasi di Lampedusa's *The Leopard* (1960): "If we want things to stay as they are, things will have to change"; or to put it in the usual misquoted form: "Everything must change so that everything can stay the same."

Visible in the brain images?

Some might think that the most compelling evidence would be to be able to 'see' these disorders in the tissues and circuits of the living human brain. So, have structural and functional brain imaging shown indisputably that psychiatric disorders are brain disorders? Since the 1970s, a range of powerful imaging technologies for exploring brain structure and function in real time in living humans has become available. Computerized tomography (CT) scanning and magnetic resonance imaging (MRI) enabled imaging of the structure of tissues, including in the brain. Positron emission technology (PET) images the uptake of certain radio-labelled elements into tissue as a proxy for brain activity in that area. Functional magnetic resonance imaging (fMRI) images changes in blood oxygenation level as a proxy for brain activity. Brain imaging has been the subject of a large body of literature in science and technology studies, notably by Anne Beaulieu and Joseph Dumit (Dumit, 1999, 2003; Burri and Dumit, 2007; Beaulieu, 2000a, 2000b, 2002).[14] What do these studies enable us to conclude with regard to the locus of mental disorders in the brain?

As Krishnan points out in his 2012 chapter on 'Structural Imaging in Psychiatric Disorders' in the *Handbook of Clinical Neurology*: "Since the advent of the ability to assess the brain in a living person, the Holy

Grail has been the attempt to find 'the pathology' in the disease. It soon became apparent that there are few visually observable findings among patients with psychiatric disorders" (2012: 90). While MRI scans do show observable vascular changes in some elderly patients with a variety of psychiatric disorders, Krishnan reports that visually observable volumetric changes are rarely observable except in dementia. When structural neuroimaging is used to explore other psychiatric conditions, Krishnan points to significant technical problems, notably diverse ways of defining and describing the brain regions of interest. As far as major depression is concerned, Krishnan reports that a number of studies claim that grey-matter loss in the hippocampus is characteristic of major depression, but "a significant number of studies have failed to find evidence of hippocampus atrophy in depressed patients" and, in general, except in elderly patients, finding are inconsistent and show considerable heterogeneity.

Krishnan is more optimistic, if that is the word, in relation to studies in patients with schizophrenia, arguing that they do show volumetric reductions in a range of regions when compared to healthy controls. However, other researchers have argued that these brain changes in patients diagnosed with schizophrenia do not reflect "an intrinsic degenerative schizophrenic process" but are a consequence of factors such as illicit drug use, cigarette smoking, obesity and diagnosis, and, in a wretched repeat of the terrible experience of long-term use of earlier neuroleptics, of antipsychotic drugs themselves, animal studies "have confirmed the effects of antipsychotics in decreasing cortical volume" (Murray et al., 2016: 362; references omitted). Robin Murray and colleagues also argue that these effects seem to be reversible on stopping antipsychotics, and conclude that there is no clear link between the changes shown in MRI studies of this sort and either cognitive decline or functional impairment. We cannot, then, conclude that structural brain imaging demonstrates that psychiatric disorders are brain disorders. On the contrary, evidence seems to suggest that the experiences of those who have a psychiatric diagnosis, together with the drug regimes utilized, are at the least a very significant cause of any changes found in the brains of diagnosed and treated psychiatric patients when compared to those who have not been so diagnosed and treated.

But if structural imaging is ambiguous, perhaps functional brain imaging might do better, actually identifying that disordered 'wiring' in neural circuits on which Josh Gordon places his bets.[15] As we would anticipate, given the popularity of fMRI in papers claiming that this or that human characteristic has its basis in this or that brain region (Logothetis, 2008), many studies have been carried out comparing individuals with a psychiatric diagnosis with those who have not been so diagnosed when they are asked to carry out a task in a scanner. As there are far too many studies to summarize here, let me refer to a recent review by Emma Sprooten and colleagues, who "undertook a systematic meta-analysis of data from task-fMRI studies to examine the effect of diagnosis and study design on the spatial distribution and direction of case-control differences on brain activation. We mapped to atlas regions coordinates of case-control differences derived from 537 task-fMRI studies in schizophrenia, bipolar disorder, major depressive disorder, anxiety disorders, and obsessive compulsive disorder comprising observations derived from 21,427 participants" (2017: 1846). They focused on the circuits proposed by the US NIMH in their RDoC project.[16] RDoC proposed that mental disorders arise from disruptions in neural circuits underpinning specific domains of mental activity, and suggested that there were at least five key circuits: reward (positive valence systems), threat sensitivity (negative valence systems), cognitive processes, interpersonal interactions (social processes), and biological activation (arousal and regulation).

While Sprooten and colleagues found that every brain region was implicated by at least one study – hence showing the kinds of variability that we found when looking at structural imaging – their main finding was that, although there were many reported group differences between cases and controls, these differences were similar across all diagnoses. They conclude: "The abnormalities in brain networks and network-regions we can observe with fMRI reflect disorder-general conditions that facilitate the emergence and persistence of symptoms but are insufficient for explaining symptomatic variability across disorders" (2017: 1857) – that is to say, they find differences between cases and controls, but do not differentiate between the very different symptoms used to classify different conditions. As 'the Neuroskeptic' puts it: "there was little or no diagnostic specificity in the fMRI results. Differences between patients and controls were seen in the same brain regions, regardless of the patients' diagnosis."[17]

Sprooten and colleagues suggest that these results reflect some neuronal circuit dysfunction, which is common to almost all psychiatric conditions and which has a causal role. But the Neuroskeptic points out that "it's notable that almost all of these top-10 regions fall within the 'limbic system' of the brain, i.e. areas which are traditionally thought to be involved in emotion." Given what we know about the actual circumstances under which brain imaging is carried out, the differences that were found may well reflect differences in anxiety and arousal experienced by the psychiatric patients, rather than the controls, when in the scanner.[18] Indeed, Simon Cohn has argued, on the basis of ethnographic work with brain imagers, that "what finally appears as an area of activation in the final brain scan of a volunteer is actually the combined response of the person in the scanner, the physical provisions of the experiment, and the thinking of the scientist who not only has to prime the volunteer, but who also establishes an essential level of intimacy with him or her in order for the experiment to be conducted in the first place" (2008: 99).

But even discounting the different experiences of the scanning situation between psychiatric patients and controls, is it not as plausible to suggest that, as with structural imaging, at least some of these differences arise from treatment with psychiatric drugs – as far as we know, none of the groups of cases were drug- or treatment-naive – and are thus *consequential* upon diagnosis and treatment, rather than being causal? Others may, and do, disagree. But my conclusion, on the basis of this review of the evidence, is that neither structural nor functional brain imaging have shown clear and incontrovertible differences between treatment-naive individuals or groups diagnosed with psychiatric disorders and so-called 'healthy controls'. To put it bluntly, brain imaging does not show indisputably that psychiatric disorders are brain disorders.

So are mental disorders brain disorders?

Let me return to the quotes with which I began this chapter. When the US Surgeon General used terms such as "mediated", "reflect" or "clearly reflect" to express the relation between mental lives and brain states, he was expressing, in a rough and ready way, something that has become the premise of contemporary neuroscience: all mental processes have a definite physical basis in the brain, or, to use the term more commonly employed by neuroscientists, they have 'neural correlates'. From this premise it follows that this must be as true for those ways of thinking, feeling and willing that we delineate as mental disorders as it is for other mental processes; hence, it is to the brain, and to these neural correlates, that we should look in order to understand these disorders. Hence, for those that reason this way, it is the neural processes in the brain that we should target if we wish to intervene in them.

At about the same time as the Surgeon General was writing his report, that is to say at the end of the 1990s, an editorial appeared in *Nature Neuroscience* entitled 'Celebrating a Decade of Progress', which explicitly linked the need for brain-based explanations of mental disorder to the data on burden discussed in the last chapter:

> The expansion of neuroscience has been driven by two major factors. One has been a growing awareness of the social and economic burden of brain disease, which seems certain to increase in most industrialized countries as their populations age ... The second factor, set against these grim statistics, is the increasing confidence of the research community that brain disease is now a tractable problem. Conditions such as depression, schizophrenia, stroke and age-related cognitive decline, once considered inevitable features of the human condition, are now seen as specific diseases whose causes can be identified and which it will some day be possible to prevent or cure. (*Nature Neuroscience*, 1999: 487)

Thus, by 1999 the editors of *Nature Neuroscience* also believed that these conditions – both those conventionally understood as mental disorders such as depression, and those thought of as neurological, such as stroke – were 'specific' diseases, that they all lay within a domain termed 'brain disease' and, because they were now 'specific brain diseases', they had become 'tractable' – that is to say, according to the *Oxford English Dictionary*, docile, compliant, manageable, governable.

In large part, this was because of the view of the brain that had taken shape in the previous 35 years, since the birth of neuroscience in 1962 (Rose and Abi-Rached, 2013). In this style of thought, a particular way of seeing the brain had taken shape, in which the brain was an organ in principle like any other. Although, of course, it was highly complex, vastly more so than, say, the heart or the liver, and more an assemblage of different parts than a single organ, it too was made of cells with familiar features such as nuclei, cell membranes, ion channels and so forth, interacting with one another in intelligible ways. In this 'neuromolecular gaze', the molecular scale seemed the obvious starting point for any understanding of the brain and how it works (Purves, 2010). One would start with the cell, for what was the brain but a collection of cells of different sorts, connected to one another in various ways? One could understand the cell in terms of its molecular properties and these could be explained in terms of biochemistry and biophysics – that is to say, in terms of physical laws, notably those related to the chemical and electrical phenomena that govern its operations. One could anatomize the brain, in terms of the different kinds of cells in different regions and layers, glia, astrocytes, neurons of various configurations, synapses, receptor sites, ion channels, and how they were influenced by their surrounding milieu. One could tease out the ways these cells connected to one another across short, medium and long distances, and so how they built into circuits with specific functions. And, at least in principle, once one knew these basic features of cells and the ways they connected and communicated with one another, one could move up the scale from the cell, to the circuits, to the organ, to the organism. Mystery had given way to mechanism. We are all materialists now.

It was not just that all mental disorders were disturbances with a basis in the cells, circuits, tissues of the brain, but also that, in principle, both normal and abnormal mental states were to be explained in exactly the same terms: mental disorders would be constituted as anomalies or malfunctions within molecular systems, and normal variations in emotion, cognition and volition would also be explained in molecular terms of variations within those same systems. In short, pathological mental states and processes would both be seen as emerging directly from cerebral events. It therefore was anticipated that neuropsychiatry would be able to identify these organic anomalies, or, at the very least, to discover biological markers that would identify them, and that these biomarkers would differ between different conditions, assisting in the problematic craft of diagnosis. Further, once one had identified these anomalous molecular underpinnings, one would be able to develop more effective treatments – more effective because these would target the neuromolecular bases of specific disorders in the brain.

Now, of course, there are many logical flaws in this line of reasoning, most crucially the assumption that the key direction of causation is from brain processes to mental life and behaviour, and hence that to intervene in abnormal – or even normal – mental life and behaviour, one should intervene in those brain processes. While this seems to be the premise of the position articulated by Josh Gordon in the quote at the start of this chapter, there are perfectly plausible arguments that go in exactly the other direction.

Undoubtedly, we have learnt more about the brain in the last 30 years than ever before. But to use the cliché, the more we know, the more we know we don't know. Despite the arguments of Michael Trimble, and of White, Rickards and Zeman that we discussed earlier in this chapter, we are no closer to making the link between genetic sequences, molecular events, patterns of neural activity and mental states. While some believe that we simply need more time, and better tools to achieve this level of understanding, many serious researchers recognize that the task of connecting up these different levels of explanation is currently beyond our capacities. So, is neuropsychiatry at the start of a long journey, but on the right path? Will we finally get to these underlying mechanisms? Do symptoms, as the Surgeon General put it, clearly reflect abnormality in neural processes? Or is this path somehow leading us astray? Even if there are neural correlates of the disorders, should the whole emphasis of our research strategy focus on those? How shall we understand the causal webs here? Are these brain anomalies with a genetic basis, which are just triggered by an environment, leading to the disorder? Or is the reverse more plausible – that what is causal is a form of life, an embodied person in an interpersonal, cultural, social and material environment in which the disorder is produced, which has neural conditions and has neural correlates? Perhaps, when it comes to such a continually transforming heterogeneous complex of tissues and milieu, in which seemingly similar forms of distress can arise in multiple different ways, and in which similar experiences may give rise to very different responses in different individuals and groups, we must abandon linear ideas of causality altogether and learn to think in a new way.

There are, of course, some neuroscientists who are trying to think differently. Take this statement by Anthony Damasio, for example:

(1) The human brain and the rest of the body constitute an indissociable organism, integrated by means of mutually interactive biochemical and neural regulatory circuits (including endocrine, immune and autonomic neural components); (2) The organism interacts with the environment as an ensemble: the interaction is neither of the body alone nor of the brain alone; (3) The physiological operations that we call mind are derived from the structural and functional ensemble rather than from the brain alone: mental phenomena can be fully understood only in the context of an organism's interacting in an environment. That the environment is, in part, a product of the organism's activity itself merely underscores the complexity of interactions we must take into account. (1995: xvi–xvii)

As I have said repeatedly, no one would doubt that mental distress, and mild, moderate and severe mental disorders involve brains. But these are not 'brains in vats'. We do not need the authority of Damasio to realize that brains are part of complex bodily systems, so disorders are of organisms – human beings – and human beings in particular and sometimes stressful social contexts.

Does it matter if we start from the brain rather than from the social? Of course, we need to conceptualize the complex interactions between social factors and neurobiology, but I doubt that we can understand the rise in such conditions from a perspective that starts with the brain and merely adds in 'the environment' as a provoking or protective factor. As with diabetes, hypertension, coronary disease or lung cancer, while these are indeed conditions of bodily tissues, it would be rash to claim that either causes or treatments can focus on those tissues alone. As we have seen in earlier chapters, even for severe mental disorders there is growing evidence about the role of childhood adversity and trauma in the development of psychosis (for one example, see Frissen et al., 2015). But even if not, we must be rather cautious with the powerful rhetoric about 'the burden of brain disorders', because – as I have argued earlier – many of these conditions could equally well be called 'social adversity disorders'.

When it comes to psychiatry, we have scarcely even begun to really tackle the question of the complexity of the entanglements that lead any individual to mental distress, either mild or severe. And, I suggest that if we focus the whole of our research endeavour on the brain, we will limit our capacity to understand these complex processes. One of the things that we do know from contemporary neuroscience is that the brain is the most highly modulated, the most open, the most transactional organ, of the whole body, modulated from the moment of conception by its engagement with its milieu. Unless we are prepared to grasp that, and to take the implications seriously for knowledge, for research and for the prevention of mental distress and interventions for those who experience it, whether mildly or severely, we will go round and round the same circles.

I do not want to deny the importance of neuroscientific research for psychiatry. But it is not enough to simply acknowledge that social and environmental factors are important, and then to maintain that the research and explanation must focus on the neuronal architecture of the brain. A collaborative approach to research is necessary to put the brain back into the organism and the organism – the human – back into the interpersonal, cultural and physical milieu for which it has evolved, in which it develops from the moment of conception, if not before, and without which it would be unable to perform the most basic of its functions. To accept this requires us to go beyond gestural references to 'the environment', and to acknowledge that sociality is fundamental to the development of human neural and mental capacities from conception, if not before, and hence fundamental to understanding and treating human mental disorders.

6

Does Psychopharmacology Have a Future?

[W]hat has been designated 'the catecholamine hypothesis of affective disorders,' proposes that some, if not all, depressions are associated with an absolute or relative deficiency of catecholamines, particularly norepinephrine, at functionally important adrenergic receptor sites in the brain. Elation, conversely, may be associated with an excess of such amines ... This hypothesis is undoubtedly, at best, a reductionist over-simplification of a very complex biochemical state and that the simultaneous effects of the indoleamines, other biogenic amines, hormones and ionic changed will ultimately have to be included in any comprehensive formulation of the biochemistry of affective disorders.

Schildkraut (1965: 509, 517)

The number of antidepressants given to patients in England has doubled in a decade, official figures show. In 2015 there were 61m such drugs prescribed and dispensed outside of hospitals. They are used to treat clinical depression as well as other conditions such as generalised anxiety disorder, obsessive compulsive disorder and panic attacks. The total was 31.6m more than in 2005 and up 3.9m, or 6.8% on 2014, according to a report from the Health and Social Care Information Centre (HSCIC). The net cost of ingredients of antidepressants, before taking account of any money reclaimed by the NHS, was nearly £285m last year. About nine in 10 of all medicines are dispensed to people eligible for free prescriptions, including older people and children.

Guardian, 5 July 2016

It may seem strange to ask if psychopharmacology – that is to say, the development, prescribing and utilization of drugs that act on mental states and behaviour, and the related forms of knowledge – has a future. For psychiatric drugs certainly have a presence in our present

– and one that is growing globally. Psychiatric drugs – from tranquillizers, to antidepressants, to antipsychotics – have become integral to many practices for the government of mental states and human conduct. They are prescribed by general practitioners to millions of people experiencing problems managing their everyday lives. Many seek them out, in the hope that, at the least, the drugs will provide them with relief and help them cope, and perhaps even restore them to a feeling of normality, to enable them to "feel like themselves again".[1] They are used in hospitals and clinics – often as first line treatment – for those experiencing major disruptions in their moods, sudden swings in emotions, hearing voices or afflicted by strange beliefs. They are used to regulate disorders of attention in children, with the rise and rise of the diagnoses of attention and hyperactivity disorders. High volumes of these drugs are given in institutions, not just to control conduct in prisons but also to manage behaviour problems in homes for the elderly and those with dementia. Over the last 50 years of the twentieth century, the development, manufacture and marketing of these drugs became a highly profitable part of the portfolio of pharmaceutical companies. And both within those companies, and in universities and laboratories across the world, research on the neurobiological underpinnings of psychiatric disorders has gone hand in hand with strategies for drug development, in the belief that if one understood the anomalies in neural mechanisms leading to mental disorders, one would be able to develop pharmaceuticals to target and rectify them.

Further, it is hard to imagine a world without these drugs, because of the growing belief that some of these pharmaceuticals can improve 'normal' mental functioning, enhancing memory or attentiveness in a range of areas, from university students to the military.[2] And, at a first glance, the future for psychopharmacology looks bright. Despite the increasingly global use of these drugs, there remain many markets to exploit, not least in China, India and Southeast Asia, where we can observe the rapid growth of indigenous pharmaceutical corporations. And, as life expectancy across the globe increases, and more and more people live into old age, the numbers who will be diagnosed with neurodegenerative disorders such as Parkinson's disease and the various dementias will inevitably increase, along with a growing demand for drugs to treat these conditions.

Yet, in another sense, as we shall see, the question for this chapter is not so strange. For the future for psychopharmacology is not quite that which was predicted for it. The dream of specificity, of smart, targeted drugs, effective and with minimal side-effects because they rectify the faulty neurobiology at the root of the problem, or personalized drugs that are tailored precisely to match the problems of each specific individual – well, these remain dreams, or promises that fewer and fewer experts believe. Indeed, when it comes to psychopharmacology, our present is paradoxical. More and more people are taking such medication at the very time when the hypotheses that underpinned the development of that medication have proved wrong, or, at the least, partial. As discussed in a previous chapter, the drugs we have today are, in almost all cases, no more effective than those we had 40 years ago. We still have no effective drugs for the treatment of dementia. And, as we shall see, when it comes to psychiatric drugs, there is a crisis of confidence, not only among many of the funders of research, but also among the commercial drug companies themselves. So is there a future for psychopharmacology, and, if so, what will it look like? These are the hard questions that we will explore in this chapter.

How did we get here?

The story of the rise of psychopharmaceuticals is well known.[3] The 'neuroleptics' such as chlorpromazine (known as Largactil or Thorazine) were invented in the 1950s and initially used for control within the asylum, gradually becoming part of the rationale for treatment of patients outside hospitals. Also in the 1950s, we saw the invention of the first 'tranquillizers' (Miltown, Librium and Valium), which rapidly became part of every doctor's pharmacopoeia. They were joined by the antidepressants, imipramine in the late 1950s, amitriptyline in the 1960s: the promotion of these drugs as antidepressants went hand in hand with increasing diagnosis of depression among people outside hospital. The selective serotonin reuptake inhibitors such as Prozac and its sisters came onto the market in the 1980s claiming that they were more effective than older antidepressants because they targeted the neurobiological pathways of the disorders in the neurotransmitter system. They rapidly broadened their scope to panic disorders, anxiety, shyness and much more, claiming not simply to help people cope, but to enable sufferers to 'become themselves again'. Some figures will illustrate the scale and scope.

Let me begin with the UK, where the National Health Service enables us to obtain very good data on prescribing rates. Throughout this discussion, we need to be aware that, as many studies have shown, being *prescribed* drugs is not equivalent to *taking* those drugs and many patients fail to 'comply' or 'adhere' with their drug regime, choosing – often because of the unpleasant consequences that experts call 'side-effects' – not to take their medication (Patel and David, 2004). Putting this issue to one side for now, the Council for Evidence-Based Psychiatry reported: "In 2013 there were over 80m prescriptions of psychiatric drugs in England alone. Almost 10m people in the UK – around 15% of the population – are taking benzodiazepines (tranquilizers), antidepressants or other psychiatric medications at any given time . . . In 2013 in England alone over 53 million prescriptions were issued for antidepressants, a 6% increase on the previous year and a 92% increase since 2003."[4] Stephen Ilyas and Joanna Moncrieff (2012) used data from the UK's Prescription Cost Analysis from 1998 to 2010 to show the rising use and costs of prescriptions in the four major classes usually used to classify psychiatric drugs. They found that, in fact, prescriptions of drugs for mental disorders rose at around the same rate as those for other drugs – about 7 per cent each year, and that there were "rising trends in prescriptions of all classes of psychiatric drugs, except anxiolytics and hypnotics (which did not change). Antidepressant prescriptions increased by 10% . . . per year on average, and antipsychotics by 5.1%" – as shown in Figure 6.1.

These trends, notably the increase in prescribing of the class of drugs known as antidepressants, are repeated in almost every region where we have data: "Antidepressant prescribing in Spain, Germany, Denmark, UK and the Netherlands has shown an increasing trend from 2001–2009, with a higher rate for women" (Abbing-Karahagopian et al., 2014); "In Italy there was a twofold increase in Antidepressant consumption between 2001 and 2007" (Damiani et al., 2013); "In The Netherlands there was an increase in prescriptions of psychotropic drugs, with the exception of anxiolytic drugs from 2001–2006" (Wittkampf et al., 2010); "Canada, USA, Greece and Ireland have all shown an increase from 2007–2011, in the use of antidepressants, with a noticeably higher rate in North America when compared to Greece and Ireland" (Wilby et al., 2013). And data from the OECD, reproduced in Figure 6.2, shows rises in antidepressant prescribing in every OECD country from Korea to Iceland[5] in the first decade of this century, with Denmark, Canada and Australia leading the way. As for the United States, "[b]etween 1988–1994 and 2007–2010, among adults aged 18 or over, the use of antidepressants increased more than four-fold, from 2.4% to 10.8%", with the use of prescription antidepressants being higher for women than for men (Office of Public Health and Human Services Department, 2015: 26).

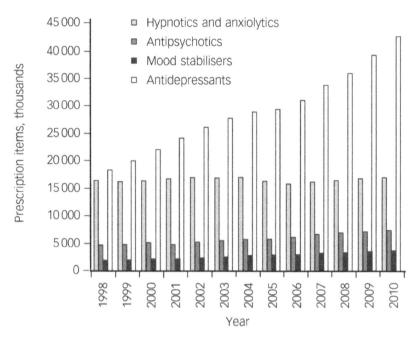

Figure 6.1 Trends in prescriptions of major classes of psychiatric drugs 1998–2010

Source: Ilyas and Moncrieff (2012)

As for China, India and Southeast Asia, with the exception of South Korea, which is within the OECD, robust data is hard to find. China has a recent history of high use of pharmaceuticals, to some extent explained by the system whereby hospitals and doctors obtained a mark-up on any drugs they prescribed. For instance, it has been reported that the "average Chinese citizen consumes ten times as many antibiotics as the average American", which has led to considerable distrust of doctors, and worries over corruption at all levels, and confusion about the roles of the many different agencies involved in pharmaceutical strategy (Burki, 2017). It is also clear that many potential patients make use of non-prescription drugs, traditional remedies available from pharmacies, or drugs purchased on the grey market. Yet at the same time, there is a widespread view, to quote a recent headline in the *South China Morning Post*,[6] that "[m]illions of people with mental illness in China, India go untreated" – a report that draws on a study published in *The Lancet* that claims that less than 6 per cent of those with anxiety, depression and other mental afflictions

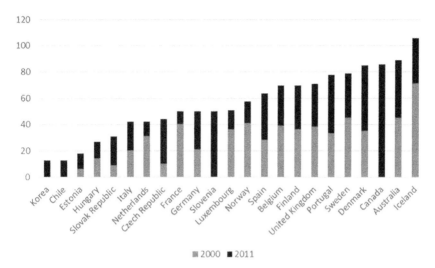

Figure 6.2 Antidepressant consumption (defined daily dosage per 1000 people per day), 2000 (light grey bar, if data available) and 2011 or nearest year (total bar height)

Source: Compiled with data from OECD (2013)

seek help due to stigma or lack of access to resources (Charlson et al., 2016).[7]

The Research in East Asia Psychotropic Prescription Pattern on Antidepressants (REAP-AD) studied the prescription patterns in the use of antidepressants at selected clinics in China, Hong Kong, India, Indonesia, Japan, Korea, Malaysia, Singapore, Taiwan and Thailand and found an increasing use of SSRI antidepressants in the ten years since 2003–4, but it was not possible to estimate national uses given the paucity of data (Chee et al., 2015). In 2012, a market data company Research and Markets suggested that there was recent growth in China's market for antidepressants, estimating the market for antidepressants in hospital medicines at about CNY3.2 billion, though with an increase of over 22 per cent year on year, and predicted that the future annual growth would be of the order of 20 per cent year on year.[8]

We should be wary about taking these estimates literally, as they are subject to many cautions. However, some general patterns emerge. First, the growth in the global market for drugs is focused on the class termed antidepressants, and in particular the SSRIs.[9] Second, where we have evidence of the rates of prescribing of other classes of drug, we can see that these SSRIs are not displacing other drugs, as was initially expected – in particular, that they would displace the tranquillizers. In fact, prescribing rates for hypnotics and anxiolytics have remained stable, so clearly new populations are being recruited into psychiatric drug use. Third, we need to bear in mind the point that I made earlier: while many reports suggest that the rising rate of prescribing of these SSRI-type drugs points to an epidemic of depression, this class of drugs has spread its net far beyond mild to moderate depression – the diagnoses that formed its initial target – to a range of other 'common mental disorders' – that is to say, to diagnoses such as anxiety disorders and panic disorders.

Whatever the limitations of the data, the trend is clear – more and more of our fellow citizens across the globe are being prescribed psychopharmaceuticals for a range of 'common mental disorders' such as depression, anxiety, panic, shyness, phobias, post-traumatic disorders and obsessive-compulsive disorder. Which, of course, raises the question 'why?' Or, to put it in more researchable terms, *how* has psycho-pharmaceuticalization arisen? And, of course, a further question: do the drugs work?

The drugs don't do nothing, but . . .

Once we could have put the spread of these drugs down to the ambitions of the drug companies, and many did blame 'big pharma' – direct-to-consumer advertising, suborning of psychiatrists, publication of misleading results from clinical trials, wilful misinterpretation of evidence, the laxity of the regulators and so forth (Whitaker, 2010; Healy, 2004; Angell, 2004, 2011). This would not be completely misleading, although it is not an entirely satisfactory explanation. Thus, for example, the increasing use of psychopharmaceuticals is not confined to countries which allow 'direct-to-consumer' advertising of the drugs, and there is no correlation between the rates of increase and the presence or absence of such advertising (Rose, 2003b, 2006b). There is certainly plenty of evidence, especially in the United States, of close financial links between some psychiatrists, thought to be 'Key Opinion Leaders', and the pharmaceutical companies, shaping their advocacy for particular drugs, and indeed for the prevalence of the disorders that the drugs purport to treat (Moynihan, 2008).[10] More generally, there have been many critical accounts of the ways that pharmaceutical companies sell their products to clinicians, from sponsoring trips to conferences in exotic locations, honoraria for lectures, even ghost-writing articles that evaluate (positively) their products (Moynihan and Cassels, 2005; Goldacre, 2012). Pharmaceutical companies, especially in the United States, also give financial support to patient advocacy groups and others involved in patient and family education on the nature and treatment of mental disorders (McCoy et al., 2017). More directly however, it is important to consider the question of clinical trials and their adequacy.

At the risk of some repetition, let us spend some time directly on this question. Randomized control trials (RCTs) are of importance, in part because most of those who evaluate research findings, including the proponents of 'evidence-based medicine', place the results of RCTs, in particular double-blind RCTs, at the top of their hierarchy of evidence (Guyatt et al., 1995). However, the problems with RCTs are well known. As Trish Greenhalgh pointed out in a paper published soon after such 'hierarchies' of evidence became popular, the results of RCTs may be "of limited applicability" – somewhat of an understatement – "as a result of exclusion criteria (rules about how may not be entered into the study), inclusion bias (selection of subjects from a group unrepresentative of everyone with the condition), refusal of certain patient groups to give consent to be included in the trial, analysis of only predefined 'objective' endpoints which may exclude important qualitative aspects of the intervention, and publication bias (the selective publication of positive results)" (Greenhalgh, 1998: 244).[11]

Such problems throw claims for efficacy of psychiatric pharmaceuticals based on RCTs into doubt.[12] Many trials exclude exactly the subjects for whom the drug is intended (people above or below a certain age, people who have previously attempted suicide, people who are not 'drug-naive' and have already used, or are currently using, one or more psychiatric drugs). Many trials evaluate results only on the basis of the use of standardized scales, and do not explore other consequences of the drugs in question for the subjects (weight gain, sexual dysfunction, etc.). And there is strong evidence of publication bias, especially in trials funded by pharmaceutical companies – that is to say, publication of trials that show favourable results for 'their' drug, and nonpublication of those that show no difference between the drug and placebo or treatment as usual, let alone a negative result.[13] These issues are made more problematic by the fact that the conduct of many drug trials is now 'outsourced' to commercial organizations which commonly do the trial in the Global South, for reasons of economy and in the search for drug-naive subjects, often paying hospitals and doctors for their participation, who in their turn will make spurious promises to potential subjects in order to recruit them, and, according to some investigations, report spurious results (Drain et al., 2014; Woodhead, 2016; Kamat, 2014). For psychiatric drugs, these problems are further compounded by the fact that trials are usually short – lasting for a few weeks – while in practice the drugs will often be given for months if not for years: such trials do not evaluate long-term effects. Randomization tends to be compromised in trials where clinicians recommend patients for participation who they think will respond well to the treatment, or by patients actively seeking out trial participation for reasons of dissatisfaction with existing treatments, or because they hope this 'new' drug will work where others have not.[14] Further, RCTs for psychopharmaceuticals are supposed to be 'double-blind', with neither the subjects nor the investigators knowing who is on the active drug. This aims to avoid both the placebo effect, where those being given a drug report improvements even where the substance is inactive, and experimenter effects, where experimenters, non-consciously, find favourable results for the drug they are investigating. However, in many cases the blinds are imaginary, with both subjects and investigators working out who is taking the active drug on the basis of 'side-effects' such as dry mouths or muscle aches.

I have already briefly noted the consequences of these issues in chapter 5. Irving Kirsch undertook a meticulous analysis of clinical trial evidence concerning the efficacy of drugs marketed as antidepressants, including access to the many clinical trials of drugs that were not published, presumably because they showed no advantage to the trial drugs. On the basis of this research, he argues that there is no evidence that these antidepressant drugs are any more effective than placebos in reducing symptoms; indeed, placebos are hardly less effective in reducing symptoms than the active drugs. Further, when the placebos simulate some of the 'side-effects' of the active drug that the patients had been told they may experience – for example, dry mouth – then efficacy is shown whether the drug is an antidepressant or a placebo, or whether it increases, decreases or has no effect on serotonin (Kirsch, 2009).

Irving Kirsch's work is controversial, but his arguments are supported by others who have explored evidence on efficacy, based not on the selected 'positive' trials that have been published, but on an analysis of all conducted trials whether or not they were published. Tim Kendall and his colleagues at the National Collaborating Centre for Mental Health, responsible for developing guidelines on psychiatric drug use for NICE, the UK's regulator of treatment provided on the NHS, have shown that, when publication bias is overcome and unpublished trials are included in their analysis, the risk profiles of the drugs under consideration change considerably (Whittington et al., 2004; Tyrer and Kendall, 2009; Kendall, 2011).[15] For instance, the risk profile for SSRIs for the treatment of depression in children was evaluated and it was concluded that "[p]ublished data suggest a favourable risk-benefit profile for some SSRIs; however, addition of unpublished data indicates that risks could outweigh benefits of these drugs (except fluoxetine) to treat depression in children and young people" (Whittington et al., 2004: 1341).

While it is certainly true that global sales for psychiatric drugs have generated very substantial revenues for pharmaceutical companies, 'big pharma' alone has not been responsible for the global rise in the use of these drugs, although it has no doubt played a vital role (Rose, 2006a; Conrad, 2005). Perhaps as important are the beliefs of both doctors and patients. The types of psychiatric medication that show a rising trend, in particular the so-called antidepressants, are largely prescribed not by specialist psychiatrists but by general practitioners. Their reasons for using the drugs are no doubt complex. While some critics argue that doctors are unduly influenced by the promotional activities of pharmaceutical companies, evidence on this is ambiguous and varies from country to country (Ali and Zurina, 2017). The reasons no doubt include the genuine belief that the drugs will 'work', at least help to cope better with the stresses, strains and adversities that threaten to overwhelm the patient, as well as the wish not to send a patient away empty handed, or with a promise of an appointment for some talking therapy weeks or even months in the future.

But just as important are the hopes and beliefs of potential and actual patients. As anthropological studies have demonstrated, the belief in the efficacy of medication as a cure for one's ills is by no means novel: medicines are full of meaning for those who seek them and those who take them (as well as for those who prescribe them); cultural beliefs in the efficacy of medicine are widespread, have a long history, and are deeply embedded in the explanatory models of illness and cure held by individuals (Sjaak van der Geest et al., 1996). While the argument that psychiatric drugs work, at least in part, through a 'placebo' effect is rightly used in the critique of clinical trials, the placebo effect is real, and the effects of consuming any drug – as with any food or drink – inescapably entangle the physiological and symbolic (Wahlberg, 2008). People use medication in their own self-making practices. Their beliefs and expectations about the drugs they are taking cannot simply be 'subtracted' from the picture to show the 'real' effects of the medication; nor can their hopes for drugs that will treat them, ease what ails them, even cure them be derided as a shallow or ideologically moulded wish for a 'quick fix'. Of course, these beliefs, hopes and expectations are shaped by 'culture' – or, to be more precise, by beliefs in families and communities, by the stories they and others tell of their illnesses and treatments, by their relations with the language and explanations of medics and other experts, as well as by images and narratives in the mass media. Thus, in our own times, it is not only the generic names of the drugs that carry meaning for those who take them, but also – whether that be ibuprofen for a headache or an antidepressant for sadness – the brand names themselves, and even the packaging in which they come: Neurofen™ is surely better for aches and pains than generic ibuprofen; Benylin™ works better than generic cough linctus; and Prozac™ is surely better than fluoxetine, and so on (see also Martin, 2006).[16] But the hopes, beliefs and expectations of those who consume pharmaceuticals, and who actively use them to manage their lives, are no more naive or 'culturally specific' than are those of the funders of pharmaceutical research or the prescribers of the medication itself.

We should certainly reflect on the many intersecting reasons for the epidemic of drug use. But we should also reflect on the failure to create more effective psychopharmaceuticals. It is not just 'the usual suspects' who assert this failure, not just those radicals who have always been critical of drug treatment in psychiatry and do not believe the rhetoric that claims the current generation of drugs to be smarter, more effective and less damaging than the 'chemical coshes' that they have partially displaced. In 2012, Steven Hyman, for example, pointed out that "in the period from 1993 to 2004, only 8% of central nervous system (CNS) drug candidates that reached the stage of initial human testing (Phase 1) eventually achieved regulatory approval". He argued that the most common reason was not the emergence of evidence of toxicity in clinical trials, but, more fundamentally, "an inability to demonstrate efficacy", pointing to the fact that "European regulators have begun to demand either improvement in efficacy over existing drugs or biomarkers that identify patient subgroups for whom a new drug would be advantageous . . . [and despite] concerted sales campaigns that attempt to recast 'me-too drugs' as innovative", many pharmaceutical companies do not believe they have the scientific knowledge of the basis of mental disorders to achieve the necessary increases in efficacy to bring new drugs to market. In relation to depression, Hyman points to the inadequacy of animal models, which have only a tenuous connection with the human conditions they seek to model, to the waste of scarce research resources on underpowered trials focused on a target of existing drugs that are barely effective, notably serotonin-related genetics and molecular mechanisms, and in general to the failure of research to tackle "[t]he best-recognized obstacles to effective clinical translation in psychiatry include the key obstacle to translation to the clinic", which lies in the challenge of moving "from molecules, to cells, synapses, circuits, and thence to higher cognition, emotion regulation, and executive function".

Hyman's verdict on the efficacy of existing drugs was also damning: none of the antidepressants developed since the 1950s has improved on the efficacy of the first drugs to be marketed under that description – imipramine and the monoamine oxidase inhibitors. The only true 'atypical' antipsychotic was clozapine, and no other drugs in this category have equalled its efficacy; but clozapine is accompanied by very severe toxicity in a significant number of patients.[17] Lithium remains the mainstay of mood stabilizers for bipolar disorder, despite its toxicity and the uncertainty over its molecular targets, and despite the use of other anticonvulsants for the same purpose. There are no useful drug treatments for the core symptoms of autism or the negative and cognitive symptoms of schizophrenia. "The molecular targets of all today's approved psychiatric drugs are the same as the targets of their pre-1960 prototypes [and] their mechanisms of action are not understood beyond a few initial molecular events" (Hyman, 2012: 1). Indeed, Hyman argues, the drug discoveries made between 1949 and 1957, far from being pointers to the future for drug development, have so captured the imagination of researchers that they may have proved to be a scientific curse.

Almost all current pharmaceuticals used in psychiatry are rationalized on the basis that they work on what they take to be the underpinning molecular mechanism of mental disorders: an anomaly in the neurotransmitter system.[18] Too much or too little of one or other neurotransmitter – serotonin for depression, dopamine for schizophrenia, for example, or, later, some combination of these neurotransmitter anomalies – was responsible. Mental disorders were neurochemical disorders, drugs worked by correcting the problematic neurochemistry and drug development strategies were grounded in this belief. It is not just that, as Hyman and others argue, the drugs we have are only moderately effective for some people, and hardly more effective than a placebo for many, especially for the mild to moderate conditions for which they are mostly prescribed. It is not only that clinical trials are too short and artificial to understand the ways that drugs or any of these other therapies work long term in the everyday world of those who experience them. It is also that most people now agree that if these drugs work at all, it is not because they correct a pre-existing anomaly in the levels of neurochemicals available in the synapses. The neurotransmitter theory of disorders – and reciprocally the molecular theory of the mechanisms underpinning non-disordered brain functions – has proved misleading. The vision of the 'synaptic self' is fading before our eyes.

The drugs don't do nothing, of course. Drugs that mess with our neurotransmitters – usually *en masse* and rather unselectively – such as alcohol, LSD and psilocybin, do transform experiences, sometimes in ways that seem to mimic psychiatric distress. This was one of the observations that led to the neurotransmitter hypothesis in the first place. But these drugs also teach another lesson – that of set and setting. The effects of a given quantum of alcohol or cannabis depend not only on the drug, but on the context in which it is consumed – at a party or coping with the end of a relationship, for example – and on the expectations of the user. Psychiatric drugs are similar – consider, for example, the different 'effects' of amphetamine when used to treat ADHD or when used by sex workers. Further, because a drug helps to alleviate symptoms, it does not mean that it acts on the pathway that has generated those symptoms. The trite example is aspirin and headaches. Some critics, notably Joanna Moncrieff, have developed this into a theory of why some find some drugs helpful – not because they act on the pathways that lead to distress, but because they act independently, and sometimes in a damaging way, on other neural processes, thereby mitigating some of the symptoms and experiences, for example by blunting emotions, or muting perception. As it happens, this was the view of the discoverers of neuroleptics – they thought they caused minor damage to nerves, but that this was a price worth paying for their therapeutic effects.[19]

So this is the psychopharmaceutical paradox. The drugs don't do nothing, although how they do what they do is not fully understood. They are not specific to some underlying molecular mechanisms of the disorder, their therapeutic capacities are limited, and what they do to thought, emotion and desire is shaped by expectations, beliefs and interactional and social settings and is not inherent in the drugs themselves. The hypotheses that underpinned them have proven partial at best, misleading at worse, and the drug development pathway arising from them has run into the sand. While some drugs produce short-term relief for some patients with some conditions, it is debatable whether long-term outcomes for most patients are better now than they were before the rise of psychopharmaceuticals.[20] What psychiatrists think of as relapse among those who come off long-term treatment with antipsychotic drugs may in fact be the consequence of drug withdrawal itself (Moncrieff, 2008a). Indeed, evidence is growing that chronic use of some widely prescribed drugs may itself be harmful, both to the brain – especially the developing brains of children – and to other organs (Murray et al., 2016). This may have some role in the fact that those diagnosed with severe mental health problems have a reduction in life expectancy of some 20 years, although this may also reflect high levels of smoking and poor general medical care for those with mental illness diagnoses.

No wonder that many biological psychiatrists are exploring other mechanisms. There is a revival of research on the potential of psyche-delics and drugs such as ketamine.[21] Others are exploring direct inter-ventions into the brain with electricity and magnetism – as in Deep Brain Stimulation. Non-drug therapies are widely deployed, notably cognitive behaviour therapies, although some argue that if these 'psy-chological' interventions actually work, this must be through changes in neural functioning (Porto et al., 2009) – as if the brain was the only ground for objectivity. But the paradox remains – more and more people are taking drugs whose mode of action is unclear and whose efficacy is debatable. Not all agree: researchers are exploring the role of many other chemicals that can act as neurotransmitters – glutamate for example. But prospects are far from bright, at least if one is looking towards investment in R&D from the pharmaceutical companies.

The pipeline is empty!

By the end of the first decade of the new millennium, despite the worldwide growth in the use of these drugs, and the size of the potential market, the major multinational pharmaceutical companies began to announce their withdrawal from this sector of the market. As reported by Greg Miller in *Science*, "On 4 February 2010, in announcing the move to investors and analysts, GSK Chief Executive Andrew Witty explained that pain, depression, and anxiety were areas where 'we believe the probability of success is relatively low, [and] we think the cost of attaining success is disproportionately high.' Ceasing research in these areas would save GSK £250 million ($387 million) by 2012. A few weeks later, news came that AstraZeneca was closing research facilities in the United States and Europe and ceasing drug-discovery work in schizophrenia, bipolar disorder, depression, and anxiety"

(Miller, 2010: 503). Thomas Insel, then still Director of the US NIMH, remarked: "The biggest problem isn't the announcements by GSK and AstraZeneca, it's when you look at the pipeline and see what companies are actually doing in psychiatric drug development . . . There are very few new molecular entities, very few novel ideas, and almost nothing that gives any hope for a transformation in the treatment of mental illness" (quoted in Miller, 2010: 502).[22]

Later reports confirmed the predictions. In 2011, an article in the *Wall Street Journal* quoted Patrick Vallance, chief of medicine R&D at GlaxoSmithKline: neuroscience research "is currently one of those of highest risk for the industry – the identification of targets, the animal models, the nature of experimental medicine and the development programs for these disease areas are amongst the least predictive and most costly of any area . . . Neuroscience research in many areas is very exciting but in some areas is not mature enough to make drug discovery efficient or effective today – which is why I believe that further investment is needed, and have argued the case for public-sector funding in this area." Nigel Gaymond, chief executive of the UK's BioIndustry Association, a lobby group for British biotechnol-ogy companies, was of the view that "[n]euroscience has largely been a burial ground for drug development", and Hakan Bjorklund, chief executive of privately owned Nycomed of Switzerland, told the *Wall Street Journal*: "It all has to do with R&D productivity . . . Investors are demanding that drug companies now justify the billions of dollars they spend on research and development" (Stovall, 2011).

In 2012, H. Christian Fibiger, writing from the psychiatrist's per-spective in the *Schizophrenia Bulletin*, put it frankly:

> Psychopharmacology is in crisis. The data are in, and it is clear that a massive experiment has failed: despite decades of research and bil-lions of dollars invested, not a single mechanistically novel drug has reached the psychiatric market in more than 30 years. Indeed, despite enormous effort, the field has not been able to escape the 'me too/me (questionably) better' straightjacket. In recent years, the appreciation of this reality has had profound consequences for innovation in psy-chopharmacology because nearly every major pharmaceutical company has either reduced greatly or abandoned research and development of mechanistically novel psychiatric drugs. This decision is understandable because pharmaceutical and biotechnology executives see less risky opportunities in other therapeutic areas, cancer and immunology being the current pipeline favorites. Indeed, in retrospect, one can wonder why it took so long for industry to abandon psychiatry therapeutics. (2012: 649)

Fibiger argued that none of the three major classes of psychiatric drugs that were currently being prescribed would have been discovered using the drug discovery strategies currently in use, because there was no genetic data suggesting that the receptor sites they supposedly targeted were expressed differently in those individuals with the disorders in question, and no preclinical data pointing to these receptor sites as interesting therapeutic targets. His view was stark: that there was simply insufficient basic knowledge of normal brain function and the ways that disturbances in those functions led to disease, and hence that it was just too early to attempt rational drug design in psychiatry. This did not, however, lead him to the view that the molecular route should be abandoned; rather, that we needed much more basic neuroscience.

In 2013, a paper in *American Health and Drug Benefits*[23] confirmed the reduction in the numbers of CNS drugs in the pipeline: in 2008 the number was similar to that for cancer drugs, between 270 and 280, but by 2013 the number was 50 per cent lower. And although CNS drugs were still second to cancer drugs in terms of sheer numbers in the pipeline, many of these were approved drugs being trialled for new conditions, others were 'atypical' psychotics whose mode of action is disputed, and others were drugs approved for other conditions that have effects on neurotransmitters.[24] Other studies echo the now familiar story: many existing CNS drugs are going out of patent, the costs of R&D are rising, few drugs currently being tested differ significantly from existing pharmaceuticals and, in general, CNS drugs take longer to bring to market than other drugs, partly because CNS drugs tend to fail in late stage clinical trials and so companies are investing in other areas such as oncology and autoimmune disease (Kaddis, 2013; Hodgkin et al., 2016). This may have some advantages – for example, the move to generics may lower prices and hence costs for insurance companies or other payers (O'Brien et al., 2014), but there seems little in prospect to change this gloomy picture for those who place their hopes in drugs for the treatment of mental health problems.

Beyond psychopharmacology?

What, then, of the future? Some, like Steven Hyman, remain hopeful that, in the longer term, new tools such as rapid and cheap DNA sequencing, capacity to make stem cell disease models and imaging technologies such as optogenetics, together with epigenetics, transcriptomics and proteomics, will lead to the advances in molecular understanding and molecular level modelling necessary to develop new and effective treatments. Still others see the future in terms that have become familiar – personalized or precision medicine: the belief if we discard the beguiling but misleading superficial indicators of mental ill health – those symptoms so laboriously and objectively classified in manuals like the *DSM* and *ICD* – and go straight to the brain, we will avoid the confusion of the superficial, and be able to find specific neurobiological patterns that have clinical relevance, even though they may cut across existing diagnostic criteria. For who could doubt that it is the brain that is at the root of these disorders, and hence to the brain that we should look to identify the pathological lesion and rectify it?

Other key players, however, seem to recognize that the psychopharmacological experiment, costly in terms of research funds, researchers' time and – most crucially – human misery – has failed. I have already quoted Thomas Insel, former Director of the NIMH, who insisted for so long on the potential benefits to patients of the vastly expensive programme of neurobiological research that he funded: "I don't think we moved the needle in reducing suicide, reducing hospitalizations, improving recovery for the tens of millions of people who have mental illness. I hold myself accountable for that" (cited in Rogers, 2017). But who will be accountable for the many millions of individuals throughout the world taking medicines of dubious value for conditions of dubious diagnostic validity, while key figures who determine funding and shape research in psychiatric neuroscience still cling to the dream of molecular explanations and molecular interventions? When is it time to say 'enough', and to admit that this pathway of thinking about, and intervening upon, mental ill health has run into the sand? That the faith that so many doctors, and so many patients, have in the efficacy of psychiatric drugs is misplaced? That the drugs that have been developed, at so much cost and with so much marketing hype, have never done much more than damp down symptoms of distress – in some circumstances as much for the benefit of the medics as of the patients? That they sometimes provide temporary solace to those who take them, but fail to address the root causes of their complaints, and often cause unpleasant and sometimes dangerous adverse effects? And who, rather than taking this as a counsel of despair, will really seek to initiate, support and fund alternatives that recognize that the pathway to mental ill health, for many if not all of those so afflicted, starts not in the brain, but in the social world? For to really accept this is also to recognize that the route to mitigating so much mental distress must start with under-standing the pathogenic forms of social adversity, not just as brute facts but as they are understood and made meaningful by individuals, the mechanisms through which they act to exacerbate and amplify distress, the conditions and resources that promote individual and collective resilience, and hence the kinds of social interventions that might mitigate adversities and their effects.

7

Who Needs Global Mental Health?

It is telling that published studies of non-Western populations often refer to participants' 'limited knowledge of mental disorders,' their lack of 'mental health literacy,' or the need to 'teach' health workers and the people they serve about mental health ... Western psychological discourse is setting out to instruct, regulate, and modernise, presenting as definitive the contemporary Western way of being a person. It is unclear why this should be good for mental health in Africa or Asia. This is medical imperialism, similar to the marginalisation of indigenous knowledge systems in the colonial era, and is generally to the disadvantage of local populations.

Summerfield (2008)

Thousands of people with mental disorders turn up each day in health centres around the world only to receive inappropriate treatments, or die prematurely, or face discrimination and human rights abuses – we must not allow the false prophets, hiding behind the duplicitous cloak of protecting the 'natives' from a profiteering and self-serving 'Western biomedical imperialism' – to distract global mental health practitioners from their duty and responsibility to reduce this suffering.

Patel (2014b)

The Movement for Global Mental Health (MGMH) has achieved both practical and conceptual prominence.[1] By 2012, it was being described as one of the top ten research advances of the year (Insel, 2012), and the most exciting development in relations between psychiatry and social science (Kleinman, 2012). There has, of course, been a long and somewhat ignoble history of colonial psychiatry. More recently, many would-be psychiatrists from the Global South have travelled to Europe or the United States for their training and returned to practise the Euro-American psychiatry that they learned in their own countries. But this new Movement – I'll use the capitalized initial letters to differentiate it from other transnational and transcultural concerns in psychiatry – seems to be rather different. The MGMH takes its impetus, in part, from the way in which the WHO has come to give such weight to 'the global burden of mental disorders', painting a picture of high levels of such disorders in low resource settings where there are few psychiatrists or mental health facilities. Framed in terms of a 'mental health gap' with large numbers suffering and untreated, and given added urgency by images of mentally distressed persons locked in outbuildings or crude cages, or chained to beds or trees, the advocates of global mental health have an evangelical commitment to doing good by bringing the healing benefits of Western psychiatry to those who lack it.

The MGMH took shape during the first decade of this millennium. In 2011, in a high-profile 'Comment' in *Nature*, it was framed in terms of the need to address "the grand challenges in global mental health" (see Collins et al., 2011). The 'Comment', illustrated by a photograph of a young girl in Somalia "with mental illness" chained to a tree, and another of some sad looking women standing in a bare room in a psychiatric hospital in Ukraine, focused specifically on what were termed the MNS (mental, neurological and substance) disorders – schizophrenia, depression, epilepsy, dementia, alcohol dependence and other mental, neurological and substance-use disorders. It reported data from the WHO's report *The Global Burden of Disease: 2004 Update* (2008a), suggesting that these disorders constituted 13 per cent of the total global burden of disease, and were not merely a growing problem in wealthy industrialized nations, but also a major if largely unrecognized cause of undiagnosed illness and untreated suffering in low- and middle-income countries. Collins et al. (2011) set out 25 challenges, established by Delphi methodology involving consultations with a panel of experts,[2] to outline key global challenges in improving the lives of people living with 'neuropsychiatric illnesses' ranging from those concerned with identifying the biological basis of disorder to those of redesigning health systems to give adequate attention to mental disorders (Collins et al., 2011).[3]

While some hailed this as the application of the principles of global health – "improving health and achieving equity in health for all people worldwide" – to the "domain of mental ill health" (Patel and Prince, 2010), others deemed it "an oxymoron and medical imperialism" (Summerfield, 2013). Critics suggested that the MGMH was based upon a culturally specific Euro-American model of mental health problems, that it failed to appreciate approaches to mental distress in other cultures, and mistakenly assumed that 'Western' definitions of illness and practices of intervention could be generalized to the radically different societies in the Global South. Some went to far as to view it as a new wave of psychiatric colonization, that wittingly or unwittingly serves the interests of big pharma (Summerfield, 2008; Summerfield, 2012; Watters, 2010; Bracken et al., 2016; Ingleby, 2014).[4]

This debate is not only important in itself; it can also tell us a great deal about the politics of mental health today. For the issues raised – for example, about the universality of diagnoses, the interpretation of clinical trials claiming to show the efficacy of particular treatments, the ways in which social, economic, political and cultural factors shape the emergence, expression, experience and consequences of mental ill health – do not merely have relevance for the psychiatric future in low- and middle-income countries. The implications go beyond psychiatry: they concern the ways in which we understand and respond to vital problems, problems of life itself, both in the Global South and in the Global North.

Grand challenge: No health without mental health?

As Alex Cohen, Vikram Patel and Harry Minas point out, "Before the year 2001, the term global mental health was used to denote a measure of the overall level of stress (primarily depression and anxiety) in a given population" (2014: 3). They suggest that the first use of the term in its current meaning, as a field within public health, was by the then US Surgeon General David Satcher, in a commentary, 'Global Mental Health: Its Time Has Come' (2001), which was to highlight the forthcoming campaign on mental health launched by the WHO – a campaign that would see the publication of the organization's influential report *Mental Health: New Understanding, New Hope* (2001). In fact, in his one-page commentary, Satcher picked out many of the themes that would become central to the MGMH: the prevalence of mental health problems globally; the impact they had on many other medical conditions; the burden in medical, social and economic terms; the barriers to effective services; the lack of policies and practitioners in many countries; and the small proportion of the overall health budget that many countries spend on mental health care despite the need. He argued for advocacy, for mental health to be an equal partner in health policies and for funding to reflect the magnitude of the problem, and for research in both neuroscience and health services research that was linked to effective practice.

In an insightful commentary on ethnographic critiques of global mental health, Stefan Ecks point out that global mental health emerges through linking together "a set of disparate fields and concerns in a new way" (2016: 804). We've explored many of these in the previous chapters. First, perhaps, was the established belief within transcultural psychiatry by the 1980s that, although psychiatric anthropology since the early twentieth century had drawn attention to 'disorders specific to particular cultures' such as Amok, Koro and Piblokto, and while the manifestations of mental disorders vary culturally, these were to be considered merely as different expressions of a small number of underlying disorders that are universal across human societies (Rack, 1982).[5] Second was the shift in psychiatric epidemiology made possible by the symptom checklist-based diagnostic approach in *DSM-III* and its successors, and, to a lesser extent, in *ICD*.[6] Used by skilled psychiatrists, who could read through these culturally variable expressions to underlying disorders, these were argued to be applicable in any region. Their standardized categorical form lent itself to the compilation of numbers which could then be transformed into prevalence rates in populations, and hence to comparisons between numbers affected by mental disorders and those affected by cancers or other high-profile conditions. Third, the new ways of calculating burden in terms of DALYs that was adopted by the WHO in the 1990s enabled the economic and social cost of different medical conditions to be placed side by side on a single scale, enabling rhetorically powerful arguments to be made about the comparative importance of mental disorders. Fourth, the rise of 'evidence-based medicine', along with its belief that there was a hierarchy of evidence in which randomized controlled trials were the gold standard, enabled claims to be made for the efficacy of psychopharmaceuticals on the basis of published data from clinical trials – data that we now know to be selective, flawed and often inflected by the aspirations of the pharmaceutical companies that funded the research. Fifth were the claims that the 'stigma' of madness, especially in low-resource regions, not only leads to social exclusion and discrimination, but deters many from seeking treatment, supported by pointing to the discrepancy between the numbers of those that psychiatrists estimate are diagnosable with a mental disorder and those actually receiving treatment (WHO, 2003). As we have seen, each of these 'pillars' is, to say the least, problematic.

As Bemme and D'souza point out, the DALY that was developed by the Harvard School of Public Health, and first used in the *World Development Report: Investing in Health*, was fundamental to the new way of calculating the 'Global Burden of Disease', bringing together mortality (years of life lost from disease) with morbidity (years lived with disability) in a single measure: "DALYs established a style of reasoning that expressed the health status of a population in the unit of 'time' [and] have become a 'common international language' . . . a shared mode of conceptualizing health disparities, expressed in the currency of one DALY signifying 'one year of healthy life' lost" (2014: 854). This measure was used in the 1995 volume, *World Mental Health: Problems and Priorities* (Desjarlais, 1995), whose reviews of mental health issues in low-income countries, and recommendations, inspired a wave of activities from the World Bank and the WHO, leading to the comments I have already cited from David Satcher and to the WHO's 2001 *World Health Report*. According to Cohen et al. (2014), these and related activities inspired funding agencies such as the UK's Department for International Development and the Wellcome Trust to fund projects of research and policy development for mental health in low-resource settings. Frustration with the slow pace of action on the ground led to the emergence of the group that created the 2007 *Lancet* series on global mental health, "bringing together leading experts from the Institute of Psychiatry, King's College London, UK, The London School of Hygiene and Tropical Medicine, UK, and WHO, to highlight the gaps in mental-health services worldwide, and to formulate a clear call to action".[7]

Launching the series, Richard Horton, editor of *The Lancet*, argued that the WHO had not converted the fine words in its 2001 report into tangible actions: it had not only failed to provide resources but, more important, it had "failed to build a sustainable mechanism across global and country institutions to hold itself and others accountable for its recommendations. This paralysis is surprising. Many low-income countries and civil society groups are crying out for help." Horton urged his readers to join "the broad new social movement" for global mental health (2007: 806). Authors in the *Lancet* series argued that mental health had been largely neglected in global health agendas, and, once more, pointed to epidemiological estimates showing the extent of the burden of the MNS (mental, neurological and substance) disorders on families, communities, nations and international economic systems.

In the first paper in the series, whose title echoed the WHO call for "No Health Without Mental Health", Martin Prince, Vikram Patel and others argued that, on the basis of WHO's 2005 data, neuropsychiatric diseases accounted for 28 per cent of DALYs worldwide – roughly equivalent to cardiovascular disease, and over twice that of cancer (11 per cent) (Prince et al., 2007). Given that mental disorders increase the risk of developing many other diseases, both communicable and noncommunicable, including disorders of reproduction, sexual health, and maternal and child health, that they may affect adherence to treatment regimes in conditions such as HIV, increase risks of injury and violence which are themselves risk factors for mental disorder, and may have a causal role in the high proportion of medically unexplained symptoms, Prince et al. argued that the case for increased awareness, and for policy changes, seems overwhelming. However, they point out, mental health "is missing from the policy framework for health improvement – and poverty reduction; missing from health and social research; and missing from targets for interventions. Moreover, mental health has not been acknowledged as an obstacle to achievement of several Millennium Development Goals . . . Mental health awareness needs to be integrated into all elements of health and social policy, health-system planning, and health-care delivery" (2007: 870). Acknowledging that much of the evidence base for the role of mental ill health in other medical conditions came from high-income countries, the authors called for more research in low- and middle-income countries, more research on mechanisms, and more research on psychosocial interventions to improve outcomes in these conditions: the "moral and ethical case for redressing the imbalance in provision for people with mental disorders can brook no delay" (Prince et al., 2007: 871).

The numbers have thus been crucial in making the moral and ethical claim for a 'social movement' for global mental health, both in *The Lancet* series and in the high-profile 'comment' in *Nature* four years later that I have already mentioned (Collins et al., 2011). But, of course, many assumptions were made in generating the figures. Consider, for instance, the 2007 *Lancet* paper by Prince et al.: in making the case for the economic gains of suicide prevention strategies in China, "we based our calculations on a 4.3% prevalence of major depression . . . and a relative risk of 14.6 for the association of depression with suicide. . . We predicted that a maximum of 6% of suicides would be averted at 25% coverage of the intervention, rising to 15% at 75% coverage. . . Since 325 581 suicides happen every year in China, we estimated that if 50% coverage with the intervention could be achieved, a maximum of 32 558 suicides would be averted every year. The potential economic effect could be substantial, with 5.8 million productive life years lost nationally, which would translate to lost productivity of US$10.2 billion per year because of suicide (on the basis of GDP per head of US$1740 in 2006). If 50% treatment coverage was achieved, a 10% reduction in the suicide rate would save 580 000 productive years of life, or US$1.0 billion per year" (2007: 870). So many estimates, so many ifs and coulds. But to say the figures are constructed is to miss the point that all such estimates in social epidemiology are the product of specific, and questionable, practices of calculation. The key point here is not about accuracy – for that would simply set one way of calculating against another – but about what the numbers are intended to do: in this form of politico-moral argument, it is hoped that the sheer weight of numbers will do important rhetorical work in demonstrating that here is scandalous neglect of suffering and 'something must be done'.

The moral argument for urgent action to counter the human tragedies brought about by the prevalence of mental disease was further supported by data from the WHO, showing the DALYs worldwide (in high-income countries, and in low- and middle-income countries) for disorders ranging from unipolar depressive disorders (10.0 million in high-income countries, 55.5 million in low- and middle-income countries) through alcohol-use disorders (4.2/19.5 million) , schizophrenia (1.6/15.2 million), bipolar affective disorder (1.5/12.9 million) epilepsy (0.5/7.3 million), migraine (1.4/6.3 million) and multiple sclerosis (0.3/1.2 million). However, the figures alone were not sufficient. What had to be demonstrated was that those who suffered from these conditions, or from other medical conditions intertwined with mental ill health, were 'unserved' – unable to access appropriate treatment, perhaps unaware that what ailed them was a mental health problem, perhaps suffering even more because of stigma or worse, such as inhumane treatment in their local communities. Hence, proponents argued that there was a large 'treatment gap' between need for and availability of mental health services and pointed to the individual and social costs of undiagnosed and untreated mental disorder and the need for effective and accessible interventions, especially in low- and middle-income countries (Patel et al., 2008; Patel et al., 2014).

These psychiatrists and policymakers hoped to create what actor-network theorists would think of as an assemblage of heterogeneous objects and people that stabilizes a particular pattern of power to change mental health care in low- and middle-income countries (see Law, 1992). And indeed the *Lancet* series did help give shape to the MGMH, initially as a web-based entity, and to further its aim to transform mental health into a globally recognized subfield of global health, to mobilize international and national political will for mental health, and to compete with other disease-based groups of experts for scarce funds and resources.

The MGMH stimulated "the global vision" of the WHO's Department of Mental Health: in 2008, WHO initiated its 'mental health Gap Action Programme' (mhGAP) committed to the idea that "there cannot be health without mental health" and aimed to garner support for the "scaling up" of cost-effective interventions for MNS disorders (WHO, 2008b). In 2011, *The Lancet* published a second major series in mental health, as a way of ensuring continued support to mental health and tracking progress in closing the so-called "treatment gap" (Patel et al., 2011), and, as noted earlier, the "Grand Challenges in Mental Health" was announced (Collins et al., 2011).

The MGMH has indeed succeeded in creating a global network of committed institutions and individuals. By 2017, the Movement had "grown to a membership of around 200 institutions and 10,000 individuals, many of who are actively involved. Members of the Movement include individuals and families affected by mental health problems, health care providers, activists, decision makers and researchers worldwide"[8] and courses in global mental health had been developed in many universities worldwide.[9] Implicit in the rationale and strategy of all these activities is the premise that standard transcultural modes of diagnosis, forms of treatment and packages of intervention can be formulated and implemented, mainly based on evidence from developed countries, and 'scaled up' for application in different cultural contexts, at least for more severe disorders, backed by the strong claim that this is a matter of protecting and promoting basic and universal human rights (Patel, 2012; WHO, 2013).

The debate

From the earliest years of the MGMH, a number of vociferous critics have disputed its conceptual, therapeutic and political bases, and it has become the subject of acrimonious controversy.[10] Critics accuse it of exporting a Western model of disorder and treatment, neglecting cultural variability in understanding and responding to mental suffering, and medicalizing distress. In regarding mental distress as a biomedical pathology, critics argue that MGMH diverts attention from the underlying social and economic determinants of mental illness in low- and middle-income countries. They doubt that Euro-American psychiatry is such a success that it must be exported at the expense of other approaches to problems of mental distress. They dispute the MNS framework, which combines mental distress with neurological disorders and substance abuse and assumes all are underpinned by pathological neurobiology. They raise concerns about the influence of the pharmaceutical industry, given that pharmaceuticals are often the first and often the only line of MGMH intervention. They question the validity of standardized diagnostic instruments across diverse national contexts, the reliability of epidemiological estimates of the global prevalence of mental disorders, and the applicability of 'evidence-based' programmes. They claim that local communities are marginalized by the global mental health agenda, that global mental health activists use misleading images of the malign treatment of the mentally disordered in poor countries to garner support, and that thoughtful local practices of caregiving and traditional healers are undermined as standardized 'packages of care' are implemented. They suggest that effective interventions must be shaped to the specificities of local cultures, existing local health care systems, and the needs of specific population (Summerfield, 2008, 2012, 2013; Kirmayer, 2012; Kirmayer and Crafa, 2014; Kirmayer and Pedersen, 2014; Kirmayer and Swartz, 2013; Watters, 2010; Campbell and Burgess, 2012).[11]

Leaders of the Movement, notably Vikram Patel, responded to this wave of criticism by arguing that global mental health is, in fact, pervaded by a concern for human rights and a postcolonial sensibility. While critics feel the MGMH has adopted a facile understanding of 'culture' to explain the *failure* of health initiatives, these global mental health activists claim they adopt a nuanced notion of culture that applies not only to the life-worlds of patient populations, but also to those of experts and policymakers. They point to collaborations with traditional healers in programmes that are sensitive to local cultural traditions. They reference the literature on socioeconomic determinants of mental disorders produced by leading researchers within the Movement, and argue that this has established a multidisciplinary empirical basis to inform interventions. They argue that critiques are based on an inappropriate equation of global mental health with 'biopsychiatry', a lack of knowledge about programmes being developed on the ground and a failure to recognize the need for a unified policy approach to underpin global mental health's credibility as a subfield of global health. The focus on treatment, they argue, does not preclude either investigations of socioeconomic determinants of mental illness or use of multidisciplinary case studies to inform locally developed social interventions. Given longstanding polarizations in global health more generally, some see the MGMH as one of the most comprehensive and least technocratic global health movements (e.g., Patel, 2014b; Cohen et al., 2012a, 2012b; Patel and Kleinman, 2003; Araya et al., 2006). Nonetheless, they argue, the pragmatics of addressing a challenge of this magnitude requires standardized, cost-effective and globally scalable packages of intervention that appear feasible and fundable to donors and governments.

Beyond the conflict?

Not surprisingly, those responses did not end the controversy, in most cases merely provoking the critics to reassert their former positions: for example, in a paper entitled 'Primum Non Nocere' – 'first do no harm' – Pat Bracken and colleagues (2016) restate the same criticisms, arguing that the Movement only pays lip service to engagement with local communities, is driven by Western experts, and that, in the face of the real problem of poverty and global inequality, the psychiatry offered by global mental health is a technocratic and reductionist answer that does more harm than good.

Is there a way forward? While, as I have argued earlier, there is little doubt that poverty, violence, famine and other forms of adversity are bad for mental health, that does not imply that, until we have peace and social justice, nothing can be done. Further, critiques such as those above are usually framed in a high level of generality, and often show a lack of knowledge of the complexities of mental distress and responses to it in the very countries they seek to protect from the harms that they attribute to global mental health. The most thoughtful assessments of the dilemmas of mental ill-health in low- and middle-income countries come from anthropologists who have conducted detailed local studies of beliefs, policies and evolving practices in relation to mental distress.

Reviewing many of these studies, Stefan Ecks argues that local ethnographic work casts doubt on many of the claims for success made by proponents of the MGMH. These studies show that many of the changes in mental health care in Kashmir, in central India, in South Africa, in Tonga and elsewhere that are claimed by the Movement actually predate its activities, and have occurred in response to local issues and campaigns, rather than global mental health policies or interventions. On the basis of his own research in India (Ecks, 2005, 2013; Ecks and Basu, 2014), he questions the way the data on the mental health gap is constructed, pointing to the fact that there are "thousands of generic brands of psychopharmaceuticals on sale in the country's private medicine shops. Thousands of companies are producing these drugs, and millions of patients are taking these drugs, but they never show up in any of the treatment gap calculations because they operate in the private market" (2016: 806). While the Movement advocates 'task shifting', he points out that the work of diagnosing and prescribing in India is already being done by millions of non-psychiatrically trained individuals, driven not by evidence from the Movement, but by all manner of local factors, including education from pharmaceutical sales representatives. One finds similar complexities in China, Brazil and, indeed, in many, if not all, the countries where the MGMH is working. To recognize this is not simply to pit the virtues of localism against the vices of universalism. Nor is it to reject the aspirations of the MGMH and the sense of outrage that mobilizes its advocates. But it is to suggest that there are some fundamental problems with the idea of scaling up: seeking to introduce standard packages of mental health care without a full understanding of local policies and conditions, and with only a rudimentary and often stereotyped view of the situation 'on the ground', is almost certain to fail.

Without denying the need for better and more effective responses to mental distress in low- and middle-income countries – in order to understand what works where and for whom – it is necessary to take apart those key pillars of global mental health that I outlined earlier: the dependence of psychiatric epidemiology on the highly problematic symptom-based diagnostic approach of *DSM*; the conception of burden adopted by the WHO; the validity of the clinical trials that are taken to have demonstrated the efficacy of psychopharmaceuticals; the naive ideas of stigma and stigma reduction that are supported by decontextualized images of the apparent ill-treatment of those deemed mad; and even the commitment to rights as the best way to counter discrimination and reform practices on the ground. Further, it is necessary to recognize that long-term success in reducing mental distress will not come from more psychiatry and psychiatrists. Psychiatry, here, may be useful in patching up some distressed people, though often at the price of distributing psychopharmaceuticals of limited effectiveness and with significant adverse effects. But – as in the Global North – genuine reductions of mental ill health in the Global South will only come from large-scale sociopolitical reforms to attack the social determinants of mental distress.

Indeed, as Ecks points out, one of the key proponents of global mental health, Vikram Patel, while sometimes crudely stereotyping those whom he takes to be 'ideological' critics (2014ba), has himself begun to cast doubt on some of these 'pillars' of the movement, and to reframe it in a way that avoids some of the key pitfalls. Patel, who, as we have seen, has been an author on most of the key publications in the history of the Movement, is currently Professor of Global Health and Social Medicine at Harvard Medical School, was the Co-Founder and first Director of the Centre for Global Mental Health at the London School of Hygiene and Tropical Medicine; in addition to a senior role in the Public Health Foundation of India, he was the Co-Founder of Sangath, an Indian NGO dedicated to research in the areas of child development, adolescent health and mental health. In a commentary titled 'Rethinking Mental Health Care: Bridging the Credibility Gap', published in a journal called *Interventions*,[12] in the same year as his attack on the MGMH critics, Patel begins the task of 'rethinking' (2014a). Without directly mentioning the universal applicability of the diagnostic categories of *DSM* or *ICD*, he argues that "the privileged status of biomedical diagnostic categories" such as depression and schizophrenia "and their associated biomedical explanations" is not only not necessary but may also be counterproductive, and that, instead, "[i]ntegrating culturally appropriate explanatory models and nonspecialist labels" and even dispensing completely with terms such as depression "[are] the hallmark of accessible and effective mental health care interventions" (2014a: 15).

Interventions, argues Patel, should "target the outcomes that matter to people" rather than psychiatric symptom reduction, and mental health interventions must go beyond biomedical constructs and treatments to "address the practical social determinants and consequences of mental disorders" (2014a: 16). Mental health care should be provided – and indeed often is provided – in many non-health settings, such as schools and homes, and often by lay people (although Patel somewhat undercuts his focus on integrating locally specific knowledge practices by insisting that they should be trained by specialists, use programmes designed by specialists and overseen by specialists, who would then be free to deal with complex or treatment resistant cases). Centrally, he accepts that there is a huge gap "between the understanding of mental disorder that mental health specialists use, best illustrated through the diagnostic systems and the epidemiological instruments arising from them, and how the rest of the world conceptualises psychological suffering" (2014a: 16) arguing that we need "to abandon the use of prevalence estimates generated by epidemiological surveys" in claims about the 'mental health gap' because the diagnostic categories and estimates used to construct such a gap lack credibility. This is because they are radically distinct from how the majority of people who would fall into those categories understand their problems. They do not see them as the distinct diseases discussed in arcane terms by those mental health practitioners who aspire to membership in "the powerful guild of medicine" but as forms of distress "inextricably linked to their personal lives". Patel thus wishes to move the MGMH away from "the medicalization of emotional worlds . . . the imposition of [normative] artificial dichotomies on dimensions of everyday experiences, the use of ever more complex jargon terms [such as Disruptive Mood Disregulation Disorder] and the increasing emphasis on a biomedically oriented mental health care as the primary solution to these problems" (2014a: 16).

So have the critics won the global mental health wars? It might seem so, when such a significant figure as Patel wishes to abandon top-down biomedical, psychiatric constructs and therapeutic paradigms (2014a: 18), to replace the label of disorder with distress, to recognize that most of those who are distressed can be better helped outside the formal health care system by dealing with economic difficulties, developing befriending, using culturally embedded sources of help and other methods that are consistent with how individuals themselves understand their problems and the outcomes they themselves desire. But things are not so simple! In a paper published in *The Lancet* at about the same time as the piece in *Interventions*, Patel, writing with K. S. Jacob, reframes his argument. He steps back from the wholesale rejection of the pillars of global mental health that he articulated so forcefully in his *Interventions* piece, and now turns the issue into a pragmatic question rather than a fundamental one: primary care workers do not find the classifications in *DSM* or *ICD* particularly useful, and should be encouraged to "devise a classification for mental distress and disorder that is usable in routine clinical practice", one that "needs to be led and owned" by them, and for that purpose they need to engage with communities and policy-makers (Jacob and Patel, 2014). And indeed, the comprehensive critique presented in *Interventions* does not inform the chapters collected in the textbook *Global Mental Health: Principles and Practice*, which Patel, along with Harry Minas, Alex Cohen and Martin Prince, edited for publication in the same year (Patel et al., 2014). And it is not the version of global mental health used to mobilize resources, taught in the many training programmes for global mental health, and embodied in the very principles that underpinned the Grand Challenge and in the mhGAP programmes which arise from it. We appear, that is to say, to encounter two very different faces of the MGMH articulated at the same time, each seemingly strategically framed towards the audience to which they are directed.[13] What then of the future?

All our futures?

What do we learn from this heated debate over the MGMH, about the nature of diagnosis and the culturally specific character of the diagnostic categories in use in the Global North, about the tensions between a recognition of the social determinants of mental distress and the need for immediate individual interventions for those in need of care and support, about whether interventions that seem to work in one context can be 'scaled up' and used effectively in other situations, and about the uses and limits of biomedical and pharmaceutical interventions and whether 'other psychiatries' are possible? In a 2015 piece in a Lancet Psychiatry series on 'Future Directions for Global Mental Health', a number of authors, including Dan Stein, a psychiatrist from Cape Town, South Africa, He Yanling from the Shanghai Mental Health Centre, and the neuroscientist turned neuroethicist Barbara Sahakian, together with Vikram Patel, reflect on the possible relations between global mental health and neuroscience (Stein et al., 2015). Few of the critics would be content with the compromises they suggest between these two conflicting understandings of the nature, origins, definitions and treatments of mental distress. They suggest developing new diagnostic classifications that aim for validity and utility, merely reactivating the recurrent dream of categorical specificity. They propose evaluating whether one might reliably use dimensional assessments in bio-behavioural domains, which hardly addresses the basic issues of cultural variations in the very meaning of distress and hence in how it does or does not 'get under the skin'. They wish to incorporate measures of structural factors such as economic inequality into diagnosis, but give no indication of how they think this might be done. They think it is important to assess and incorporate measures of the environment – seemingly understood as a set of components or factors – in genetic and neuroscientific research, but it is hardly a novel insight to gesture to the importance of 'the environment'. They would like to include a focus on cultural context in neuroscientific studies, rehabilitating transcultural psychiatry but only to the extent that it can be given a neuroscientific basis. And they suggest incorporating measures from neuroscience and social risks into randomized controlled trials in different settings, working on the assumption that RCTs are still the gold standard despite so many criticisms of the applicability of their outcomes in real-life settings. They think it is important to learn lessons about pharmacotherapy and psychotherapy from low- and middle-income countries for high-income countries, and vice versa, which is a somewhat vacuous hope, as lessons concerning efficacy or its absence have certainly not been learned so far. And they propose undertaking neuroethics research. But surely ethics is not the point here, except the ethical obligation to seek to mitigate mental distress.

This paper on potential synergies between global mental health and neuroscience, however well-meaning, illustrates clearly how difficult it is for researchers in psychiatry who have placed their faith, and their careers, in molecular neuroscience to recognize that their bio-medical paradigm has run out of steam. Or that diagnoses, whether symptomatic or brain-based, are merely rough and ready first steps to deciding on effective clinical intervention. Or that the forms of mental distress with which they deal are transindividual and neither their origins nor their effective treatments are to be found by focusing on the brains of isolated sufferers, let alone in animal models. Or that their search for biomarkers has failed not merely because of technical difficulties, but because calculable and clinically usable markers or 'brain signatures' for psychiatric disorders do not exist. This is not a counsel of despair: indeed, what we can learn from the experience of those working with mental distress in low-resource settings applies equally to high-resource settings. Categorical diagnosis is unhelp-ful and epistemologically misleading in its belief in an underlying biological universality merely given different culturally shaped forms of expression. Prevalence estimates based upon categories such as those in the list of MNS disorders or the categories of the *DSM* are disingenuous in their gross overestimation of the territory of mental disorder. Pharmacotherapy may be of short-term palliative use, but – in low-, middle- and high-income countries alike – is not a solution to the experience of mental distress. Most forms of mental distress are inextricably linked to problems of poverty, precarity, violence, exclusion and other forms of adversity in people's personal and social experiences, and are best addressed not by medicalization, but by low intensity but committed and durable social interventions guided by outcomes that are not measured in terms of symptom reduction, but by the capacities that people themselves desire in their everyday lives.

If at least some of the leaders of the Movement for Global Mental Health have learned these lessons over the past decades, and if they were willing to make these the central premises of their activities, then a path could be opened up for a different psychiatry, and indeed a different biopolitics, not just in the Global South but also in the Global North.

8

Experts By Experience?

The constitution of madness as a mental illness thrusts into oblivion all those stammered imperfect words without fixed syntax in which the exchange between madness and reason was made. The language of psychiatry, which is a monologue of reason about madness, has been established only on the basis of that silence.

Foucault (1967)

Thus far, in our examination of psychiatry, I have by and large focused on those who would be traditionally considered 'experts': medical specialists, scientific researchers, policymakers, academics.[1] Given what we know about the prevalence of diagnosed mental disorders and the use of psychopharmaceuticals, we can assume that many of them are also, often undeclared, users of mental health services. But nonetheless, they do not speak and write as patients, or as persons experiencing mental distress, panicking in public places, tormented by overwhelming sadness, hearing voices, self-harming or subject to any of the other phenomena on which they pronounce. Even the critics that I have drawn upon, or at least most of them, write in the dispassionate language that we have come to associate with reason and objectivity and publish their arguments in the scholarly journals. But what of the voices of those who are the subjects of psychiatry: the patients, the users of mental health services, the survivors of compulsory confinement, involuntary treatment, or long-term medication?[2] Should they not be the people who should judge the benefits of psychiatry?[3]

While at university in the middle of the 1960s, I picked up a copy of Michel Foucault's book *Madness and Civilization* – the much abbreviated translation of his *History of Madness* – and I read the words that I have reproduced at the head of this chapter, words which I still find rather moving. A monologue of reason about madness. If I have been drawn to reason in this book, it has been to reason, not about madness, but about psychiatry. But it is well past time to turn in the other direction. Psychiatry and the associated psy professions all stake their claim to legitimacy not merely on their objectivity, but also because they are committed to help and not to harm those whom they analyse, diagnose and treat. Surely then, at a minimum, those to whom they minister gain the right to speak, to give their own views on the treatment meted out to them.

Have those designated mad, by doctors, by the courts, by their neighbours, by their families or by themselves, spoken of their experience, and, if they have, have those words been written on the wind? The answer, of course, is yes, they have spoken and written, and no, those words have not – or not all – disappeared into the air. Even by the 1960s when Foucault's book was first published in French, some of the writings of those deemed mad would have been available to him and other scholars.[4] Dale Peterson published his selection of these writings in his *Mad People's History of Madness* (1982), ranging from the 1436 Book of Margery Kemp, through memoirs of life in private madhouses in the eighteenth century and the lunatic asylums of the nineteenth century, to excerpts from better known writings closer to our own times, such as *The Snake Pit*, published by Mary Jane Ward in 1946 and *I Never Promised you a Rose Garden*, by Joanne Greenberg, published in 1964. Roy Porter's *Social History of Madness* (1987) collected together writings from 28 of those deemed mad, seeking – in the words of the subtitle to the US edition – to picture 'the world through the eyes of the insane' – a project Porter continued in his editorship of *The Faber Book of Madness* (1991). And we have other famous memoirs, such as Clifford Beers's 1908 autobiographical account of his own journey to madness and back, *A Mind That Found Itself*, which was so influential in the early mental hygiene movement in the United States. But while some of these writings had an impact, as did Beers's book and the book and movie of *The Snake Pit*, they hardly amount to a concerted movement to make audible the voices of those deemed insane.

When it comes to madness, then, what has been the experience of those deemed mad? And what has been, what is, and what could be their role in challenging that monologue of reason about madness? Might that experience give rise to another knowledge of madness, another set of practices for understanding and managing mental distress? Given that what we have available from our mental health experts – from drugs to talking cures – is, to put it generously, of limited efficacy, might a radical re-evaluation of the respective powers and knowledges of experts and patients lay the basis for another psychiatry, and another biopolitics of mental health?

Is psychiatry still a monologue of reason about madness, or have things changed since the mid-twentieth century? In some quite obvious ways, they have. One might have expected the first signs of such a change to be found in the radical critiques of psychiatry, and the movement that became known as anti-psychiatry, but in fact these criticisms were mainly made by people who did not self-identify as users of psychiatric services, but who spoke on their behalf. While Laing, Cooper and others drew attention to the meaningful nature of the narratives and symptoms of psychiatric patients, they seldom provided forums for those who were the recipients of psychiatry to express their own views about their treatment, except in a therapeutic context. That is to say, the voice of the patient was to be interpreted by experts, whether in the therapeutic communities that began to flourish in the aftermath of the Second World War, the 'concept houses' set up by groups of radical psychiatrists, social workers and philanthropists, such as *The Philadelphia Association* and *The Richmond Fellowship*, or the therapy groups that were increasingly established in hospital settings.[5] And while Basaglia and his fellow reformers in Italy sought to free asylum inmates from the ghastly conditions of their incarceration, their own voices are seldom heard in his writings (Basaglia, 1968; Basaglia et al., 1987).

Nonetheless, these group encounters, which became almost inescapable for those who were inpatients or who attended day centres from the 1960s on, did, in some cases, generate resistance from patients and a sense that they had something in common. Patients had to speak, had to be involved, had to give voice to their experience and their understanding of their condition, as part of the process of therapy and the production of 'insight' – this term usually meaning that the patient has accepted the doctor's view of the problem at hand. However, to be required to speak is not necessarily to be heard. It is no doubt good to 'give voice', to 'get it off one's chest', to be able to speak out about one's experiences, to bear witness to them. But it requires more than 'giving voice' for the words of the mental patient to be heard as other than a symptom to be interpreted by someone who knows so much more about their meaning than the speaker does. To challenge the monopoly of professionals over madness, some kind of sustained action, some kind of durable organization, some kind of politics is required.

Mental patient movements

Perhaps the first step towards creating something like a political movement of those who were the subjects of psychiatry, at least in the Anglophone world, occurred in the early 1970s and grew out of the group experiences described above. In the UK, the Scottish Union of Mental Patients was formed in July 1971, and the Mental Patients Union (MPU), which arose out of group encounters at the Paddington Day Hospital, was formed in March 1973. One of the founders, Andrew Roberts, describes its genesis:

> The idea of a Mental Patients Union was first developed by a small group of mental patients and supporters back in December 1972. A pamphlet was produced – which came to be known as the Fish Pamphlet (it had a picture of a fish struggling on a hook on the cover) – that was strongly Marxist in its analysis. Its argument was that psychiatry was a form of social control of the working classes in a capitalist state, and that the psychiatrist was the "high priest" of technological society, exorcising the "devils" of social distress through electroconvulsive therapy (ECT), lobotomy and medication. The thinking was that, in the same way that workers formed trade unions, mental patients also needed a union to fight for their rights against political oppression and social control.[6]

This is not the place for a detailed history of the proliferation and fate of local branches of the MPU in the UK; much material on this and other developments in the user and survivor movement can be found in the webpages established by Andrew Roberts,[7] and Peter Campbell has provided illuminating accounts of the history of the movement in the UK (Barker et al., 1999; Campbell, 1985; Campbell, 1996).

Things were similar, though not identical, in the United States.[8] As in the UK, the rise of feminist activism, 'consciousness raising', disability politics and the general spirit of activism that pervaded students, young people and many others in the 1960s and 1970s was important: organizing, demonstrating, protesting, publishing newssheets and small independent magazines. These movements advocated for change outside the conventional party system, many questioned the requirement for long abstract political programmes, and the need to wait for the election of governments to implement them; they argued for local control and for making change in the here and now. In the US, there was also the example of the civil rights movement, of legal activism and a pervasive belief in the sanctity of rights and the efficacy of rights-based claims in countering oppression and promoting liberation from unjust constraints.

The Mental Patients' Liberation Front was founded in 1971. Judi Chamberlin describes her encounter with it at that time, after she had undergone a whole series of rather unsuccessful treatments during and after numerous admissions to psychiatric hospitals. "There was this sense of doing something new and different. I mean, a lot of people had been involved in one way or another in the civil rights movement, the women's movement or whatever. It was like, 'Okay, here's something for MY people'."[9] In the next few years, there was a Conference on Human Rights and Psychiatric Oppression and the growth of small movements of 'ex-inmates', mostly focused on the role of involuntary detention in mental hospitals, deliberately using the words 'mental patient' and 'ex-mental patient' in their campaigning, and deploying the language of liberation and civil rights,[10] often linked up with radical lawyers contesting involuntary detention, coerced treatment and forced seclusion and forced medication.

Chamberlin's book, *On Our Own: Patient Controlled Alternatives to the Mental Health System* (1978) came out of that background. After describing her own experiences of hospitalization and of various institutions run by nonmedical personnel, and recounting the similar experiences of others, Chamberlin's manifesto comes down firmly against what she terms the 'partnership' model, where trained professionals work in partnership with patients in a programme of rehabilitation. She believes that these projects, even if they are less autocratic, less restrictive and less demeaning for the patients, are actually infused by a language and ideology of mental illness as a disorder or an illness – something which – often referring to the work of Thomas Szasz – she rejects.[11] Indeed, following Goffman, Chamberlin argues that mental patients suffer from 'contingencies'; she argues against the claims by the authors of the *Midtown Manhattan Study* (Srole et al., 1962) that there were large numbers of mentally ill people in the population who need mental health services but do not receive them. For Chamberlin, what makes mental patients different from others "is not the nature and severity of their problems but that their difficulties have been redefined as 'psychiatric symptoms,' requiring professional help. Since more and more kinds of behavior are being redefined as psychiatric in nature, psychiatry is creating an ever greater 'need' for its services" (1978).

Further, she argues that these 'community' projects, despite thinking of themselves as 'partnerships', are always structured by professional authority, no matter how much this is disguised: the inmates are only given those powers that professionals choose to grant them, and these can be withdrawn or overruled at any time: "[T]he role played by ex-patients is the crucial variable. When they are excluded from any meaningful role in planning the service, it becomes an alternative in name only. The same attitudes of condescension and distancing that are found in mental hospitals are also found in many of the halfway houses, rehabilitation services, and social clubs that are the supposed alternatives" (1978).¹² Chamberlin gives many examples of the ways in which clients of any mental health service are degraded, overtly or subtly, by what she terms 'psychiatric elitism' that focuses on and maximizes the inadequacies of people having difficulties in living, and ignores their strengths. Instead, as the title of her book indicates, she argues strongly for alternatives that are fully established, run and controlled by patients and ex-patients, "who are not merely passive recipients of a service but who are actively involved in running it. Role distinctions between service providers and service recipients blur and disappear . . . True alternatives are threatening because they do away with the need for professionals" (1978). By the time she wrote her book, there were a number of these true alternatives in (precarious) existence in the USA and Canada that she could cite – notably Project Release in New York, the Elizabeth Stone House in Boston, the Vancouver Emotional Emergency Centre and some drop-in facilities and other services run by the Mental Patients' Association, also in Vancouver – and 'Alternatives' became the name for a series of conferences that were run by mental patients and ex-mental patients themselves.

By 1990, Chamberlin still believed that the best path was for those who had experienced psychiatric treatment and hospitalization to develop their own self-help alternatives, and to do so alone and not with, represented by or spoken for by allies who had not had such experiences; these alternatives would not be medically based and would be controlled by ex-patients (Chamberlin, 1990). Further, Chamberlin invokes Thomas Szasz as an ally, not only for his arguments for absolute freedom of choice and against any involuntary confinement or treatment, but also because of his opposition to affirmative action and other strategies to give mental patients rights *as mental patients* – quoting Szasz's critique of the role of "professional civil libertarians, special-interest-mongering attorneys, and the relatives of mental patients [who have] joined conventional psychiatrists demanding rights for mental patients – qua mental patients . . . The phrase 'rights of mental patients' has meant everything but according persons called 'mental patients' the same rights (and duties) as are accorded all adults qua citizens or persons" (Szasz, 1989). She remained optimistic, arguing that, despite formidable obstacles, notably the entrenchment of psychiatry in the courts, the prisons, the schools, in the beliefs of the general public and in patient advocacy groups, there were hopeful signs for the movement "because ex-patient groups speak to a truth of the patienthood experience . . . that only by speaking out can individuals who have been harmed by the entrenched power of psychiatry mount a challenge against it" (Chamberlin, 1990).

Around the time that Chamberlin was writing this, in 1987, a meeting was held in the UK of those who were then describing themselves as *survivors* of the psychiatric system. 'Survivor' is a much-hated word by many – it seems to lump those who have been recipients of mental health services with those who have suffered from assaults such as rape or child abuse. But at this meeting of 'Survivors Speak Out', held on 18–20 September, these most radical activists unanimously agreed their charter of needs and demands:[13]

- That mental health service providers recognise and use people's first hand experience of emotional distress for the good of others.
- Provision of refuge, planned and under the control of survivors of psychiatry.
- Provision of free counselling for all.
- Choice of services including self-help alternatives.
- Government review of services, with recipients sharing their views.
- Provision of resources to implement self-advocacy for users.
- Adequate funding for non-medical community services, especially crisis intervention.
- Facility for representation of users and ex-users of services on statutory bodies.
- Full and free access to all personal medical records.
- Legal protection and means of redress for all psychiatric patients.
- Establishment of the democratic right of staff to refuse to administer any treatment without risk of sanction or prejudice.
- The phasing out of electro-convulsive therapy and psychosurgery.
- Independent monitoring of drug use and its consequences.
- Provision for all psychiatric patients of full written and verbal information on treatments, including adverse research findings.
- An end to discrimination against people who receive, or have received, psychiatric services: with particular regard to housing, employment, insurance etc.

In 1987, those demands, coming from probably the most radical section of the psychiatric patients' movement in the UK, seemed outrageous, a challenge to the very basis of a professionally organized and run mental health system whose treatments were underpinned by knowledge and where decisions were properly made by trained professionals. But today, many mainstream mental health organizations would support most of those objectives. Indeed, across the decade of the 1980s, the radicalism of these movements, in the United States, the UK and elsewhere, had already begun to transmute into a focus on actually trying to implement some changes through new collaborations with more mainstream organizations, and recommendations for changes rather than – or alongside – alternatives such as 'drop-in' centres run by former mental patients – which were themselves sometimes supported by funds from local or national government. In the US, the National Institute for Mental Health allocated funds to organizations running such centres, and the Carter Administration legislated for a 'consumer-run facility' in every state and set up a service use evaluation team headed by Jean Campbell (Campbell, 2005).[14] Activism had been reframed: no doubt in part as a result of the fact that long-term institutionalization, the mental hospital and the demeaned status of mental patients no longer delimited the territory of psychiatry and its subjects. But has this move from alternatives to engagement transformed the power relations of psychiatry? Let me turn to examine these changes in more detail.

From 'on our own' to 'nothing about us without us'

From the 1980s onwards, there was a gradual change in the strategies of many activists. Emphasis shifted from the objective of independent, alternative services 'on our own' – though this was never completely abandoned, especially in movements of black and ethnic minorities – to the engagement of psychiatric service users in the formal psychiatric and mental health apparatus. One of the conditions for such a shift was a surprising 'side-effect' of the 'consumerization' of professional services under the new right governments of Margaret Thatcher in the UK, Ronald Reagan in the US, and similar political developments elsewhere in Europe and in Australia, Canada and New Zealand. Among the components in these strategies, later believed by many to mark the birth of an egregious 'neoliberalism', was an attack on the enclaves of professional power in education, in the law and elsewhere, and policies to open them to the stringent rigours of the market. Clients were to be transformed into consumers, and professionals into suppliers of services who had to compete for business like any others with products to sell.[15] And consumers, unlike passengers on nationalized railways, or residents locked into monopolistic suppliers of basic utilities, had choice and had voice. The consumers of health services, in this dream, were no longer mere patients required to wait passively until an expert deigned to deliver an opinion based on incontrovertible knowledge. They too were to have choice and voice, no longer a patient patient, but 'free to choose' among the services offered by health professionals.

This is not the place to evaluate this dream or its consequences (see Rose, 1999b). But in psychiatry and mental health services too, the voice of the patient began to achieve a certain limited legitimacy: no longer merely heard as a symptom, provided it was expressed rationally and constructively and without too much passion, the voices of users of psychiatric services now were seen as essential elements in the management of a mental health system.[16] Peter Campbell and Diana Rose, pioneers of service user activism in the UK, argue that "service user activists first rode into the corridors of power in the United Kingdom on the back of health service consumerism" (2010: 455). Peter Beresford, one of the most acute participants and analysts of these developments, has pointed out that there were, and remain, tensions between the involvement of users as consumers of services that remain organized and controlled by others, and the aspirations of what he calls 'democratic' involvement which entails "personal and political empowerment" (2002: 97). However, the reality probably lay in a grey area between these two poles, with psychiatric service users seeking to transform existing services through their involvement, yet at the same time arguing that, by means of multiple small changes, a more radical transformation of power relations within the mental health system could be achieved. Thus many service users participated in advocacy groups, such as the United Kingdom Self Advocacy Network and the National Self Harm Network, and also actively engaged with the development of government policy, notably in the development of a National Service Framework for Mental Health published in 1999.[17] Almost all service users found these experiences of participation unsatisfactory, and some found them positively traumatizing.

'Nothing about us without us' was a slogan first adopted in the disability movement and transformed into a manifesto by James Charlton (1998), an America disability rights activist. He locates the origins of its philosophy in liberation movements in South Africa,[18] and in the movement for disability rights in the United States. For Charlton, this slogan encapsulated a demand for control of services by those with disabilities that resonated with Chamberlin's belief that when others speak for you, you lose. It challenges not only the powerlessness of those with disabilities, but the paternalism of those who placed them into conditions of dependency: "For the first time in recorded human history politically active people with disabilities are beginning to proclaim that they know what is best for themselves and their community. This is a militant, revelational claim aptly capsualized in 'Nothing About Us Without Us'" (Charlton, 1998: 4).[19]

But if 'nothing about us without us' became a favourite slogan, and its model of self-advocacy was taken up by activists in mental health, their strategies were not always framed in Charlton's radical dialectics of oppression and empowerment. As I have already suggested, more frequently they took the form of a less radical demand for those who were subject to paternalistic management – whether they were people with disabilities, the elderly, substance users or those using mental health services – to have a seat at the table and a voice in decisions that affected them. Patient councils and patient advocacy were introduced into many hospital settings. Conforming to the logic of the new public management, new public/private alliances were formed in which publicly funded mental health services contracted with user-run organizations to provide support groups, and even – occasionally – to run day centres and supported housing schemes.

Psychiatric service users found themselves invited to professional debates on planning and shaping local and national mental health services, although again their experience was often uncomfortable. If patient involvement was a watchword in so many areas of medicine and health, it was a particular challenge to professional authority where those patients had long been disqualified by the very condition which had led them into the medical arena. Thus, there were persistent disagreements about the extent to which those users were 'representative'. Professionals who wished to delegitimize their arguments contended that these were the views of a small, articulate, politically motivated minority, not those of the majority of inarticulate but grateful beneficiaries of services. Others claimed that they failed to represent highly stigmatized users, especially those from ethnic minorities. And, from the other side, as it were, those who did take up the challenges of engagement with the evaluation and reform of mental health services were often accused of tokenism and incorporation by those who considered themselves more radical. Engagement often led to what Beresford (2002: 102) termed 'consultation fatigue', producing only small changes in relation to the efforts involved, which were sometimes no more than an exercise in legitimation so that the right boxes could be ticked by the professionals in charge.

The risk, of course, was that those who took up positions in such institutions would themselves become 'bureaucratized' quasi-professionals, in the uncomfortable position of being neither 'proper professionals' nor 'normal patients' (Epstein, 2008, 2011).[20] At the same time, all too often, their arguments were rapidly recuperated, domesticated, and became part of the toolbox of those very professionals who were the subject of challenge. Advocacy, for example, was one of the initial means by which excluded or demeaned groups sought to make their own voices heard: psychiatric services users would advocate *by themselves* and *for themselves*. However, within a decade, mental health professionals and policymakers began to see advocacy as a mechanism for engaging hard-to-reach patients in their own care, and managing grievances. Advocates were soon to be a requirement of almost all mental health institutions, and advocacy, rather than a process of speaking *for oneself* became a professionalized mechanism in which others were given the role of speaking for you, advocating 'on your behalf', mediating between parties all of whom were considered to have the best interests of the patient at heart.[21]

Similarly, the term 'empowerment' was initially used to support and sustain service users in finding their own voice and their own authority against a system that consistently denies these values. Patricia Deegan, herself a service user, argued passionately that changing systems was not enough: each person who had been psychiatrically labelled needed to "take up the wondrously terrifying work of changing ourselves and opening ourselves up to be transformed", and that was a process of "empowerment [embodying a] profound reverence for the fundamental value of each human being. Empowerment is founded on the value that each human being is a subject who can act. Human beings are not objects to be acted upon. Any act on the part of social workers or other health professionals which enhances the opportunity for human beings to act on their own behalf is empowering social work praxis. Any act on the part of social workers or other health professionals which reduces the human subject to an object that is acted upon, is an oppressive act. It is an act of violence. It is a transgression. It is dehumanizing. It is fundamentally disempowering" (Deegan, 1997: 14). Growing out of her moving account of her own disempowering treatment at the hands of professionals who deemed her a chronic sufferer from an incurable disease and asked her to give up her dreams for her future, forget her belief that she might live a meaningful life, and accept the limits imposed upon her by her unfortunate, disabling medical condition, Deegan argues that empowerment embodies the need for professionals and patients to share power and to support individuals to regain hope and act to transform their future.

However, empowerment rapidly freed itself from the passions grounded in experience that imbued it at the start and became another tool in the toolbox of well-meaning caring professionals – something for professionals to use on unfortunate individuals suffering from mental illness (Cruikshank, 1999). They became professional 'empower-ers', trained by experts of empowerment, educated by textbooks of empowerment, even gaining qualifications in empowerment. It now became a part of their role to 'empower' those who were their clients, though seldom by giving up their own powers or those of their fellow professionals, and seldom by enacting the systematic and structural changes needed to support capacities for independent action to those whom they 'empowered' (Baistow, 1994). Indeed, 'empowerment' became one of the key terms in the politics of welfare state reform of the 1980s, for if the welfare system created 'dependency' among those who benefited from it, destroying their independence, their will and their incentives to fight for themselves in the marketplace of life, empowerment was one of the antidotes, one of the key modes for 'governing subjectivity' – the resubjectification of welfare recipients as freedom-loving entrepreneurs of their own existence, equipped with 'self-esteem' whatever their external or internal circumstances (Cruikshank, 1993).

The politics of recovery

The movement for 'recovery' has suffered a similar fate. The recovery movement was initially a radical alternative to conventional psychiat-ric norms and practices, stressing the right, and the capacity, of those with mental health problems not to be defined by their illness. Once more, Patricia Deegan was one of the first to argue, not for treatment or cure, but for recovery, not as an end point, but as a journey, an attitude, "a way of approaching the day and the challenges I face. Being in recovery means that I know that I have certain limitations and things I can't do. But rather than letting these limitations be an occasion for despair and giving up, I have learned that in knowing what I can't do, I also open up the possibilities of all the things I can do" (1997: 20–1). Each individual must find their own way to do this, helped by conversation with others making their own journey. "Your life and your dreams may have been shattered but I say that from such ruins you can build a new life full of value and purpose. The task is not to become normal. The task is to take up your journey of recovery and to become who you are called to be" (1997: 24).

In New Zealand, Mary O'Hagan, one of the initiators of the psychiatric service user movement in that country, the first chair of the World Network of Users and Survivors of Psychiatry, who has also been a Mental Health Commissioner for New Zealand, was a powerful advocate of what she termed 'the recovery framework'. In this framework, madness is seen as a legitimate human experience, the subjectivity of the individual is to be respected and understood, and services are designed to support people to recover their well-being, to lead their own recovery, emphasizing hope, self-determination over life, their personal choices of services and their valued place in the world.[22] She was one of the architects of the New Zealand Mental Health Commission's *Blueprint for Mental Health Services* (1998), which required all mental health services to adopt a 'recovery approach' loosely defined as 'living well in the presence or absence of one's mental illness' and has tried to set out the competences required by mental health professionals to implement this approach (O'Hagan, 2004). While recognizing that the recovery approach can be 'abused', O'Hagan and her fellow advocates of recovery set out a range of key principles for a genuine use of recovery, which includes the use of peer support workers, encouraging individuals to make advance directives as to their treatment if they become ill, developing wellness recovery action planning, appropriate illness management, recovery interventions focused on strengths and the development of recovery colleges and recovery education programmes (Slade et al., 2014).

It is certainly true that a recovery approach "is a hopeful one that believes people with a mental illness diagnosis can come to terms with their difficulties and live a meaningful life", and it does so in a way that recognizes that much of the support to enable individuals to create a form of life for themselves comes not from mental health professionals, but from others, including fellow service users (Campbell and Rose, 2010: 467). However, as with empowerment, recovery rapidly transmogrified into a professional practice with a particular form. Recovery came to be seen as an antidote to service dependency, and the aim of recovery professionals – together with peer support workers who had often themselves gone through a 'recovery journey' – was to promote practices of self-reflection and other forms of 'experiential learning' to inculcate the capacity for self-management and self-reliance into those who had given up hope, or forgotten the techniques, to make a life for themselves (Voronka, 2017). While the initial ideas of recovery embodied the principle "that each person should be allowed and encouraged to set their own goals and outcomes" this was now undermined by the professional 'recovery approach' that set out "key stages of recovery and lists of desired outcomes" (Campbell and Rose, 2010: 467).

By the 1990s, professionals were already hailing the 'recovery approach' as the guiding vision for mental health services after the asylum: mental health professionals needed to lessen their focus on symptom reduction and develop a new way of thinking of services in terms of supporting and facilitating those 'patients in the community' to develop their self-esteem, to adjust to their disabilities, to be empowered, to exercise self-determination, to live with their mental health condition and – like those with physical disabilities or who have spinal cord injuries because of accidents – to find new ways to make meaning in their lives (Anthony, 1993). Such attitudes were taken up by mental health service managers in many countries, and by many professionals, notably psychiatrists and social workers, who retrained or relabelled themselves as 'experts in recovery', researching recovery, writing manuals and programmes for recovery, drafting in former mental health services users as 'peer support workers', and indeed rebranding day centres and outpatient clinics as 'recovery houses' (Perkins and Repper, 2003; Slade, 2009).

In this process, the idea of recovery often became linked with an idea of resilience, taken from debates about child development in situations of adversity (Werner, 1993), and about the trajectory of those who had experienced 'life-changing' injuries, or undergone natural disaster, fires, explosions or terrorist incidents. Resilience arguments stressed the ways in which human beings, as living creatures, had a natural capacity to survive and thrive even in the most difficult of circumstances, characteristically making use of informal networks of support and care to 'bounce back' after devastating events, and finding the resources within themselves and their communities to make a new life for themselves (Masten, 2015). However, this apparently 'natural' capacity could be enhanced and nurtured by experts, and resilience too developed its body of professional expertise (Grotberg, 1995; Flett and Hewitt, 2014; Robertson et al., 2015). One could, it seemed, learn the ways to cast off one's feelings of hopelessness in the face of adversity, and learn to be resilient.

Unsurprisingly, many psychiatric service users find such language deeply patronizing: they do not need the sympathy and facilitation of 'experts', and they do not wish to be compared with heroic paraplegics making a new life after injury. Indeed, quite the reverse. They not only regard the recovery movement, in its professionalized form, as highly normative, actually maintaining and sustaining a 'deficit' model of mental disorder, ignoring the fundamental questions of poverty and social justice that drive so many to mental distress, and promoting a particular vision of a normal life, with a focus on gaining and maintaining employment as a key index of recovery (Harper and Speed, 2012). They not only point to the fact that, despite the protestations of its many supporters (Slade et al., 2014), there is little evidence that these kinds of recovery approaches 'work' or even that they address the issues that those they wish to 'empower' consider most important (Rose, 2014). Far from it: they also argue that, by accident or design, this version of recovery finds its ecological niche in a context where an ideology of welfare reduction of services and of budgets has taken hold, where former welfare services are privatized and marketized, where resilience is seen as an individual trait to be promoted by experts, not a collective capacity grounded upon a range of material and cultural resources (Rose and Lentzos, 2017), and where new norms of personhood have been disseminated in which citizens are reimagined as entrepreneurial managers of their own existence and held responsible for their own destinies. In other words, the professionalized recovery movement has flourished in so many countries because it fits perfectly with the rationalities and technologies of neoliberalism.

There is indeed a certain 'elective affinity' between ideas of recovery and resilience and the fear of dependency that stalks contemporary welfare and social work practices. Practices of 'responsibilization' stress 'self-management' and translate these ideas – each of which stressed that these capabilities grew out of particular forms of social relationships – into psychological capacities of individuals that, on the one hand, are natural and essential elements of human nature – to wish to recover, to be resilient – and, on the other, can be brought forth from them, shaped and developed by expert practices for fashioning the self. In mental health policies in Canada, for example, Teghtsoonian argued that "individuals, families, communities and workplaces – rather than publicly-funded services – appear as key resources in responding to experiences of mental distress" (2009: 28). In Australia, Brijnath and Antoniades (2016) demonstrated that while professionals seek to train patients in the arts of self-management and responsibility, it is often the patients themselves who have to work out how to cope with the challenges of self-care and self-management in response to their unsatisfactory experiences with the formal mental health system. As Howell and Voronka put it:

> Whereas twenty years ago resilience and recovery were harnessed as organized frameworks for psychiatric survivors to avert the medical system through alternate means (including peer knowledge and support), they are now harnessed to incorporate psychiatric survivors into medical systems. They now work in ways that attempt to make psychiatric survivors responsible for their own adherence to prescribed ways of governing their interior lives, while at the same time leaving medical authority intact, since psychologist and psychiatrists have become experts in recovery and resilience. (2012: 2)

A new epistemology of mental distress

Despite these challenges, and despite the persistence of the long-standing association between mental illness, risk, difference and dangerousness,[23] collaboration between psychiatric service users and mental health services started the long process of reconfiguring power relations within the mental health apparatus, and articulating a different conception of the rights and capacities of service users. By 2003, a survey conducted by the Sainsbury Centre for Mental Health found around 300 local service user groups, mostly small, undoubtedly providing support for those in their local area, often being consulted in local policy development, but fragmented and hardly amounting to a radical movement for changing power relations in mental health (Wallcraft et al., 2003). Nonetheless, by 2014 it was estimated that there were 800 service user researchers involved in these activities in the UK, undertaking user-led evaluation of services, helping develop guidelines for treatment and clinical practice, sitting on committees deliberating on mental health policy at local and national level and consulting on service development.[24]

Judi Chamberlin, in an overview of user/consumer involvement in mental health services in the United States – one of the last pieces that she wrote before her untimely death – argued that although much had been achieved, the power differential between 'patients' and professionals was a major stumbling block to getting the voice of the user heard at all, "let alone making real and substantive changes in the conditions of their lives" (Chamberlin, 2005: 11).[25] She argued that this would remain "so long as users can be subjected to involuntary interventions in supposedly voluntary services", but nonetheless she points to the rise and achievements of the organized user/survivor movement in the United States that echo those in the UK. She singled out their role in campaigning for limitations on involuntary commitment, achieving improvement of institutional conditions, developing user-controlled alternative services, combatting discrimination and promoting services for recovery. And for the future, she argued that reducing power differentials and meaningful involvement can be realized by service users taking a key role in training mental health professionals, the design and operation of mental health programmes, the evaluation of services, in mental health research and in the provision of alternative user-run programmes (2005: 12) as well as the practice of joint decision-making and the use of advance directives when a person is "in an emotional state that presents difficulties [so that] difficult emotional states can be seen as natural life events rather than as medical crises" (2005: 14). And she supported genuine discussion among users and professionals who may hold different, and equally valid, views on the role of involuntary commitment and treatment, but where all can have a 'seat at the table' as long as those power differentials are openly acknowledged and agreed by all.

But perhaps the most radical development came from those psychiatric service users who sought to go beyond engagement and collaboration to develop an alternative knowledge basis for the transformation of mental health systems. Thus in 1998, Diana Rose and colleagues at the UK's Sainsbury Centre for Mental Health published *In Our Experience* (Rose et al., 1998), followed shortly by *Users' Voices* (Rose, 2001b) in which psychiatric service users themselves developed a methodology – user focused monitoring, or UFM – for researching and evaluating the mental health services that they were experiencing. Analogous research was carried out by Alison Faulkner and colleagues at the Mental Health Foundation (Faulkner and Layzell, 2000; Faulkner and Thomas, 2002). Together with developments in the National Self Harm Network, and the Hearing Voices Network,[26] these research projects led to a radically new practice, in which psychiatric service users challenged the *epistemological* authority of psychiatry and psychiatrists in evaluating different kinds of treatment interventions for those living with a psychiatric diagnosis.

These mental health service users and researchers argued that the apparent objectivity of psychiatric research masked the position from which it emanated, and the power relations and value systems it upheld. They showed how this shaped the questions being asked, the methods used to answer them and the criteria by which evidence and outcomes were to be assessed. Some believed that this psychiatric epistemology should be countered by an epistemology of 'lived experience' which needed no randomized controlled trials to demonstrate that it was 'evidence-based' – patients were 'experts by experience'. For others, however, it was insufficient to simply refer to experience to refute the truth claims of psychiatry. User-led research had to be rigorous, both using, modifying and supplementing the standards of rigour in conventional research practices. Thus, both Faulkner and Rose used rigorous research methods to show the discrepancies between many of the claims made in the published literature, and the experience of those who had been subject to those treatments, developing user-identified measures for evaluating the outcome of interventions and much more. This, then, was not simply a matter of incorporating service users and 'consumers' as one group among many that had the authority to set up and evaluate services. It was to argue that knowledge from the perspective of the patient, from those traditionally thought to 'lack insight' and hence to have limited ability to make appropriate decisions because of their illness, provided an alternative, and perhaps a better, basis for developing effective practices to support those experiencing mental distress, even those diagnosed as suffering from a serious mental disorder. Conventional psychiatric knowledge claims could be challenged on their own grounds, and the epistemologies of psychiatry could be denied their claims to universality, and located in their time, place and epistemic community.

Peter Beresford was one of the first service user researchers to argue explicitly for the need for a new paradigm in research from the psychiatric service users movement, drawing on the experience and achievements of research by those in the radical movements of disabled people (Beresford and Wallcraft, 1997; Beresford, 2002). For him, the key point at issue was that such research had to be explicitly political and emancipatory in orientation, but it also had to address issues raised in feminist epistemology about hierarchies of credibility, standpoints of knowledge production, the relationships of knowledge and direct experience, and the nature of evidence in claims about 'evidence-based' arguments (Beresford, 2000).

Diana Rose took this argument further, arguing for the need for a new epistemology for psychiatric user and survivor research.[27] Drawing on Donna Haraway's critique of 'the god trick', by which the views of particular communities of scientists are presented as if they are 'views from nowhere' and simultaneously 'views from everywhere', Rose argued that the truth status of claims to scientific objectivity are inescapably arbitrated upon by particular scientific communities bound by time, space and professional allegiance. Such an argument finds support from key figures in the philosophy of scientific knowledge. For example, Gaston Bachelard argued that truth in scientific reason is never the work of the isolated *cogito* but of the communal *cogitamus* – a community of truth that sets what counts as epistemological norms and assures the validity of knowledge claims (see Cutting, 1987). Karl Popper too argued that, ultimately, the scientific community must be the guarantor of truth, though his belief in the 'openness' of real science runs counter to the recognition, from Ludwik Fleck (1979 [1935]) to Thomas Kuhn (1962), that such communities are not open, but are demarcated by some fundamental, though far from universal and timeless, agreements on what counts as problems, explanations, evidence and proof. And this argument is taken up by sociologists of science, for example by Shapin and Schaffer's (1985) highly influential account of the 'invisible college' necessary to support Robert Boyle's practice of scientific experimentation in the mid-seventeenth century, or Knorr Cetina's (1999) ethnographic description of contemporary epistemic cultures in high energy physics and molecular biology.

What then happens when the collective and consensual judgement of a scientific community is challenged? When anomalies accumulate, when validation proves hard to maintain? This is indeed the condition of much psychiatry today, with its focus on mental disorders as brain disorders, its incessant references to anomalies in neurotransmitter systems, its recurrently failing attempts to identify genetic sequences and biomarkers for specific form of mental distress, and its highly questionable claims about the efficacy and specificity of pharmaceutical intervention (Faulkner, 2017b). In the face of this crisis, can users and survivors of psychiatry create an alternative epistemic culture, that can challenge the truth claims of conventional psychiatry, and articulate an alternative set of rigorous claims, based on a different set of fundamental questions about mental distress, different kinds of evidence and different forms of validation?

Rose argues that an appeal to 'lived experience' is not enough (in press). As Joan Scott (1991) argued long ago, experience is constructed, vision is never naive, but shaped by a system of thought, profoundly structured by the categories of language and meaning in operation at a particular time and place, hence not an individual but a collective production.[28] In the case of the movement of users and survivors of psychiatry, that experience is structured by collective action, by practices of resistance, by the sharing of accounts and the gradual assembling of an alternative style of thought, and alternative way of rendering experience into thought, making encounters with the mental health apparatus and its practices of knowledge and power intelligible in a different way. From this standpoint, the knowledge claims of users and survivors of psychiatry depend for their objectivity on a different and newly emerging epistemic culture, a new community of knowledge and practice that is formed by those who experience mental and emotional distress, and who experience the forms of treatment available within the psychiatric and mental health systems.[29] To end the monologue of reason about madness thus means to free madness from its Siamese twin of unreason, to argue that rigorous forms of knowledge can be created by those deemed mad, can be rendered objective through the creation of a new epistemic community, and can challenge the knowledge claims of psychiatry at their heart.

Have we moved beyond the monologue?

Over the last few years, at least in the countries of the Global North, we have witnessed a paradoxical development. We have a plethora of voices of those who have experienced mental distress, especially celebrities, speaking out about their conditions and how they have suffered, overcome or lived with them. Anti-stigma campaigns have used all the devices of marketing, such as films, posters and celebrity endorsements, to seek to break down the barriers between 'us' and 'them' – mental ill health, it now seems, is something that we all can understand, on a continuum with everyone's normal experiences of depression, anxiety, fears and phobias, feelings of unworthiness and despair. These feelings are not shameful weaknesses that must be hidden, but human experiences to which we can bear witness, and which call for understanding and counselling. 'Mental health issues' are no longer in the shadows; they now dare to speak their name.

And yet, at the same time, provision of user-run services is minimal. Professional mental health services in the community, now justified because they are more economical than inpatient treatment, are being cut to the bone. Police complain that they are being used to fill gaps in mental health provision, and each year, thousands of people considered to be 'mentally ill' are detained under mental health legislation in police cells for considerable periods before they can access any form of treatment.[30] Inpatient care, sometimes a vital sanctuary for those in mental distress, is hard to access, restricted to those experiencing major crises. It seldom offers an environment of respite and sanctuary, and is used merely as an interim measure until the person is stabilized enough by drugs to be released into the community to be managed – again with drugs – by a home treatment team. A growing number of patients are detained under the Mental Health Act, in many cases because this is the only way in which their mental health professionals can ensure that they can access a place in a hospital. Increasingly, wards are kept locked. As I write, a report from the Care Quality Commission in England reports that more than 3,500 patients in 248 mental health wards are under lock and key. In 2015–16, while some patients were in locked wards for up to 45 days, others had been there for up to 1,744 days – four and a half years. Two-thirds of these beds are run by private providers, who are increasingly used by the NHS.[31] Given the quality of care, or lack of it, in these wards, it is no wonder that many patients become agitated and that staff, lacking the skills, choose to restrain them with drugs or with physical methods. The same report finds that "[o]n too many wards the combination of a high number of detained patients who pose a risk to themselves and sometimes to others, old and unsuitable buildings, staff shortages and a lack of basic training, make it more likely that patients and staff are at risk of suffering harm."

So, have all the anti-stigma campaigns, the fun-runs, the celebrities speaking out, the argument that mental ill-health is, on the one hand, part of everyday experience and, on the other, just an illness like any other: have these led to a transformation of the fundamental power relations in psychiatry? On the basis of this recent evidence from England, the answer can hardly be a resounding yes. Indeed, Flick Grey, as a result of her study of such campaigns in Australia, refers to these as "benevolent othering . . . in which others are spoken of in ways that are ostensibly positive, but that function to maintain the subordination of mental health service users" (2016: 241). Grey extends this gloomy conclusion to what she calls "consumer participation" and "co-production" discourses – that is to say, those developments I have described in this chapter in which psychiatric service users and survivors have actively engaged with mental health professionals and policymakers in the reshaping of the services to which they are subject. She suggests that while they "have the potential to transform the relationship between service users and service providers [they] also have the potential to re-inscribe existing power relations, with services continuing to be delivered according to service provider priorities, while service providers can pat themselves on the back for being such 'giving beings,' allowing service users to participate. Ongoing participation may be conditional upon service users remaining both useful and harmless, including cooperating with service provider agendas and contributing unpaid or underpaid labor" (2016: 248).

Must we accept such a depressing conclusion? Or should we, as Errol Francis suggests, referring to the work of Susan Sontag, recognize the limits of 'compassion' as an emotion to engender change unless compassion is tied to action? As Francis puts it, we must "come to terms with . . . the limited potential of photography and social marketing campaigns that rely on challenging stereotypes to change attitudes toward mental health or any other social or health issue" and recognize that concrete actions to transform authority relations in specific practices are much more likely to achieve some success in combatting discrimination and exclusion (2016: 259).

This is not the place to analyse the entirely predictable weaknesses of anti-stigma campaigns based on the assumption that changing attitudes will ameliorate disadvantages held in place by social and structural inequalities. But it would be a mistake to suggest that the activities of the psychiatric user and survivor movement over the last decade or more has been limited to support for anti-stigma campaigns and the stimulation of compassion. Indeed, many of those user/survivor activists whom I have discussed in this chapter have explicitly drawn attention both to the damaging consequences of the lived experience of stigmatization and discrimination – which certainly call for compassion if not anger – and to the limits of any campaigns seeking to wring compassion but failing to challenge the social and structural determinants of practices of exclusion and marginalization. They have pointed to the hypocrisy when, for example, 'anti-stigma' campaigns supported by various governments go hand in hand with transformations in welfare services based on the premise that many of those receiving social support are in fact scroungers who must be not merely demeaned, but subject to repeated and often risible evaluations of job readiness by private and for-profit agencies incentivized by payments based on the numbers of people they return to work, and offered the option of either entering into unsuitable and often unrealistic employment or losing all their benefits (Faulkner, 2017a). Further, they often ignore the fact that stigma and discrimination do not only exist 'in the general public', but also among health care practitioners, especially in relation to certain diagnoses such as 'borderline personality disorder' (Bonnington and Rose, 2014), or for individuals from ethnic minorities or other demeaned groups.[32]

Thus we should not conflate developments in the psychiatric user movement with these strategies to normalize the experience of mental ill health and to stimulate sympathy for those unfortunate individuals who are afflicted, and which sidestep the more difficult social, structural and political practices that operate to sustain and sometimes to accentuate discrimination and exclusion. The psychiatric user/survivor movement has offered a more fundamental challenge to the power of psychiatry, not only because of the criticisms that it, along with many others, has made of the claims to objective knowledge of mental disorder and effective treatments for it, not only because of its well-founded criticisms of the actual practices of care experienced by those living under a psychiatric diagnosis, but also because of its articulation of alternative forms of knowledge of mental distress, linked to alternative modes of intervention and support for those experiencing profound crises in their lives. These arguments chime closely with others that I have made throughout this book, and they lead us to a final hard question, perhaps the most important of all: is another psychiatry, a different psychiatry, possible? It is to this question that I turn in my final chapter.

9
Is Another Psychiatry Possible?

What is the future for psychiatry? A recent Lancet Commission report with that title argued that what was needed was nothing less than a revolution (Bhugra et al., 2017). I agree. But my manifesto for that revolution, though it has some points in common, differs from theirs in many ways. What I argue in this chapter is not 'anti-psychiatry' but for a different psychiatry, one that is *as* research-based, *as* supported by objective evidence, as is the psychiatry that I have discussed so critically in this book. In particular, my alternative draws on current research in biology and neurobiology, but does so in a different way, starting not with a brain in the lab, but with human organisms in their milieu. Further, my approach is not anti-psychiatrist, though I do call for a fundamental revision in the role that medically trained person- nel should have in helping those who experience mental distress, and a radical shift in their ways of working so that they can address the social determinants of mental distress and not merely seek to manage the effects. And, in consequence of these shifts, I suggest, psychiatry and psychiatrists will have a different relation to politics: another psychiatry is also part of a very different biopolitics.

Manifestoes for the future

We are, of course, not short of manifestoes. For some, what is required is a wholesale rejection of psychiatry. This was the view expressed forcefully by Judi Chamberlin (1978), who argued four decades ago that psychiatry should be replaced by something that mental patients, ex-mental patients and service users do 'on their own'. Some have reactivated the term 'anti-psychiatry' for this approach. The original cultural movement often termed anti-psychiatry was something of a confection created by commentators, bringing together incompatible bedfellows with different assessments of psychiatry proposing very different alternatives. These included radical psychiatrists who wished to transform the asylum, such as R. D. Laing, David Cooper, Franco Basaglia and Felix Guattari; historians of psychiatry and the conceptions of madness that underpinned it, such as Michel Foucault; sociologists who had analysed pathways to the asylum, the total institution, labelling, stigma and the moral career of the mental patient, such as Erving Goffman and Thomas Scheff; and right-wing libertarians, such as Thomas Szasz, for whom mental illness was a myth to perpetuate state control over troublesome people, and who argued that those who clung to their illness label were malingerers who should take responsibility for their own problems in living. Most of those dubbed anti-psychiatrists in the 1960s and 1970s vigorously denied that they were either anti-psychiatry or anti-psychiatrists. But some in the fledgling movement for 'Mad Studies' embrace this term for a position that is anti-both. For example, Bonnie Burstow, a radical feminist therapist based in Toronto, allies herself with Thomas Szasz, arguing that mental illness is a myth invented by psychiatrists, that psychiatric methods, from treatment with psychopharmaceuticals to the use of ECT, are damaging; that psychiatry is an instrument of 'the state' exercising police powers on behalf of 'the state'; that it is a 'business', in cahoots with the pharmaceutical companies; and that psychiatric powers are oppressive and violate human rights (Burstow, 2015).[1] These arguments are sadly simplistic, not least because of their portrayal of political power in terms of a calculating 'state', their homogenizing conception of 'psychiatry' and their unquestioned adoption of Szasz's myth of the autonomous individual free to choose. Nonetheless they contain enough nuggets of truth to attract some psychiatric service users, especially in the United States, who have been treated badly in the mental health system, and who are very critical of the medicalization of everyday life, the overuse of ineffective and damaging pharmaceuticals and the egregious links between the psychiatric profession and 'big pharma' – all points made more thoughtfully in a number of widely read articles by the former editor of the *New England Journal of Medicine* Marcia Angell (Relman and Angell, 2002; Angell, 2004, 2011).

However, perhaps the key attraction of this reborn, rights-based anti-psychiatry is that it seems to address the sense of coercion that many have experienced in their encounters with the mental health system, outside as much as inside the mental institution, even if formal powers are not invoked. As we saw in the previous chapter, the focus on civil and human rights goes back to the early mental patients movements in the United States, and is, in many ways, similar to that made by other largely US-based radical libertarian organizations such as MindFreedom.[2] Further, some of the propositions of these radical libertarians, in particular their implacable opposition to any involuntary treatment – with the reciprocal valorization of the freedom of each individual to choose – have found their way into perhaps the most consequential of all interventions into mental health practices, the Convention on the Rights of Persons with Disabilities (CRPD),[3] which, some argue, prohibits both involuntary detention of an individual where mental disorder or mental illness is one of the grounds for such detention, and prohibits involuntary treatment.[4] Autonomy, freedom, choice, individual rights and a belief in the powers and virtues of the law – such American values! But one does not have to be a rabid socialist to realize their limitations, to recognize that there is such a thing as 'society' and that each and all of us exist only within this matrix of social bonds, to understand the reality of mutual dependency and obligation, sadly so often etiolated for those with longstanding and serious mental health problems, and to acknowledge the fact that individuals are never 'free to choose', and far less so when they are in states of anguish, despair or tormented by voices telling them they are worthless and should die. Sometimes, compulsory admission to a place of safety for a short period of respite and care, even where conditions are far from ideal, together with the short-term, even involuntary, administration of some sedative medication, can be a way of returning an individual in such a state of extreme distress to a condition where they can make thoughtful decisions about their own lives.[5]

Rights are a powerful way of saying no to undesirable practices and are sorely needed in those countries and regions where confinement in mental hospitals, often in appalling conditions, is the norm. However, their capacity to deliver positive improvements in mental health care is exceptionally restricted (Rose, 1985b). Transferring authority to lawyers and legal institutions in the name of civil or human rights is an inadequate strategy for generating radical reform of a contemporary mental health apparatus in which involuntary confinement and treatment play only a limited role. A strategy focused on prohibiting compulsion would have no traction on the powers of most of the psychiatrists, medical practitioners, psychologists, therapists and others who manage those in distress on the new territory of mental health. The rapid worldwide increase in the use of psychopharmaceuticals has occurred outside the legal domain, except as it pertains to licensing or, in rare cases, to litigation for adverse effects.[6] Most fundamentally, as we have seen in all civil rights- and human rights-based movements, they have very limited powers in shaping, funding and implementing desirable policies and practices, or in transforming the ethos of professionals.[7] For a realistic but radical revolution in contemporary mental health practices, we must look elsewhere.

What, then, of the revolution that is called for by the Lancet Commission on the Future of Psychiatry? The Commission was set up by the World Psychiatric Association and *Lancet Psychiatry* to "stimulate thought, debate, and the change necessary for psychiatry to fulfil its potential as an innovative, effective, and inclusive medical specialty in the 21st century" (Bhugra et al., 2017: 776). The limitations of the proposals made by the Commission were inscribed in this aim. The report states boldly that "[p]sychiatry in the first quarter of the 21st century is on the cusp of major changes", but while some of these are hinted at in the report, most of its concerns are about how to keep things more or less the same in a changing world. Yes, it is important for psychiatry to be able to work with an ageing population, to learn to use digital technologies and to retain – if it has ever truly had it – cultural sensitivity and a focus on the therapeutic alliance. Yes, it is important for mental health legislation to be updated in the light of the Convention of the Rights of Persons with Disabilities, although the implications of the potential prohibition in that convention on compulsion of any sort are not properly addressed. And yes, I am sure that the training of psychiatrists should be focused less on acquisition of information and more on lifelong learning and quality improvement. If psychiatry is to stay much the same in a changing world, who could disagree? Yet at points in the document, which shows clearly that it has been written by many authors with a diversity of views, a more radical transformation of psychiatry is hinted at. Let me try to pull out those strands.

At the very start of the introduction to the report, an intriguing question is raised: "Psychiatry has always been a medical discipline, but was this development inevitable, and will it always be this way?" (Bhugra et al., 2017: 776). Actually, an affirmative answer is written into the very aims of the report, and this question remains unanswered in the text that follows. But at points we can find some hints of alternatives. For example, the report acknowledges that the "dramatic neuroscience research advances in psychiatry" have not led to substantial advances in patient care, and that, at the same time, the "increasing recognition of the social determinants of health has clearly led to increased appreciation of demographic, economic and sociocultural aspects of risk for development of psychiatric disorders" (2017: 776). It points to the large-scale demographic changes – ageing, urbanization, migration and digital connectivity – and to the importance of 'cultural variables' "such as help-seeking patterns, causal attributions, explanatory models of illness, and severity assessment", which require further refinement of the ways in which "idioms of distress and cultural syndromes" figure in psychiatric diagnosis (2017: 776). It suggests changes in diagnostic practice, pointing towards the use of 'formulation' which "takes into account the social context, contributory risk and protective factors, and developmental change" in order to plan treatment, and asserts that this approach "is unlikely to be replaced by a purely biological or investigative approach and in its ideal form should continue to be based on an integrative biopsychosocialcultural formulation" (2017: 776) – although it goes on to talk approvingly about the NIMH's adoption of the RDoC approach, which is far from biopsychosociocultural, stresses the importance of psychiatrists having proper measuring and monitoring technologies in their toolkit, and is somewhat ambiguous about the potential for identifying and using biomarkers. And while it raises anxieties about the possibility, utility and consequences of 'precision medicine' in psychiatry and stresses the importance of the therapeutic alliance between patient and doctor involving a caring professional using all their skills and subjective capacities, many would question whether psychiatry, historically and today, has exemplified this alliance in its relations with the majority of its service users.

What then of the suggestion that psychiatry might not inevitably be a medical specialty? At various points, the report suggests that in many situations and many countries, it might be more appropriate to integrate mental health care into primary health care, and for psychiatrists to work as public health practitioners, rather than medical subspecialists. This requires building alliances and "collaborative linkages with colleagues from different specialties, and close interactions with other sectors beyond health, including a much more broadly defined social care sector – for instance, comprising social welfare, education, and justice" (2017: 786; references omitted). Indeed, it suggests that this is actually a better way for psychiatrists to maintain their professional identity than stressing their unique professional authority, for example by the use of jargon and esoteric language. But while it recognizes that psychiatrists "are not the only experts in mental disorders", and claims to have involved service users in its development, their expertise and their potential role is rarely mentioned.[8]

Of course, we should not expect coherence from a report written by so many hands, and at times, for instance in relation to mental health legislation, the failure to reach consensus is acknowledged. However, on some other issues the internal conflicts are clear to see. On the one hand, the report argues that as "mental disorders emerge from disruptions in normal brain function, the 'psychiatrist of the future will need to be a brain scientist'" (Bhugra et al., 2017: 886, quoting Insel and Quirion, 2005), yet it takes a different approach in its conclusion, arguing that "social determinants of mental illness and the role of social discrimination in the causation of mental illness deserve study, but adequate financial resources need to be committed to carry out this research. Both advocacy against poverty and unemployment and equitable funding into neurosciences and social research is needed. Psychiatrists need to be skilled, competent, professional, and collaborative" (2017: 810).

What is one to conclude about how psychiatrists see their future? Clearly, contemporary psychiatry is torn between those who wish to maintain its status as an elite profession, grounded in biomedicine, with all the tools and techniques – and social status – of other medical specialisms, and those who recognize that a real revolution is required, in which psychiatrists develop different explanatory models and engage in a very different kind of practice, in relation both to those in mental distress who come to them for help and to the societies of which they are a part. Intriguingly, some clearer glimpses of this alternative are provided in a paper published a few months before the release of the report, coauthored by the Lancet Commission report's lead author Dinesh Bhugra (Ventriglio et al., 2016). I will return to this presently. But first let me consider how the future looks from the perspective of psychiatry's sometimes collaborators, but traditional competitors, the psychologists.

In May 2013, just as the fifth edition of the APA's *DSM* was about to be launched, the division of clinical psychology of the British Psychological Society issued a position statement: "*Classification of behaviour and experience in relation to functional psychiatric diagnoses: Time for a paradigm shift*" (Awenat et al., 2013). This was widely reported as a fundamental attack on "psychiatry's predominantly biomedical model of mental distress – the idea that people are suffering from illnesses that are treatable by doctors using drugs"; one of the authors, Lucy Johnstone, was quoted as asserting it was unhelpful to see mental health issues as illnesses with biological causes:

"On the contrary, there is now overwhelming evidence that people break down as a result of a complex mix of social and psychological circumstances – bereavement and loss, poverty and discrimination, trauma and abuse."[9] Much of its criticism was organized around the new edition of the *DSM*, and raised concerns about the lack of validity of diagnostic categories, about the interpretive work which these categories' purported objectivity disguises and about their links with medicalization and stigmatization, and their decontextualization and ethnocentricity. However, the BPS statement did not argue against classification per se, but asserted that "diagnoses such as schizophrenia, bipolar disorder, personality disorder, attention deficit hyperactivity disorder, conduct disorders and so on, due to their limited reliability and questionable validity, provide a flawed basis for evidence-based practice, research, intervention guidelines and the various administrative and nonclinical uses of diagnosis". Further, the psychologists did not want to deny the role of biology "in mediating and enabling all forms of human experience, behaviour and distress", but called for "an approach that fully acknowledges the growing amount of evidence for psychosocial causal factors, but which does not assign an unevidenced role for biology as a primary cause, and that is transparent about the very limited support for the 'disease' model in such conditions. Such an approach would need to be multi-factorial, to contextualise distress and behaviour, and to acknowledge the complexity of the interactions involved, in keeping with the core principles of formulation in clinical psychology" (Awenat et al., 2013: 3). And, while clearly wishing to advocate for a leading role for their own profession, the psychologists argued that the needs and wishes of service users should be central, that their knowledge from their own experience should be key, and their capacity to make active choices in relation to their recovery should be recognized and supported.[10]

For those who have followed my discussion in the previous chapters of this book, nothing in this will be surprising, let alone shocking. Many of the elements, such as the call for formulations rather than categorical diagnoses, are certainly not new, and indeed many chime with parts of the Lancet Commission report in seeking not to abolish psychiatry or deny that mental disorders exist, but to relocate these disorders in their social context and argue that psychiatrists and others need to address these, working in equal partnerships with other professions and service users themselves. In many ways, this argument restates some of the central elements of a proposal made more than a decade earlier by two psychiatrists, Patrick Bracken and

Phillip Thomas, for something they termed 'postpsychiatry'. Bracken and Thomas (2001) argue that psychiatry, with its belief in reason, truth and the power of science and technology to resolve social and human problems, is – or was – a 'modernist' enterprise, and needs to be radically transformed in the era of postmodernity. It needs to recognize that multiple perspectives are both possible and valid, and to move beyond the conflict between two alternative claims to truth about madness – the biomedical and the social – to embrace pluralism, and centrally, to include among the multiple perspectives that of service users and their 'lived experience'. In 2012, Bracken and Thomas, now writing with a larger group of psychiatrists, psychologists and social scientists, updated their argument in a paper in the *British Journal of Psychiatry* (Bracken et al., 2012). They argued that what they called 'the technological paradigm' – the search for context-free abnormal causal mechanisms in the individual, which could be identified and studied outside social relationships, and which were the basis of mental health problems – had not served psychiatry well. Empirical evidence – the effects of placebos in drug trials, of sham ECT when compared with actual ECT, and of the relative efficacy of CBT and other psychotherapies – showed that improvement in depression and other conditions actually came from the nonspecific aspects of intervention, from the therapeutic alliance, that is, the belief among those suffering from mental ill health that someone cared about their problems, was on their side, engendering hope. While drugs can give limited short-term benefits, their long-term effects are equivocal and often damaging: overreliance upon them and blindness to their adverse effects arise from "a shameful collusion with the pharmaceutical industry's marketing campaign that sold the illusion of major innovations in antipsychotic drugs" (Bracken et al., 2012: 432).[11] Recovery from serious mental disorder, they tentatively suggest, also grows from the therapeutic context, in particular helping the individual to re-establish a positive self-identity. Medical knowledge and expertise remain relevant, but, as Kirmayer and Gold (2012) have argued, psychiatry is not "applied neuroscience", while Bracken and colleagues argue for "an approach to mental health problems that is genuinely sensitive to the complex interplay of forces (biological, psychological, social and cultural) that underlie them and that can be used therapeutically" (2012: 432). In particular, they argue for collaboration with the service user movement, large sections of which value the human aspects of their encounters with professionals – being listened to, taken seriously and treated with dignity, kindness and respect – and "seek to reframe experiences of mental illness, distress and alienation by turning them into human, rather than technical, challenges" (2012: 432).

But how can we both recognize the neurobiological dimensions of mental health problems and also "reach beyond the brain to involve social, cultural and psychological dimensions" (Bracken et al., 2012: 432)? There is, in fact, a growing sense of how this can and should be done. For example, if we turn to the paper coauthored by Dinesh Bhugra that I mentioned earlier, we can begin to see the lineaments of an alternative. In this paper titled 'Why Do We Need a Social Psychiatry?', Bhugra, Antonio Ventriglio and Shusham Gupta argue that psychiatry needs to begin from the recognition that human beings "grow up and develop within society and specific cultures and their upbringing and learnt interactions define their behaviours that in turn affect brain structures leading to dysfunction" (Ventriglio et al., 2016: 1). While one's hackles may be raised by some of the phrasing here, at its root their argument recognizes that social determinants play a major role – perhaps the major role – in mental ill health. Theirs is, in essence, an argument for an approach to mental ill health in terms of 'social medicine', recognizing not only that norms of adequate social functioning are socially and historically variable, but also that social factors shape neural development from birth onwards, and that the mechanisms for the shaping of human biology – for example, epigenetics and stress pathways – need to be understood if psychiatry is to be able to take the lead on an agenda for public mental health, and to highlight the impact of social inequalities and other social factors on mental health. And this provides a good starting point for my own suggestions for another, a different, psychiatry.

Seven answers to seven hard questions

Let me start to conclude this book by returning to the 'hard questions' that have framed my arguments.[12]

Question One: Is there really an 'epidemic' of mental disorder? My answer to this question is 'no'. We must treat figures that rely on estimates by psychiatric experts about undiagnosed mental disorder, and that use very broad ideas about diagnosable conditions, with a great deal of caution.[13] There are undoubtedly very many people experiencing forms of mental distress, but most of these arise from experiences of adversity, and many of these forms of adversity can and should be tackled directly, without the need for individualized diagnosis requiring treatment by medically trained specialists. And where people do need more structured and direct support, much of that can also be carried out without a diagnosis, and outside the formal mental health system. This is not to dispute the repeated claims that governments need to address the challenges posed by the prevalence of mental distress and provide more resources so that people can get quicker access to support. But it is to suggest that such resources should not be directed, solely or mainly, to specialized medical or psychiatric services, picking up the casualties of adversity and reinforcing the view that they are suffering from a condition rooted in their neurobiology. Undoubtedly, inpatient facilities for crisis care are needed, and in many countries these are shockingly underfunded, understaffed and quite the reverse of the sanctuary that those in severe crisis require. A better model is one in which community mental health centres, often staffed largely by peer support workers, have a small number of short-term beds for people in crisis, to enable them to feel safe and supported while other measures are put in place to alleviate their distress. More generally, funds should be directed towards community-based services, facilitating pathways to support centres and groups and to teams that can help people in their own homes. Such community-based services would help people address whatever conditions might be exacerbating their distress, whether these be the bullying of children and young people at school or on social media, pressures at work or financial and housing problems. They would also help enable rapid access to the kinds of nonspecialist counselling services that evidence suggests can be very supportive.

Question Two: Is it all the fault of neoliberal capitalism? We should be cautious about sweeping generalizations about the reasons for the rise in mental distress – individualization, marketization, the fetishizing of competition and economic success and so forth – and about the figures used to support these claims. However, the more general point concerning the social determinants of mental ill health – both in the recent life of individuals and in their past – are well founded in evidence and cannot be denied. We are beginning to understand the mechanisms through which such adversity acts, notably via stress pathways, and other pathways leading to epigenetic changes that affect neurogenesis and neuroplasticity.[14] There is also growing evidence that these changes are reversible, not by drugs but by addressing the proximal causes of these changes, such as violence – whether actual, threatened or feared – social exclusion and isolation. The fuzzy term 'social capital' is one not very satisfactory way of trying to encapsulate these, but the evidence does point to the ways in which social exclusion and loneliness are provoking factors, and that some forms of collective engagement are protective, including the opportunities to share experiences with others who have been through similar difficulties. Given the current rise of self-harm among young people and young women in particular, we also need to think of the consequences of the oversaturation of our lives by social media and its normativity, not to mention the various unpleasant ways in which it is used to target, bully or shame individuals. And more generally, we need to redress the balance of research, away from neurobiology and towards the social sciences and social theory, so that we can explore and understand these processes with the necessary evidence base, rigour and intensity, to examine what can be learnt from the work that has already been done in cities such as Trieste to develop a "whole system, whole community" approach (Mezzina, 2014), and to evaluate the various programmes that seek to encourage and develop 'mental health friendly' cities and workplaces.[15]

Question Three: If mental disorders exist, how shall we know them? I have argued strongly that current diagnostic approaches are misguided, not merely because of diagnostic expansionism, which is transforming many of the ordinary vicissitudes of life – sadness, shyness, childhood irritability and so forth – into psychiatric categories, but also because of the belief that the ultimate truth of such disorders is to be found in 'the brain' and hence it is towards the brain that such diagnoses should be targeted. I have argued instead for an approach developed from the old-fashioned idea of formulation, and I will say more about this presently.

Further, I have argued strongly against the way in which psychiatry has sought to overcome its diagnostic uncertainties through the search for genetic or neural 'biomarkers' that would enable precise and objective diagnosis, enable early identification of those at risk of future mental pathology and allow us to develop 'precision medicine' in psychiatry. I have argued that this search is probably futile, in that clinically reliable and valid biomarkers are unlikely to be found, certainly not for depression, anxiety, self-harm or trauma, and almost certainly not for conditions such as bipolar disorder, or even for neurodegenerative disorders such as Alzheimer's and other dementias. I have also argued that, when it comes to psychiatry, as in many other 'common, complex conditions', the use of biomarkers, which are always probabilistic and population-based, is undesirable in any event, given the likely problems of overdiagnosis, of false positives and false negatives in such strategies of 'screen and intervene'. Biomarker-based diagnoses of potential mental health problems in presymptomatic or asymptomatic individuals are liable to generate stigma, overintervention and anxiety – 'managed fear', to use Charles Rosenberg's (2009) term – without significantly affecting individual or population outcomes.

Question Four: This leads us to perhaps the central conceptual question in this book: Are mental disorders 'brain disorders'? While, of course, brains are involved in the mental distress, anxiety, despair, thought disruption, voice hearing and all the other symptoms now placed in the category of mental disorder, brains are also involved in almost everything that humans think, feel and do. So the question is whether disorders of 'the brain', either of any of the components whether these be 'molecular' or cellular – ion channels, receptor sites, neurotransmitter synthesis or metabolism and so forth – or in 'neural circuits', are either the 'causes' – in the sense of the necessary preconditions for – of mental ill health, or whether they establish 'susceptibilities' that can then be provoked or activated by an external event – such as an environmental insult, or a biographical experience. When researchers have sought a genetic basis for mental disorders, as we have seen, it is because they believe that a genomic anomaly has consequences through its effects on such 'causes' or 'susceptibilities'. Our review of this issue in chapter 5 suggests, as I put it there, that "we are no closer to making the link between genetic sequences, molecular events, patterns of neural activity and mental states". We need to learn to think in a new way, beyond ideas that mental health problems from depression to dementia are 'specific diseases' with neurobiological causes, to recognize that even conditions currently diagnosed as schizophrenia and dementia arise from complex interactions across the life course between the individual and his or her milieu, as that is made meaningful and understood in particular social and cultural circumstances. We will never be able to understand, let alone ameliorate, the incidence of such conditions if we maintain a style of thought that begins from the idea that these are disorders of the brain in which 'the environment' is merely a set of factors that can provoke or protect. Let me leave it at that for now, as I shall return in the final section of this chapter to the question of what an alternative approach might look like.

Question Five: What about drugs? While rates of prescription of psychiatric drugs seem inexorably to be rising worldwide, evidence shows increasing doubts about the efficacy of these drugs, the founding hypotheses as to their modes of action are now discredited and the large pharmaceutical companies are withdrawing from psychiatric drug development as they have had little success in bringing new and more effective drugs to market for any psychiatric condition; instead, they are moving to invest in more profitable products. While, for some, this is an argument for more and deeper research to find new and better drugs, I take a different view. It is now time to admit that this attempt to identify precise molecular targets underpinning mental ill health, and to create psychopharmaceuticals that will be more effective and with fewer unwanted effects because they target them, has been a failure. We need to admit that while the psychiatric medications that millions of people are taking may ameliorate some of the symptoms of distress for some people for a relatively short period of time, they do not have these effects because they act on the neurobiological pathway underlying the distress. We need to acknowledge that much of their supposed efficacy may be a result of what is disparagingly termed the placebo effect – that is to say, the culturally, medically and biographically shaped beliefs, hopes and expectations of the patients. Some effects may also come from some general 'tranquillizing' effect arising from the broad action of the drugs on multiple dimensions of neural activity and on neurotransmitters in many other bodily sites. And we need to face up to the fact that the consequences of prolonged use of such medication are likely to be damaging to both physical and mental health. Hence, the focus in psychiatric drug development and use should be on medication that provides short-term relief when individuals are in crisis – such as the much maligned benzodiazapines – and individuals should be advised to come off those drugs as soon as possible and as soon as other nonpharmaceutical forms of support can be made available. The spread of psychiatric drugs across so many regions in the world should be seen not as a success story of the increasing recognition and treatment of mental ill health, but as a story of the failure – or absence – of endeavours to reduce experiences of adversity and to provide other forms of support for those experiencing mental distress.

Question Six: How should we evaluate the Movement for Global Mental Health? While I think it is too simplistic for critics to describe the activities of this movement as psychiatric colonization, my view is that any attempt to address mental distress in 'the Global South' needs to learn from the *failures* of psychiatry in the Global North, more than from its imagined successes. These include: the problems with the conceptions of 'burden' and the lack of credibility of the estimates of the numbers of those who are suffering from undiagnosed mental illness; the failure to develop adequate diagnostic approaches or to recognize the weaknesses of either symptom-based or brain-based conceptions of diagnosis; the failure to develop more convincing explanatory models that pay more than lip-service to issues of culture and meaning; the failure of clinical trials to adequately evaluate the efficacy of psychopharmaceuticals and the consequences of their long-term use in the real world and the failure of these drugs to provide effective interventions for those in mental distress that genuinely address the outcomes that really matter to those receiving treatment; the continued failure of neurobiological research to generate findings with clinical utility, coupled with the failure adequately to invest in research to understand, let alone to address, the social determinants of mental distress and the recognition that what is often redescribed as mental disorder is often an experience of distress closely tied to people's personal biographies and the realities of their lives; the failure, to repeat the words of Vikram Patel quoted in a previous chapter, of "the increasing emphasis on a biomedically oriented mental health care as the primary solution to these problems" (2014a: 16); the reluctance to recognize that the difficulties experienced by most people in mental distress are inextricably linked to problems of poverty, violence, exclusion and adversity, and that most of those who are distressed can be better helped "outside the formal health care system by dealing with economic difficulties, developing befriending, using culturally embedded sources of help and other methods that are consistent with how individuals themselves understand their problems and the outcomes they themselves desire" (quoting myself: see p. 146). And these are lessons that should be learned for interventions not only in the Global South, but also in the Global North.

Question Seven: What is the place of the patient in the psychiatric system – that is, the place of the user, the survivor and the consumer in the mental health system? As we saw in chapter 8, there is a growing agreement that any reforms in mental health policies and provisions must give a leading role to those who have experienced the mental health system, both in the Global North and the Global South. Patients' evaluations of the services that purport to be for their benefit must be the guides for reform; users' identification of the outcomes by which mental health services should be judged must be central. Their analyses of the services that need to be put in place, and the conditions that need to be achieved to mitigate mental distress and to support those who are experiencing it, must drive reform forward. This rebalancing of power towards service users is crucial, especially when mental health care is seeking to move towards an approach that recognizes the social determinants of mental health and mental ill health. But my answer to this hard question is that we need to go further, and to accept the challenge that the psychiatric user/survivor movement has offered, not only to the 'brain disorder' conception of mental distress, or to the failures of the existing system to provide genuine care to those experiencing either minor or major mental distress, but also because of the alternative knowledge that service users have developed of the social and interpersonal foundations of mental distress, and the forms of support that might genuinely meet the needs of those experiencing profound crises in their lives.

Another psychiatry, another biopolitics

Where, then, for the future of psychiatry? As I have said repeatedly in this book, all mental disorders – or what I would prefer to call all forms of mental distress – are conditions of persons embedded in unceasing dynamic transactions with their interpersonal, social, cultural, semantic and physical milieus across their lives, from birth if not before. If one accepts this then certain propositions follow.

From diagnosis to formulation

I have argued that we should replace diagnosis, seeking to allocate individuals to particular diagnostic categories on the basis of either their symptoms or their biomarkers or brain signatures, with formulation, that is to say an account that seeks to make sense of a person's current difficulties in terms of aspects of their current situation, for example, their relationships, their experiences at work or in unemployment, their housing and financial situation, and indeed their own ways of making sense of their situation, and accounting for their distress. It would include aspects of their life history that they consider relevant, or that might be relevant in the eyes of the person making the formulation. It would lead to a mutually agreed plan of action, which may involve acting on each or any of the current conditions that seem to be linked to distress – helping resolve financial difficulties or housing problems, developing a plan to deal with difficulties in relations with partners or problems with children. It would seek, where possible, to identify local and nonprofessional forms of support, drop-in centres, self-help groups, community organizations, links with others who have experienced similar difficulties. It may include the use of medication, but with very realistic discussion of the reasons for its use – for example, to help one sleep, or to reduce anxiety – and of its likely good and bad effects, and also some indication of how long (or rather how time-limited) should be the use of this medication, and what might be experienced when 'coming off' the drugs.

Some would suggest that the key to helping individuals come to terms with their distress is to enable them to accept that they are suffering from a mental illness, which is just an illness like any other. I think there are helpful and problematic aspects of this view. It is helpful to be able to talk about distress openly, and to feel no shame or guilt in experiencing it, and for others to accept it. In this respect, the many campaigns to support those in distress who are 'speaking out' are to be welcomed, not least because they help people understand that such distress, anxiety, feelings of inability to cope, guilt, even despair and self-loathing, are actually rather common human experiences. An excellent example here is the work of the Hearing Voices network.[16] This network has established self-help groups and a range of other resources to support voice hearers outside the professionalized domain of the mental health services, not by 'task shifting', as advocated by those in the Global Mental Health Movement, where professionals train and advise lay persons to become para-professionals, but by peer support, drop-in centres, and more. As important, it has contested the traditional psychiatric view that voices should be understood as 'auditory hallucinations' which are symptoms of severe mental illness. Activists in the Hearing Voices network have drawn on research to help voice hearers to realize that they are not alone, and to establish that voice hearing is actually quite widespread in the population, is not usually a sign of psychosis, and may arise from social experiences such as stress. In this respect, in raising awareness of the diversity of human sensory experiences, this is an excellent example of the need to expand our understanding of – and our willingness to accept – the 'bandwidth' of ways of being human, contesting the myth that there is some single standard of normality of ways of being in the world, of thought, emotions, beliefs and desires, of ways of hearing, seeing, smelling, tasting, of rhythms of speed and slowness.[17] Difference is not pathology, and we have more to learn from recognizing such diversity than we gain from insistence on an ideal of normality.

There are other reasons to contest the narrative that mental distress arises from 'diseases' like any other diseases, with all the resonances that this has for how the conditions are understood by those of us experiencing it, and by others. Of course, doctors deal with many things that are not 'diseases' in the sense of a clear pathology with an identifiable and treatable organic malfunction as its cause (Rose,

2007a). For example, pain – back pain, neuropathic pain, or many other types of pain – often has no identifiable or addressable organic basis, and has to be treated by helping the patient learn a range of techniques for pain management, which may include drugs, but not because those drugs attack the roots of the pain. "A heart attack attacks the heart, of course, and lung cancer is a cancer of the lung, but it would be a rash person to claim that the causes or treatments of either can be focused on the heart or the lung alone"[18] – and indeed, while these conditions may be 'medicalized', most doctors are acutely aware of the wider social determinants of these disorders and are very involved in endeavours to counter them. Nonetheless, the 'destigmatizing' strategies that seek to convince us that mental distress is, or arises from, diseases like any other, does not, in fact, seem to liberate individuals from responsibility, guilt and blame for their condition, as one might have hoped from Talcott Parsons's classical view of 'the sick role' (1951). And, in our current cultural climate, the narrative of 'it's a disease like any other' almost always implies that this distress arises from an internal pathology, increasingly a brain pathology, that should be treated with medication, rather than by pinpointing the experiential roots of the distress in the current and past life of the individual, identifying those that are tractable, and focusing any support on those.

Begin research with the person in their milieu

A further proposition flows from the recognition that mental distress is a condition of whole persons in their milieu. That is, that research in psychiatry should begin from this recognition and not merely focus on isolated brains in laboratories, often in animal models, 'adding in' the 'environment' at a later stage. Reductionism is often a powerful research strategy, but, as Claude Bernard (1957 [1878]) recognized long ago, the whole is not simply the sum of the isolated parts.[19] It is now well past time to reverse the direction of research, and to start from the reality of the human experience that is to be understood. That is to say, to use the evidence that can be gathered from formulations, and from many other forms of epidemiological and social research, on the 'social determinants' of mental distress, and to seek to understand how – in what ways, through which pathways – for some people, in some circumstances, these adversities mark their bodies, their brains and their minds and bring them to states of severe distress, and how, for others, even very severe hardships can be undergone without such consequences.

As we saw earlier in this book, one promising pathway draws on several decades of research on stress and its consequences, recognizing that stress is not a brute fact arising from social disadvantage, overcrowding, unemployment, isolation or even violence, but is shaped by the way individuals understand and encode their experiences, in the light of their own expectations and cultural beliefs. The consequences of prolonged stress experience in humans is to increase what McEwen and Stellar termed 'allostatic load' – the "strain on the body produced by repeated ups and downs of physiologic response [to stress], as well as by the elevated activity of physiologic systems under challenge, and the changes in metabolism and the impact of wear and tear on a number of organs and tissues"; and there is increasing understanding of the mechanisms that such prolonged increases in allostatic load lead to: "specific changes in the immune and cardiovascular systems and neural and adipose tissues that produce specific disease outcomes" (1993: 2094). In the case of mental distress, such mechanisms lead to changes in both functional and structural organization of neural circuits, and affect the genesis of new neurons, through epigenetics and other processes of neuroplasticity (for a recent review, see Peedicayil, 2017). Thus, as should be clear, this approach is not hostile to the recognition that neural mechanisms are involved in mental distress. However, it recognizes that these are not themselves primary causes but are elements in complex pathways, and that other bodily systems are also involved, notably the immune system, which, when weakened by prolonged stress may predispose to the kinds of reactions traditionally thought of as symptoms of mental disorder.

A brief glance at the diagrams in the classic paper by McEwen and Stellar (1993) will demonstrate the complexity of the pathways that are hypothesized here. But why should we believe that these should simple? Complexity is not a reason for stepping aside from the challenge of rigorous research that goes beyond the correlational style of thought that has demonstrated social determinants of mental distress, to identify more precisely the mechanisms that might exacerbate such distress, and indeed the mechanisms that might 'buffer' individuals against these consequences of adversity (Galea and Link, 2013; Keyes and Galea, 2017). An evidence-based understanding of these biosocial dynamics might help us go beyond the woolly conceptions of social capital discussed earlier in this book, to be clearer about the kinds of sociopolitical strategies that might reduce the prevalence of both minor and major mental health problems.

A new role for psychiatric professionals

As I have said repeatedly, while I argue that there are crucial roles for nonprofessionals in such a changed conception of psychiatry, this does not mean there is no role for psychiatrists. Some leading psychiatrists argue that, in fact, clinical psychiatrists have never been obsessed with brain-based explanations of the ailments of their patients, and have never practised according to the logics ascribed to biomedicine, but have always seen problems as those of the whole person in his or her situation, and taken that situated complex of person and environment as the issue to be addressed in therapy. Whether or not this ideal is shared by all who practise psychiatry, it is clear that it does not represent the experiences of most of those who have been subject to their attention. But what would be the role of psychiatrists in the future to which I point?

We must, of course, recognize that for most people, most of the time, whether it be historically or in the present, and whether it be in the Global South or the Global North, support for those in mental distress has been provided outside any formal health or social care system. The much missed social historian Roy Porter (1985) has pointed out the fallacies, or at the least, the partiality, of accounts – historical or contemporary – that write of sickness, physical or mental, from the perspective of the medics. It is not only that, for most of known history, and indeed for today, what we call 'primary care' is actually 'secondary care', as it takes place only when those deemed in need of attention by themselves or others 'enter the medical arena'; it is also that many people do not call on any of these and other 'experts' at all, but treat themselves, or are treated by family and friends, with homemade remedies, herbs, patent medicines, vitamins, dietary supplements and 'natural remedies', rest or exercise, diet or fasting, prayer, meditation and now, of course, going to the gym or posting on Facebook.

Our understandings of our ailments certainly come, in part, from the dissemination of medical knowledge, probably more so today with the prominence of health in the mass media and on the internet. But today, as before, that expert knowledge appears, to most people, to be disputatious and contradictory, often deemed effective by some but nonsense by others. Thus, we should not be surprised that most people think about their distress in ways in which expert opinion is mixed with explanations and practices from other sources, so disparagingly deemed 'folk medicine' by experts. Nonetheless, I think psychiatrists do have a key role here, which is paradoxically to

support the 'demedicalization' of much mental distress, and especially to challenge the widespread and increasing long-term use of
psychopharmaceuticals. It will indeed be a challenge for psychiatrists
to reassure those in distress that they are not suffering from a disease,
that there are almost certainly stresses and strains in their current or
past form of life that have led to their current state, that they will need
help to deal with these, and to ensure that they are provided with
swift and effective support to manage their situation. It will also be a
challenge for psychiatrists to switch from advocating the use of such
drugs as effective and often first-line treatments for mental disorder,
to advocating precisely the reverse. That is to say, as is happening in
a different way with antibiotics, to advocate for a radical reduction
in the use of such drugs, for them to be used with caution for short
periods, not as pharmaceuticals that target the neurobiological bases
of mental distress, but as drugs that can, in certain circumstances,
help mitigate a crisis and assist a person to regain a state of com-
posure in which they are able to engage in discussions and actions
designed to produce the outcomes that they themselves desire.

Further, perhaps the most significant shift in the role of medically
trained psychiatrists is that many would operate outside the clinical domain, as public health professionals, as suggested at various
points in the Lancet Commission report discussed earlier. Experts
in mental health should be working alongside other professionals in
advocating for a transformation in the social conditions that underpin
mental distress, in working with policymakers to develop strategies to
promote mental health in cities, workplaces and other organizations,
and in supporting policies that fund community centres, drop-in
centres, peer support networks and other facilities, largely run by
nonprofessionals but with professional support where needed. In particular, professionals would work alongside those experiencing severe
mental distress, in developing formulations of their current predica-
ments that make sense to them, devising strategies and objectives for
regaining control over their lives, and in helping identify, coordinate
and manage the actions necessary to ameliorate the contributors to
their distress that are tractable, ranging from housing difficulties and
financial problems to troubles with partners or children.

Not least among these sociopolitical roles for psychiatrists would
be to challenge the 'other face' of psychiatry – that is to say, its
role in strategies of control. For alongside all the developments I
have discussed here, it remains the case that in many countries in
the Global North, as well as in the Global South, those considered
to be suffering from mental disorders are considered to be risky,

and are subject to programmes of risk management, often including incarceration in locked wards. As I argued in chapter 1, this pervasive link between mental disorder and risk has persisted alongside all the attempts to normalize mental distress, to destigmatize it, to encourage us all to speak out about our own mental troubles and not to shun those who are experiencing mental distress. Many psychiatrists are concerned by this (for example, Buchanan and Grounds, 2011), but far too few speak out publicly about the hypocrisy of a situation when, on the one hand, some public policies seek to normalize and destigmatize mental disorder, and, on the other, another set of policies continues, in the face of evidence to the contrary, to regard those experiencing mental distress as uniquely risky to others, and hence requiring special regimes of risk management (Szmukler and Rose, 2013). Rights-based arguments, as in the CRPD, may play a part in transforming this 'police' function of psychiatry. But such a transformation, taken together with the other proposals that I have made, requires more than rights. It requires a reformatting of the social control functions of psychiatric expertise – it requires another biopolitical role for psychiatry.

Another biopolitics is possible

Psychiatry has always been a biopolitical science, from its role in strategies to manage degeneracy and in eugenics in the nineteenth and early twentieth centuries, through the mental hygiene movement in the middle decades of the twentieth century, in its imbrication in schemes of risk management and social protection in the closing years of the twentieth century, to contemporary concerns about the economic burden of mental illness (Rose, 1996c).[20] What, then, might be the kind of psychiatric biopolitics that would flow from the arguments in this book?[21]

Such an alternative psychiatric biopolitics would draw its intellectual basis from two main sources. On the one hand from the social sciences, including social epidemiology and social psychiatry, working in alliance with the life sciences, to understand how the experience of adversity is seared into the bodies and souls of those who live it, aiming to gain a more precise understanding of the mechanisms through which different forms of adversity get transformed in ways that go beyond 'everyday unhappiness' to severe distress and sometimes to an individual's inability to manage or sustain a life for themselves. It would draw on what we are now beginning to understand about the pathways through which such diverse experiences of adversity – experiences formed through the beliefs, meanings and expectations of individuals, groups and communities – shape and reshape bodies and brains at both molar and molecular levels, engendering both physical ailments and mental distress. It would undertake the empirical research and the conceptual clarification that would give depth and precision to the rhetoric of biopsychosocial approaches to mental distress, and seek to formulate these pathways such that we might better identify potential points of intervention.

On the other hand, a new psychiatric biopolitics would ground itself in the knowledge, experience and evaluations of those who have themselves experienced mental distress and their analysis of the conditions that provoke such distress, their assessment of the kinds of policies, resources and practices of social support that are helpful, mitigating distress and its consequences and promoting resilience, and their specifications of the desirable objectives of such a complex of support mechanisms. Of course, such knowledge is neither unitary nor homogeneous, and in many cases it overlaps with and intersects with that from other epistemic communities. But a new psychiatric biopolitics must begin from the recognition that, if it claims to be for the benefit of those who are its subjects, those subjects, actual or potential recipients of mental health care, must have the leading role in judging its successes and failures.

This new psychiatry would take, as the territory on which it would work, the array of conditions – taking that term in the broadest sense to include the interpersonal, financial, occupational, environmental, sensorial and social conditions – that exacerbate mental distress. Such an approach might be described, perhaps oversimply, as ecological.[22] It would be based on the premise that humans are living creatures, inhabiting milieus that are material – homes, shops, buildings, roads, traffic, exposures to all the varieties of pollution, parks, open spaces, countryside – intersubjective – communities of support or exclusion, discrimination, racisms, exposure to actual or potential dangers and hazards from others – social – forms of work, experiences of employment or precarity, financial capabilities and limitations, forms of social support – and 'cultural' – symbolic, saturated with public and private meanings. Given that such a large and growing proportion of the world's population inhabit those sprawling and complex ecologies we term cities, the urban and its politics of physical and mental health would be a prime location for analysis and intervention in such a new biopolitics.[23] Policies of urban renewal in the name of health have historically focused largely on physical health – from sanitation and social hygiene to public housing and garden cities. A biopolitics of mental health would seek to identify – both epidemiologically and ethnographically – what it was in the urban that intensified mental distress and, correlatively, what was salutary, whether that be clean air, noise reduction, urban design, small local stores and cafés, good and affordable transport systems, accessible social services, or even apparently minor factors such as clear signage and well-maintained walkways. Such an urban biopolitics of mental health would also prioritize spatial justice (Soja, 2009), social justice in the city, affording all inhabitants – citizens, denizens, migrants, refugees – equal rights to the city – not rights as legal and justiciable, though that may be important, but rights in terms of capacities and capabilities. That is to say, central to such a new psychiatric biopolitics would be the objective of making 'the experience of city living' positive for mental health. Some may think such ambitions are utopian and unrealistic, but we should not think back only to the grand schemes of urban reform of the nineteenth century, but also to current strategies directed at other objectives ranging from the micro – dropped kerbs to facilitate movement by those in wheelchairs or using buggies – to the macro – the design of 'green' environmentally friendly cities in China (Hoffman, 2011).[24] Why not 'mental health friendly cities'?[25]

That is to say, a new psychiatric biopolitics would take up the challenge posed to psychiatry by 'social medicine' and its combination of objectivity and passion – its mode of passionate knowing[26] – in the analysis and mitigation of 'social suffering', undertaking and supporting research into those conditions and their consequences, working with other professional groups and organizations committed to understanding and reducing social disadvantage and inequity, and advocating for measures – facilities, resources, support services, legal protections – that would mitigate those conditions. In particular, it would work with others to shape a radical reimagining of welfare, not a return to the old and often paternalistic form of the welfare state, but countering the individualization and responsibilization of the welfare reforms since the 1980s, and exploring forms of provision that will meet the major social challenges of our own times – urbanization, mobility, changes in family forms and the patterns of the life course, demographic change, precarity at work. It would grasp the possibilities provided by our digital era, not only addressing the malign consequences of social media for cognitive overload, but understanding the potential of robotics and machine intelligence for transforming the lives of those living with disabilities, including what the CRPD terms 'psychosocial disabilities' and exploring the ways in which online facilities might actually be able to provide easily accessible, non-stigmatizing support for those experiencing mental distress.[27]

This would, of course, require psychiatrists to rethink the control functions that have long been part of their role – that is to say, their capacity to impose compulsory confinement in mental hospitals and involuntary treatment. These capacities are already having to be rethought in the light of the provisions of the CRPD. Thoughtful social psychiatrists are already envisaging a future in which "[r]esponse to threats of violence and actual violence would be the remit exclusively of the criminal justice system, following the same legislative framework as for anyone else in society. Consequently, offenders with mental disorders would be sent to prisons rather than hospitals" (Giacco et al., 2017: 258). Others, notably George Szmukler, have suggested that one needs no special law for the involuntary detention or treatment of those with mental health problems, rather a single set of legal provisions that would apply to "*all* persons who have a serious problem with decision-making, whatever their diagnosis – physical or mental – and in any setting – medical, surgical, psychiatric or in the community" (2017: xxii). Personal experience has convinced me that, where those in mental distress trust the specialists who are caring for them, even during periods of extreme confusion, hallucinations or despair, they will accept brief periods of confinement, and even initially unwelcome medication, to keep them secure until the crisis can be resolved. Roberto Mezzina (2014), Director of the Department of Mental Health in Trieste, has shown how, in practice, "An 'Open Door No Restraint' System of Care for Recovery and Citizenship" can be implemented in a whole city. While it is true that Trieste is a small city, of fewer than 250,000 inhabitants,[28] and that the implementation of the reforms inspired by Franco Basaglia to achieve this system took many years, this example, taken together with the arguments from within more conventional social psychiatry that I have just cited, shows that it is possible for psychiatry to overcome that tension between care and control that Basaglia argued ran through its very existence – and to resolve it on the side of care.

The objective of such a biopolitics would not be framed in terms of cure or normalization, or even of health, certainly not health as in the WHO's infamous definition of health as "a state of complete physical, mental and social well-being".[29] It would accept what I have referred to as the 'bandwidth' of ways of being human, and recognize that most human beings, most of the time, do not live their lives 'in the silence of the organs' and that 'happiness' – as currently construed as a technique for 'living well' – is a highly problematic obligation (Ahmed, 2010a, 2010b).[30] Rather, biopolitics would think of its objective in terms of something like the 'capabilities' formulated by Martha Nussbaum (2011): of life, health, bodily integrity, the ability to think and reason, to express emotions, to plan one's life, alone and with others, having control over one's environment.[31] Its objective, that is to say, would be to advocate for, and work to provide, the conditions under which people, never isolated but always enmeshed with others, have the capacities and resources to understand and manage their lives within the fluctuating circumstances in which they live, not merely to adapt to these circumstances, but to engage with them, to challenge them, to transform them, and to have the chance, at least, to become the kinds of persons they would like to be.

No doubt many will conclude that it would be impossible to transform psychiatry, root and branch, so that it becomes a part of social medicine. A future where psychiatrists are trained more in social science and ethics than in psychopharmacology and neuroscience. Where they work alongside other professionals, and with nonprofessionals, with no special or unique claims to knowledge of mental distress, not just in public health but in advocating for changes in social support systems, urban planning and the organization of work. Where they recognized that the knowledge crafted from the local and global experience of psychiatric service users might be as valid, maybe even superior, to their own. Would it ever be possible for psychiatrists themselves to help overturn the power differentials that have underpinned their relations with their patients since the nineteenth century, and to collaborate in practices that are guided and shaped by nonprofessionals on the basis of their own experiences and analyses? Could psychiatrists lead the kinds of transnational changes in policy and practice that would radically reduce the use of psychiatric drugs and accept that, not just for the present, but for the future, interventions into the human brain whether by drugs or devices, can only play a limited, short-term, palliative role in mitigating mental distress? Could psychiatrists campaign against the view that mental distress, risk and danger to others were somehow bound together, and that special legislation was required to constrain the dangers posed by 'the mentally ill'? Could psychiatrists take the risk of entering with passionate objectivity into the political domain, working alongside others to challenge injustice on the foundation of an evidence-based knowledge of its malign consequences? Could psychiatrists, and psychiatry, play a progressive role in helping chart out the kinds of societies, the kinds of policies, the kinds of practices

necessary to human well-being in the face of the rapid global transformations – demographic, social, political, ethical – that we face in
the twenty-first century? I do not know the answer to these questions,
but I do know that if psychiatry and psychiatrists turn away from
these challenges to the lure of neurobiology and the fantasies of individualized precision medicine, they will abdicate their responsibilities
to those whom they claim to serve.

Notes

Acknowledgements

1 Supported by the European Union's Horizon 2020 Research and Innovation Programme under Grant Agreement No. 720270.

Chapter 1   What Is Psychiatry?

1 This is why I do not, during most of the discussion in this book, advocate my own definition of mental illness, mental disorder or mental health. My main task is to explore the nature and implications of the various classifications and terms adopted within psychiatry. However, I do discuss this issue further in my final chapter and make some suggestions for an alternative approach. As for those who are recipients of psychiatry, I also try to avoid a single definition, for, as we shall see, we are all potentially 'suitable cases for treatment' under one or other of the definitions used. Note that following the Convention on the Rights of Persons with Disabilities (the CRPD), which came into force in May 2008, the term 'persons with psychosocial difficulties' has started to be used in policy, and by some individuals and groups. I do not adopt it here, not least because many would dispute the idea that those in mental distress are 'disabled', even if one adopts the 'social model of disability'. I discuss the CRPD in later chapters; for the text, see http://www.ohchr.org/EN/HRBodies/CRPD/Pages/ConventionRightsPersonsWithDisabilities.aspx.
2 This is the definition in the online *Oxford English Dictionary*.
3 To avoid overburdening this introductory chapter with references, all the data and papers mentioned briefly here are discussed and fully referenced in the chapters that follow. Here, I have given only a few key references and web links to nonspecialist sites to help the interested reader in advance of what is to come.

4 http://www.euro.who.int/en/health-topics/noncommunicable-diseases/
  mental-health/data-and-statistics.
5 https://www.theguardian.com/lifeandstyle/2016/sep/29/self-harm-ptsd-
  and-mental-illness-soaring-among-young-women-in-england-survey.
6 We should note that this is not just in the developed countries of the
  Global North. For example, there are not only claims that China is
  experiencing an epidemic of mental disorder, but there also is a rapid
  growth of the psy professions in China; see, for example, Wang, 2016.
7 http://www.youngminds.org.uk/training_services/policy/mental_health_
  statistics; https://www.theguardian.com/society/2017/mar/12/schools-to-
  trial-happiness-lessons-for-eight-year-olds.
8 https://www.theguardian.com/society/video/2017/jan/30/dementia-dia
  ries-its-like-trying-to-go-through-a-brick-wall-video.
9 For the list of OECD countries, see http://www.oecd.org/about/mem
  bersandpartners/list-oecd-member-countries.htm. These do not include
  countries in China, Southeast Asia, India, Latin America or Africa.
  Figures on pharmaceutical usage are notoriously difficult to interpret,
  as different countries measure different aspects (numbers of prescriptions dispensed, actual volume of drugs dispensed, numbers reporting
  that they have taken such drugs). Thus, for example, the US National
  Survey on Drug Use and Health includes 'pain-relievers' in its estimates,
  and reports: "In 2015, an estimated 119.0 million Americans aged 12
  or older used prescription psychotherapeutic drugs in the past year,
  representing 44.5 percent of the population. About 97.5 million people
  used pain relievers (36.4 percent), 39.3 million used tranquilizers (14.7
  percent), 17.2 million used stimulants (6.4 percent), and 18.6 million
  used sedatives (6.9 percent)." Surveys such as this may be more accurate
  than data on prescribing rates, as many who are prescribed the drugs
  do not take them or do not take them as prescribed. The issues will be
  discussed in more detail in a later chapter.
10 This term broadly refers to the 'anti-anxiety' drugs – Miltown, Librium,
  Valium and their cognates – that provoked heated discussion in the
  1960s and 1970s, especially in the United States, where the number
  of prescriptions filled for such drugs in US drugstores rose from 45.1
  million in 1964 to a peak of 104.5 million in 1973, before various scan-
  dals led to reluctance to prescribe them; however, prescriptions were still
  running at 71.4 million in 1980, rose further in the 1990s, and remain
  high, despite some claiming that their use has been displaced by the
  so-called antidepressants (figures up to 1980 from table 4.1 in Smith,
  1991; see also Tone, 2009). Data for the 1990s from Rose, 2004. See the
  discussion in chapter 6 for more details.
11 http://www.nytimes.com/books/first/s/slater-prozac.html;   https://www.
  nytimes.com/2016/07/10/books/review/peter-d-kramer-ordinarily-well-
  about-antidepressants.html.
12 http://www.oecd-ilibrary.org/sites/health_glance-2013-en/04/10/index.

html?itemId=/content/chapter/health_glance-2013-41-en. In the UK the number of antidepressant items dispensed has more than doubled in the last decade: in 2016, there were 64.7 million antidepressant items dispensed – 33.7 million (108.5 per cent) more than in 2006, when there were 31.0 million; see http://content.digital.nhs.uk/article/7756/Antidepressants-were-the-area-with-largest-increase-in-prescription-items-in-2016.

13 For, of course, for much of their history, psychiatrists were a somewhat demeaned professional specialism, locked away in institutions together with those they treated. As Andrew Scull put it: "Reflecting the poverty of its cognitive accomplishments, its persistently dismal therapeutic capacities, and the social undesirability and disreputability of most of its clientele, psychiatry has enjoyed a perpetually marginal and unenviable position in the social division of labour- a profession always, so it seems, but a step away from a profound crisis of legitimacy" (1989: 22). See also Rosenberg, 1975.

14 As I have noted in the Acknowledgements, at the time of writing I have been, for some six years, a member of the Steering Committee of the Human Brain Project, and Director of its 'Foresight Lab': http://www.humanbrainproject.eu/en/.

15 In the US, many credit Jon Kabat-Zinn with being the pioneer of mindfulness: he founded the Mindfulness-Based Stress Reduction programme at the University of Massachusetts in 1979, which later became the Center for Mindfulness at the University of Massachusetts Medical School: https://www.umassmed.edu/cfm/. For UK examples, see https://www.nhs.uk/Conditions/stress-anxiety-depression/Pages/mindfulness.aspx or https://bemindful.co.uk/.

16 Although Robin Murray and his colleagues have questioned this emphasis on the use of antipsychotic drugs for long-term maintenance, and suggested that some of the problems experienced by those who 'fail to adhere' to their treatment may not be a recurrence of their psychiatric condition, but the unpleasant but usually temporary effect of drug withdrawal; see Murray et al., 2016.

17 In the wake of the closure of large psychiatric institutions, many different forms of 'treatment' of patients 'in the community' were developed, although some had been advocating such an approach since the 1960s: see Little, 1961; Friedman et al., 1960.

18 There is no simple way of dividing the world up – developed, developing, underdeveloped; First World/Second World/Third World; industrialized/non-industrialized. I use the much-criticized distinction between a 'Global North', roughly comprising Europe, North America, Australia, New Zealand, Japan and South Korea, versus the 'Global South', roughly comprising Africa, India, the Middle East and some other resource-poor areas of Asia. But this is a rudimentary definition; we will need to complicate this as we get into details later in this book.

19 We shall explore the story of why this is no longer the case in a later chapter, because there is a lot that we can learn from it.

20 Thus for the previous (fourth) edition of *DSM* (APA 1994) a condition termed Oppositional Defiant Disorder is described as "A pattern of negativistic, hostile, and defiant behavior lasting at least 6 months, during which four (or more) of the following are present: often loses temper; often argues with adults; often actively defies or refuses to comply with adults' requests or rules; often deliberately annoys people; often blames others for his or her mistakes or misbehavior; is often touchy or easily annoyed by others; is often angry and resentful; is often spiteful or vindictive", although it is noted that a criterion is met only "if the behavior occurs more frequently than is typically observed in individuals of comparable age and developmental level" and if it causes clinically significant impairment in functioning.

21 As we shall see in a later chapter, these critics included not only social scientists but also psychologists, and some psychiatrists. These latter include Allen Frances, the Chair of the Task Force that produced *DSM-IV*, who later argued in many blog posts and a subsequent book that diagnostic inflation was leading to the overtreatment of children and the 'worried well' at the expense of the real vocation of psychiatry, which was to treat those with serious illnesses: see Frances, 2013.

22 https://en.wikipedia.org/wiki/Classification_of_mental_disorders. There have been repeated attempts to bring these two classification regimes into harmony, which have been partially successful. We explore classification in chapter 4.

23 For the philosopher J. L. Austin (1965), who invented the term, a performative utterance is a statement that does not just state something; when uttered in appropriate circumstances, it actually *does the thing* – his examples are utterances like "I name this ship . . ." or "I take this man to be my lawful wedded husband . . .".

24 The BBC has had a long-running series of radio programmes entitled 'Am I Normal?' (http://www.bbc.co.uk/programmes/b007v7py), which explored how doctors decide questions such as when eccentricity becomes abnormality, or what level of tiredness is normal. It was also the title of another UK TV series (https://aminormal.channel4.com/) and this issue has also been the topic of other media shows, such as Channel 4's 'Embarrassing Bodies' (http://www.channel4embarrassingillnesses.com/). It is clear that 'Am I normal?' is not only a question asked by medical professionals of their potential clients, but also one that many people ask of themselves at many points in their lives.

25 In Rose, 2010, I discuss the downsides of screening – false positives, false negatives, the number necessary to screen to avert a single occurrence, the treatment of those who would never become ill but suffer the adverse effects of the treatment itself and so forth.

26 I argued this in my first book, *The Psychological Complex* (Rose, 1985a).

27 NIH Director's Blog, 30 September 2014, at https://directorsblog.nih.
    gov/2014/09/30/brain-launching-americas-next-moonshot/
28 This was a key point in the language used in the early phases of the Human
    Brain Project; see the lecture given in 2014 by Richard Frackowiak,
    Director of the Medical Informatics Platform, at: https://www.youtube.
    com/watch?v=TaMVIACV-ek; that language was later somewhat toned
    down in the light of subsequent developments: http://www.humanbrain-
    project.eu/en/medicine/.
29 This belief is now almost ubiquitous, at least among funding agencies.
    When I gave a version of this chapter as a talk at McGill University in
    late 2016, it was just after the university had received an $84 million
    grant from the Canada First Research Excellence Fund, spread over
    seven years to support Healthy Brains for Healthy Lives, "an ambitious
    effort in neuroscience to advance understanding of the human brain and
    ease the burden of neurological and mental-health disorders." See http://
    publications.mcgill.ca/reporter/2016/09/mcgill-wins-84-million-grant-
    for-neuroscience/.
30 http://www.bps.org.uk/system/files/Public%20files/cat-1325.pdf.
31 For a textbook organized around images of this sort, see Stahl, 1996.
32 Although, as I write, these remaining powers are under challenge from
    the UN's CRPD, which I discuss in a subsequent chapter.
33 The following sentences derive directly from Rose, 2016.
34 Four centres were set up to receive individuals who satisfied the follow-
    ing criteria: (1) they are more likely than not to commit an offence within
    five years that might be expected to lead to serious physical or psycho-
    logical harm from which the victim would find it difficult or impossible
    to recover; (2) they have a significant disorder of personality; (3) the risk
    presented appears to be functionally linked to the significant personal-
    ity disorder. This scheme was controversial because it had long been
    accepted that 'personality disorders' were not 'treatable' and so those
    who were considered to be dangerous because of those disorders could
    not be compulsorily detained in psychiatric hospitals as they failed to
    meet the treatability criterion in mental health legislation, and yet they
    could only be detained in prisons when they had committed an illegal act,
    not simply because they were thought to be dangerous. There was little
    evidence that those so confined were given careful and intensive pro-
    grammes of treatment, rather than being 'warehoused' for the purposes
    of public protection, and doubt was cast not only on cost-effectiveness,
    but on the validity of the 'diagnosis' itself; see Tyrer et al., 2010.
35 Data from NHS Digital, 'Inpatients Formally Detained in Hospitals
    under the Mental Health Act 1983 and Patients Subject to Supervised
    Community Treatment: 2015/16, Annual Figures': http://digital.nhs.uk/
    catalogue/PUB22571.
36 This is the topic of chapter 3 of this book.

Chapter 2   Is There Really an 'Epidemic' of Mental Disorder?

1 A significant portion of this chapter is based on my research published as a section of a paper written with Ayo Wahlberg; I am grateful to Ayo for agreeing to its reuse in this form: see Wahlberg and Rose, 2015.

2 These figures come from the UK's Mental Health Foundation, at https:// www.mentalhealth.org.uk/statistics/mental-health-statistics-uk-and-worldwide; similar figures can be found in many other places. Thus NAMI (the National Alliance for Mental Illness) in the United States, estimates that one in four adults – approximately 61.5 million Americans – experiences mental illness in a given year. One in 17 – about 13.6 million – lives with a serious mental illness such as schizophrenia, major depression or bipolar disorder. Approximately 20 per cent of youth aged between 13 and 18 experience severe mental disorders in a given year: http://www.nami.org/factsheets/mentalillness_factsheet.pdf.

3 The statistics are rather hard to compare, because of variations in the ways they have been collected, but in England and Wales the number of inpatients peaked in the mid-1950s at around 152,000, or just under 3.5 per thousand of the population, and – in a different way of calculating – in the 1970s, when the adult population of England and Wales was around 48 million, first admissions to hospital care for mental illness in the 1970s ran at around 61,000, with a further 86,000 receiving mental health services from local health authorities; see Jones, 1972. The number of 'mental illness' beds in hospitals has continued to decline; in England it has fallen by around 72 per cent since the early 2000s to around 18,5000 in 2016/17 for a population of around 55 million; see   https://www.england.nhs.uk/statistics/statistical-work-areas/bed-availability-and-occupancy/. Across all European countries, numbers of psychiatric hospital beds vary greatly, from 1.75 beds per thousand of the population in Belgium to around 0.1 per thousand in Italy, where public hospital admission has been very severely constrained since the passage of Law 180 in the Italian Mental Health Act of 1978: data from Eurostat at   http://ec.europa.eu/eurostat/statistics-explained/index.php/Mental_health_and_related_issues_statistics#Healthcare_beds_and_personnel. In the United States, the asylum population peaked in the mid-1950s at around 560,000 at a time when the adult population was around 150 million, or around 3.7 per thousand of the population; see Grob, 1991a. While there are many technical difficulties in finding accurate figures for the current US situation, a recent estimate, albeit by an advocate for increasing bed numbers, suggested that in 2016 there were 35,000 state psychiatric beds, or about 0.11 beds per 100,000 population; see http:// www.psychiatrictimes.com/psychiatric-emergencies/dearth-psychiatric-beds.

4 Of course, in medicine and public health, the term epidemic actually applies to a spread of infectious disease, and clearly mental health prob-

lems are not infectious, so I use the term here loosely, in the sense defined in the *Oxford English Dictionary* as meaning widespread and prevalent.

5 The image is from W. Gross, 1935, "Drei Jahre rassenpolitische Aufklarungsarbeit", *Volk und Rasse*, 10 (1935): 335, and is reprinted in Proctor, 1988: 182.

6 This section derives from Wahlberg and Rose, 2015.

7 These estimates fuelled further concerns about the reliability and validity of diagnoses undertaken by psychiatrists and epidemiologists, and these were important in the process that led to the revision of the APA's *DSM*, whose third edition, published in 1980, famously attempted to define each category in its classification schema in terms of clearly specified and observable behavioural, emotional or other characteristics (estimate based on figures reported in Jones, 1972). I discuss this process, and the debates over the nature of psychiatric diagnosis, in chapter 4.

8 http://www.presidency.ucsb.edu/ws/?pid=30714.

9 This is the kind of survey that was first envisaged by the President's Commission on Mental Health in 1978.

10 Later surveys were rather more complicated but took the same basic form. The instruments used in the NCS family of surveys can be found at http://www.hcp.med.harvard.edu/ncs/instruments.php.

11 I discuss the Movement for Global Mental Health in chapter 7.

12 I am drawing here upon my argument in Rose, 1991.

Chapter 3 Is It All the Fault of Neoliberal Capitalism?

1 The report was written by a team from the Institute of Health Equity at University College London in collaboration with colleagues from the WHO and advice from an international panel of experts.

2 The Harvard Center on the Developing Child defines toxic stress as follows: "Toxic stress response can occur when a child experiences strong, frequent, and/or prolonged adversity – such as physical or emotional abuse, chronic neglect, caregiver substance abuse or mental illness, exposure to violence, and/or the accumulated burdens of family economic hardship – without adequate adult support"; see http://devel opingchild.harvard.edu/science/key-concepts/toxic-stress/.

3 The term 'social problem' group seems to have first appeared in the Report of the Departmental Committee on Mental Deficiency, published in 1929, to refer to the lowest 10 per cent in "the social scale of most communities" that contains a large proportion of "insane persons, epileptics, paupers, criminals (especially recidivists), unemployables, habitual slum-dwellers, prostitutes, inebriates and other social ineffi-cients"; see Lidbetter, 1932. It was not only eugenicists who considered that this group reproduced itself across generations.

4 See http://decal.ga.gov/HeadStart/History.aspx. See also https://obam

awhitehouse.archives.gov/blog/2015/05/18/day-history-creation-head-start?utm_medium=twitter&utm_source=twitterfeed.

5 This is a rolling panel of households interviewed either in person or by telephone.

6 https://www.theguardian.com/lifeandstyle/2016/sep/29/self-harm-ptsd-and-mental-illness-soaring-among-young-women-in-england-survey.

7 This financial crisis is often dated to the collapse of the US investment bank, Lehmann Brothers, on 15 September 2008, following on from the crisis of the US 'sub-prime' mortgage market which came to worldwide notice a year earlier. In the UK, the idea of an 'age of austerity' is often dated to a speech given by the then Conservative prime minister, David Cameron, in April 2009; see https://www.theguardian.com/politics/2009/apr/26/david-cameron-conservative-economic-policy1.

8 http://content.digital.nhs.uk/catalogue/PUB21748/apms-2014-full-rpt.pdf.

9 The same team previously reported on the rising numbers of children in the US treated for attention deficit disorders (Olfson et al., 2003), and the increasing use of antidepressant medication in the United States, especially among those aged 6–17 (Olfson and Marcus, 2009).

10 *La fabbrica dell'infelicità. New economy e movimento del cognitariato* was published by Derive Approdi in 2001: http://www.deriveapprodi.org/. Berardi, who is known as 'Bifo', is the founder of 'Radio Alice' in Bologna and a member of the Italian Autonomia Movement.

11 I have drawn here on an interview with Berardi conducted by Matthew Fuller in 2001: http://fuller.spc.org/fuller/matthew-fuller-factory-of-unhappiness-interview-with-bifo/.

12 Thomas is a proponent of a development that he and Pat Bracken (2001) call 'postpsychiatry', which I will discuss in my final chapter.

13 There is also an extensive literature on mental ill health and social exclusion, in which social exclusion – a confused term with many definitions – is seen as the obverse of social capital – the absence of social capital increases social exclusion, which is a factor in mental ill health, which itself intensifies social exclusion and reduces social capital further: see Social Exclusion Unit, 2004; Evans-Lacko et al., 2014; Wright and Stickley, 2013; Morgan et al., 2007.

14 I am quoting here from the translation of Bourdieu's *The Forms of Capital* by Richard Nice, available at: https://www.marxists.org/reference/subject/philosophy/works/fr/bourdieu-forms-capital.htm.

15 The increasing propensity of Americans to 'bowl alone' rather than as members of such clubs was, for Putnam, an index of the decline of social capital.

16 Cacioppo was the first to use the term 'social neuroscience' in the early 1990s: see Cacioppo and Berntson, 1992.

17 These were nationally representative surveys carried out by the American Association of Retired Persons (AARP).

18 See the report by The Lonely Society?, published by the Mental Health Foundation, at https://www.mentalhealth.org.uk/sites/default/files/the_lonely_society_report.pdf.

19 https://www.jocoxloneliness.org/pdf/a_call_to_action.pdf. The Jo Cox Foundation was established in memory of the UK Member of Parliament who was brutally murdered outside her Yorkshire constituency office in June 2016 by a right-wing activist.

20 I discuss the historical and present biology of the stress response and its relationship to mental ill health in more detail in my forthcoming book, coauthored with Des Fitzgerald.

21 See http://www.psy.cmu.edu/~scohen/.

22 This is popularly known as 'the inflamed brain' or sometimes 'the inflamed mind': see, for example, http://bebrainfit.com/brain-inflammation-depression/ and http://www.bbc.co.uk/news/health-37166293.

23 See, for example, https://www.cato.org/publications/commentary/ending-mass-poverty.

24 http://www.worldbank.org/en/topic/poverty/overview.

Chapter 4   If Mental Disorders Exist, How Shall We Know Them?

1 This chapter started life as a talk given in 2013 at the Institute of Psychiatry of King's College London, at an event to mark the publication of *DSM-5.0*. Thanks to Diana Rose and George Szmukler for many discussions of these issues.

2 Karl Menninger, together with his father Charles Menninger, established the Menninger Clinic in 1919, and were joined by Karl's brother William Menninger in 1925. The clinic, and a range of associated activities, led to the establishment of the Menninger Foundation. For the timeline, see https://www.menningerclinic.com/about/newsroom/quick-facts.

3 A very senior psychiatric colleague of mine remarked that there was never a time, over his long career, when psychiatry had not been 'in crisis'. His aim was to suggest that there was nothing for psychiatrists to worry about in the recent use of the term. While I am critical of this somewhat complacent attitude, I agree that one should use the 'c' word sparingly.

4 For an excellent evaluation and development of Scheff's original account, see Link et al., 1989.

5 Clare became a well-known public figure in the UK as presenter of a long-running BBC radio series *In the Psychiatrist's Chair*, in which he interviewed prominent public figures about their personal, familial and emotional lives.

6 Clare ends his discussion of the diagnosis process with a brief reference to the Task Force on Nomenclature and Statistics of the APA that was established, in September 1973, to develop a new edition of the *DSM* – *DSM-III* – which would finally be published in 1980. He wondered if

it was possible, or even desirable, to attempt to provide a single classification system that cannot only be a means for professional communication,
a guide to treatments, indications of prognosis for different conditions,
but could also reflect what is known about the causes of the disorders in
question. His doubts were prescient. We will return to this issue later in
the present chapter.

7 For a useful, and unusually dispassionate, summary of this controversy,
see https://www.nhs.uk/news/mental-health/news-analysis-controversial-
mental-health-guide-dsm-5/.

8 This, for example, was roughly the position taken by Professor Simon
Wessely of the Institute of Psychiatry at King's College London in an
article that he wrote to coincide with the launch of *DSM-5*: http://www.
guardian.co.uk/science/2013/may/12/DSM-5-conspiracy-laughable.
Wessely is now the Regius Professor of Psychiatry and was elected president of the Royal College of Psychiatry; in July 2017 he became the first
psychiatrist to be elected as President of the Royal Society of Medicine.

9 There is a growing interest in the sociology of diagnosis: see, for example,
Jutel and Nettleton, 2011; McGann, 2011; Manning, 2001.

10 As, for example, was the case when the diagnosis of Asperger syndrome
was elminated from *DSM-5*; see, for example, http://www.slate.com/
articles/health_and_science/medical_examiner/2013/05/autism_spectr
um_diagnoses_the_dsm_5_eliminates_asperger_s_and_pdd_nos.html.

11 Some psychiatrists extend the term 'anosognosia' to this 'lack of insight'.
The term was proposed for some conditions that follow brain damage by
the neurologist Joseph Babinski in 1918; see Langer, 2009. Its extension
to psychiatry is controversial. There are many examples where psychiatrists have considered individuals to 'lack insight' when they refuse to
accept that their gender orientation, political beliefs or lifestyle are symptoms of disorders requiring treatment. 'Insight' in psychiatry usually
means agreeing with the judgement of the expert psychiatrist.

12 See http://www.patientslikeme.com/.

13 Much can be learned from the history of visualizations in psychiatry –
something I am currently researching; for details, see www.neurovision.
com.

14 Thus in 1904 and 1910 special censuses of the insane largely avoided
the classification of mental disorders (psychiatric nosology) in order to
focus on the linked issues of race and immigration that were central to
the eugenic concerns that saturated US politics in the early twentieth
century.

15 Grob (1991b) reports that these were: traumatic psychoses, senile
psychoses, psychoses with cerebral arteriosclerosis, general paralysis,
psychoses with cerebral syphilis, psychoses with Huntington's chorea,
psychoses with brain tumour, psychoses with other brain or nervous diseases, alcoholic psychoses, psychoses due to drugs and other exogenous
toxins, psychoses with pellagra, psychoses with other somatic diseases,

manic-depressive psychoses, involution melancholia, dementia praecox (subsequently schizophrenia), paranoia or paranoid conditions, epileptic psychoses, psychoneuroses and neuroses, psychoses with constitutional psychopathic inferiority, and psychoses with mental deficiency.

16 While I focus here on the situation in the United States, the experience in the UK was similar; see Miller and Rose, 1988.

17 Grob (1991b) lists these as infection; drug, poison, or alcoholic intoxication; trauma; circulatory or metabolic disturbances; intercranial neoplasms; multiple sclerosis; and Huntington's chorea or other diseases of hereditary origin.

18 Many non-US psychoanalysts doubted that the kinds of psychodynamic explanations and practices of American psychiatrists, with their focus on ego and adaptation, were true to the teachings of Sigmund Freud.

19 There is a large critical literature on the history, politics and conceptual basis of *DSM-III* and the versions that followed it; see, for example, Bayer and Spitzer, 1985; Cooper, 2004; Frances and Cooper, 1981; Gaines, 1992.

20 Of course, this may be true of many other kinds of disease.

21 Part of the Broad Institute of MIT and Harvard: https://www.broadinsti tute.org/stanley.

22 http://www.nimh.nih.gov/research-funding/rdoc/nimh-research-doma in-criteria-rdoc.shtml.

23 http://www.nimh.nih.gov/about/director/index.shtml.

24 The term 'precision medicine' is now preferred to 'personalized' medicine, perhaps because the idea of personalization implies that each medical intervention should be specific to each individual, whereas the idea of precision does not embody the fantasy of medical individualization, or imply that previously medicine was 'impersonal' – an implication that irritated many clinicians.

25 https://mindstronghealth.com/.

26 http://www.nimh.nih.gov/about/director/index.shtml.

27 This approach has some similarities to the proposals for understanding 'causal architecture' made by Keyes and Galea (2017).

28 Meyer Archive Series II/353/124, quoted in Double, 2007.

29 Since early 2013, when I wrote the paper on which this chapter is based for a Conference on *DSM-5* held at the Institute of Psychiatry, Psychology and Neuroscience at King's College London, a group of British psychologists have argued strongly against diagnosis, arguing that we should 'drop the language of disorder' (Kinderman et al., 2013) and suggesting that psychologists are best placed to develop formulations that make the experience of mental distress meaningful, unlike diagnostic categories that are merely labels made up by people sitting around a table and 'slapped on' to people experiencing emotional distress as a result of their traumatic experiences; see http://www.adisorder4everyone.com/. As this book was about to go to press, these psychologists published an

extended expression of their position, staking their claim to authority in these matters (Johnstone et al., 2018). I discuss this briefly in my final chapter.

30 Of course, this does not imply that interventions on the brain and body, for example with pharmacology or by brain stimulation, cannot play an important role in alleviating particular conditions, and perhaps even allowing a return to normal functioning.

Chapter 5 Are Mental Disorders 'Brain Disorders'?

1 Ian Hacking's reflections on this issue are, as always, provocative (Hacking, 2005, 2007). Hacking suggests that we have come to think of bodies as machine-like compositions of exchangeable and replaceable parts, but although he recognizes that we can alter minds by ingesting psychoactive chemicals, and has some reflections on different ways of thinking in Japan, he is less clear as to whether we have come to think of minds as modifiable mechanisms.

2 Now, of course, each time I write a word like 'basis', I ought to write an explanatory note, for instance here pointing out that this term has a whole variety of meanings. In the online *Oxford English Dictionary*, it can mean a foundation, a support or "[t]hat on which anything is reared, constructed, or established, and by which its constitution or operation is determined; groundwork, footing".

3 On recurrent history, see especially Canguilhem, 1968.

4 Most people agree that the only true 'atypical' is clozapine, which can cause the serious, potentially fatal, condition of agranulocytosis, and so should only be used in programmes that ensure regular surveillance and blood tests. For an excellent critical discussion of other so-called 'atypicals', see Kendall, 2011.

5 Of course, few still accepted the eugenic conclusions that Kallmann drew from his research.

6 I discuss this further in chapter 4.

7 When Gottesman and Shields published their polygenic theory of schizophrenia, they claimed that around half the beds in public mental hospitals in the USA were occupied by patients diagnosed as schizophrenics, amounting to more than a quarter of a million individuals.

8 https://www.scientificamerican.com/article/first-gene-for-schizophre/#.

9 Haploinsufficiency refers to the situation where only one of the two copies of the gene is functional, leading to an insufficiency of the relevant protein.

10 "An odds ratio (OR) is a measure of association between an exposure and an outcome. The OR represents the odds that an outcome will occur given a particular exposure, compared to the odds of the outcome occurring in the absence of that exposure" (Szumilas, 2010: 227).

11 Of course, there is a very basic problem in that all studies that test so

many associations for statistical significance are liable to what statisticians term Type One errors: if one tests 1,000 associations, then one of those will appear statistically significant at the 0.001 level simply by chance.

12 For a more optimistic view, that still recognizes how far we need to go beyond current approaches, see McCarroll et al., 2014.

13 Jim van Os has also argued that we should abolish the term 'schizophrenia' and replace it with the term 'psychosis spectrum disorder' which, he believes, does not carry the connotation of a 'brain disease', is less stigmatizing, helps individuals understand the conditions they are experiencing and that they can recover from them, and hence makes it more likely that they will seek help (van Os, 2016). Some countries, notably Japan and South Korea, have already eliminated the term and devised alternatives.

14 I have discussed these technologies elsewhere; see Rose and Abi-Rached, 2013.

15 See the quote at the head of this chapter. There are many other technical and conceptual problems with the interpretation of results from fMRI, and a large literature on these both from imagers themselves, and from social scientists. These are discussed in Rose and Abi-Rached, 2013; I won't repeat that discussion here.

16 Discussed in chapter 4.

17 http://blogs.discovermagazine.com/neuroskeptic/2017/01/14/fmri-mental-illness/#.WYsNK3cjH_o.

18 This is also suggested by the Neuroskeptic in the comments cited above.

Chapter 6   Does Psychopharmacology Have a Future?

1 This was a recurrent theme on the websites and direct-to-consumer advertisements for the SSRI class of drugs in the 2000s. Some may once have believed that the drugs would, in Peter Kramer's (1992) infamous phrase, make them feel 'better than well'.

2 There is, of course, a large and largely speculative literature on 'enhancement' that I do not discuss here.

3 I have discussed this history in detail elsewhere; in this chapter I will focus largely on the period from 2000 onwards.

4 Data from the Health and Social Care Information Centre, presented by the Council for Evidence-Based Psychiatry in their Briefing Note to the All Party Parliamentary Group for Prescribed Drug Dependence, in June 2015; at http://prescribeddrug.org/wp-content/uploads/2015/10/Briefing-note-for-APPG-PDD.pdf.

5 Iceland is a special case: with such a small population, the prescribing practices of a few doctors can skew the statistics greatly.

6 http://www.scmp.com/news/china/policies-politics/article/1947236/millions-people-mental-illness-china-india-go-untreated.

7 In China, the reframing as depression of the condition previously known as neurasthenia has opened the market for the increasing use of antidepressants; see Lee, 2011; Lee et al., 2009.

8 http://www.prnewswire.com/news-releases/research-report-on-chinas-antidepressant-market-2013-2017-211159091.html. See also a report in the *Guardian* in 2013, "China starts to turn to drugs as awareness of depression spreads", at https://www.theguardian.com/world/2013/nov/20/china-depression-antidepressants-drugs.

9 Of course, in countries that have previously had very limited use of psychiatric medication, such as China, one also sees a rise in the use of antipsychotics for treating severe conditions, usually placing those conditions under the diagnostic category of schizophrenia. In Europe, North America and Australasia, there is some evidence of increasing use of the 'antipsychotic' class of drugs following the introduction of 'second generation' antipsychotics, thought to have fewer side effects, perhaps as the result of aggressive marketing campaigns for their use in the treatment of bipolar disorder, and off-label prescribing for children, adolescents and those suffering from dementia (Rose, 2003a, 2004, 2006b) – although, as I have already said, many believe this distinction between first and second generation antipsychotics is spurious: see Verdoux et al., 2010; Kendall, 2011.

10 The best-known recent case is that of Joseph Biederman's advocacy of the diagnosis of juvenile bipolar disorder: while some hailed him as a visionary for his argument that this disorder could be recognized in very young children and successfully treated with antipsychotic medication, others questioned both the diagnosis and his treatment, and pointed to his financial ties with the relevant pharmaceutical companies and hence conflicts of interest. See http://www.nytimes.com/2008/06/08/us/08conflict.html.

11 Actually, at the top of most hierarchies are meta-analyses of all the published papers on a particular question that have used RCTs.

12 Another set of problems arises when the RCT methodology is used – or attempted – in what are termed 'complex interventions' such as those involving talking, group or social therapies, where conditions cannot be held constant between those in the active arm and others, and multiple confounding issues are introduced. See Craig et al., 2008; Wolff, 2001; Oakley et al., 2006.

13 For this reason, medical journal editors now insist that before they are able to publish trial results, researchers must have preregistered the trial in a public clinical trial registry in advance of conducting it; see De Angelis et al., 2004; Laine et al., 2007.

14 There are also 'professional' guinea pigs, who volunteer repeatedly for trials in which participants are paid, or for other reasons; see Abadie, 2010.

15 These studies were conducted and published while Tim Kendall was

NHS England's National Clinical Director for Mental Health and a long-time Director of the National Collaborating Centre for Mental Health at the Royal College of Psychiatrists.

16 There is a large literature on branded versus generic for specific drugs in particular markets, but for an interesting general analysis of branded versus generic medicines, see https://www.theguardian.com/lifeandstyle/2008/apr/08/healthandwellbeing.consumeraffairs.

17 Meta-analyses have shown that the so-called 'atypicals' are no more effective than older psychiatric medications (see, for example, Leucht et al., 2009) and that they are in fact associated with a whole range of adverse effects (Haddad and Sharma, 2007).

18 This is not the place for a history of the ways in which pharmaceutical companies rationalized their drugs, but it is notable that in advertisements in the medical journals and other presentations of the drugs in the 1950s and 1960s, the focus was on their social benefits, rather than their neurochemical modes of action; the drugs made patients more amenable to therapy, more communicative, less prone to violent outbursts, more able to cope with the demands of their roles – which were always strongly gender specific. See, for example, Metzl, 2003.

19 French psychiatrist Pierre Deniker, one of those credited with the discovery of the effects of chlorpromazine in the 1950s, soon realized the problems of toxicity that increased with high doses. According to David Healy, Parisian psychiatrists thus avoided many of the problems that arose from the use of high doses of these drugs in the USA and elsewhere; see Healy, 1998, 2000.

20 As this book was going to press, a paper in *The Lancet* in February 2018 received a great deal of publicity (Cipriani et al., 2018) with press reports trumpeting that, as a headline in the *Guardian* put it, "The drugs do work: antidepressants are effective", and the authors claiming this finally put doubts to rest about these medicines, that "antidepressants are effective" and that there are many millions of people who are currently untreated to whom they should be prescribed. However, the paper itself – a systematic review and meta-analysis of 522 trials – tells a different and more complex story. First, it put together drugs whose claimed modes of action were radically different – amitriptyline, which is a tricyclic, and fluoxetine, which is a selective serotonin reuptake inhibitor – the psychiatric equivalent of conflating the efficacy of aspirin and dihydrocodeine in the treatment of headaches and then proclaiming "headache pills do work". Second, increased efficacy was only claimed to have been shown in adults with major depressive disorders, so the study has no relevance at all to the vast majority of those for whom prescriptions are currently given who are diagnosed with mild or moderate depression. Third, no increases in efficacy of trial drugs over placebo were found in children. Fourth, even taking the paper on its own terms, effect sizes were smaller in more recent and larger placebo-controlled trials – indeed, effect sizes

tended to be highest in older, smaller trials against placebo and when a drug was novel, and lower in recent larger trials and as novelty wore off, which indicates that some of the processes that I have described were in play. Fifth, the study looked at both efficacy and acceptability, but few of the drugs rated highly for efficacy were also rated high for tolerability as measured by drop-outs from the clinical trials. Sixth, as Joanna Moncrieff has pointed out in an excellent analysis, efficacy was measured using changes in numerical scores on depression scales such as the Hamilton Rating Scale for Depression (HRSD), but when the actual figures underpinning claims on efficacy are examined, "differences are trivial, amounting to around 2 points on the HRSD which has a maximum score of 54. These differences are unlikely to be clinically relevant"; see https://joannamoncrieff.com/2018/02/24/challenging-the-new-hype-about-antidepressants/. And seventh – although this is by no means the last major problem – the study focused on outcomes after only eight weeks of treatment, whereas almost everyone who is prescribed antidepressants – and who does not discontinue themselves – takes the drugs for many months; to quote Moncrieff again: "'real world' studies of people treated with antidepressants show that the proportion of people who stick to recommended treatment, recover and don't relapse within a year is staggeringly low", despite the fact that, as the study itself remarks in passing, if left untreated depressive symptoms tend to improve over time. If the debate over antidepressants has become deeply 'ideological', it would be a mistake to believe that the 'ideology' was all on one side.

21 https://www.theguardian.com/society/2017/jun/02/ketamine-help-thou sands-severe-depression-doctors.

22 For recent discussions, see the article in the *New York Times* by Richard Friedman: http://www.nytimes.com/2013/08/20/health/a-dry-pipeline-for-psychiatric-drugs.html?src=twr&_r=1; also see http://psychnews. psychiatryonline.org/doi/10.1176/appi.pn.2014.11a2.

23 http://www.ahdbonline.com/issues/2013/april-2013-vol-6-no-3-payers-guide-to-new-fda-approvals/1387-article-1387.

24 They note the five CNS drugs awaiting approval by the FDA in 2013 as examples of the problem: Levadex (dihydroergotamine), an oral inhaler for acute migraine; levomilnacipran, a serotonin norepinephrine reuptake inhibitor (SNRI) for the treatment of depression, which has shown greater potency and selectivity for norepinephrine than other SNRIs; suvorexant, with a new mechanism of action for primary insomnia; Brintellix (vortioxetine), which has shown mixed efficacy data for major depressive disorders; and cariprazine, an atypical antipsychotic for schizophrenia, with a mechanism similar to Abilify, but potentially with an improved safety profile.

Chapter 7   Who Needs Global Mental Health?

1 In this chapter I have drawn on work conducted with Nick Manning, Ilina Singh, Dominique Behague, Ricardo Araya and Francisco Ortega for a large research project on resolving controversies in the Movement for Global Mental Health, submitted to the Wellcome Trust, but not funded. Thanks to my colleagues for allowing me to draw upon it in this chapter.

2 The panel of 422 experts, working in more than 60 countries, included researchers in genetics and genomics, neuroscience, basic behavioural science and neurodevelopment, who made up just over one-third of the panel, mental health services researchers who constituted another quarter, and a further third who were clinical researchers and epidemiologists. It is not clear if any social scientists were included, and it seems that no psychiatric service users took part – except perhaps those experts who were themselves undeclared service users.

3 The authors included Pamela Y. Collins, Office for Research on Disparities and Global Mental Health, National Institute of Mental Health, Maryland, USA; Vikram Patel, Centre for Global Mental Health, London School of Hygiene & Tropical Medicine UK, Sangath, Goa, India; Sarah S. Joestl, Office for Research on Disparities and Global Mental Health, National Institute of Mental Health, USA; Dana March, Office for Research on Disparities and Global Mental Health, National Institute of Mental Health, USA; Thomas R. Insel, National Institute of Mental Health, USA; Abdallah S. Daar, University of Toronto and McLaughlin-Rotman Centre for Global Health, Toronto, Canada, and Chair, Global Alliance for Chronic Diseases.

4 A whole issue of the journal *Disability and the Global South*, entitled "Globalizing Mental Health or Pathologising the Global South? Mapping the Ethics, Theory and Practice of Global Mental Health" was devoted to these issues; see http://dgsjournal.org/volume-1-no-2/.

5 Of course, such arguments were contested within transcultural psychiatry itself. For a review of the state of the argument in the 1980s, see Kobena Mercer's chapter on racism and transcultural psychiatry in Miller and Rose, 1986.

6 Culture specific disorders were listed in the WHO's 1993 *ICD-10 Classification of Mental and Behavioural Disorders: Diagnostic Criteria for Research*, which argued for more research, but stated: "The status of these disorders is controversial: many researchers argue that they differ only in degree from disorders already included in existing psychiatric classifications, such as anxiety disorders and reactions to stress, and that they are therefore best regarded as local variations of disorders that have long been recognized" (WHO, 1993: 213) An Appendix to *DSM-IV* discusses various "idioms of distress through which symptoms or the need for social support are communicated" (APA, 1994: 844) and

gives advice to diagnosticians to help them relate these "folk categories" to *DSM* diagnoses. But note that for psychiatric anthropologists like Laurence Kirmayer, 'decoding' the meaning of somatic symptoms is not a means of recognizing underlying *DSM* disease categories; on the contrary, psychiatrists must avoid such a reduction to universality by "seeing them as part of a language of distress with interpersonal and wider social meanings"; see Kirmayer, 2001: 22.

7 http://www.thelancet.com/series/global-mental-health.
8 http://www.globalmentalhealth.org/.
9 For example, the University of Melbourne (International Mental Health Leadership Program); Sangath, Goa (Leadership in Mental Health); Universidade NOVA de Lisboa (International Master in Mental Health Policy and Services); Center for International Humanitarian Cooperation, Geneva (Mental Health in Complex Emergencies); Harvard Program in Refugee Trauma, Orvieto (Global Mental Health: Trauma and Recovery Certificate Program); London School of Hygiene and Tropical Medicine and the Institute of Psychiatry, King's College London (MSc in Global Mental Health); University of Ibadan (Mental Health Leadership and Advocacy Programme for Anglophone West Africa.
10 Many of these issues came to a head at a 2012 event at McGill University entitled 'Global Mental Health: Bridging the Perspectives of Cultural Psychiatry and Public Health'; see http://somatosphere.net/2012/07/global-mental-health-and-its-discontents.html. See also http://somatosphere.net/2011/10/a-reply-to-grand-challenges-in-mental-health.html.
11 As previously noted, the criticisms were rearticulated in a special issue of the journal *Disability and the Global South*, at http://dgsjournal.org/volume-1-no-2/.
12 There are several journals with this title; this one bears the subtitle 'Mental Health and Psychosocial Support in Conflict Affected Areas', and was apparently started by the War Trauma Foundation; see http://www.interventionjournal.org/.
13 Indeed, according to Bemme and D'souza, at the McGill conference in 2012 (see above, note 10), Patel referred specifically to the strategic use of language and arguments: "What bothers people is the word 'global.' But we need to see it is completely strategic. One uses labels for particular purposes. GMH is about generating resources and we have to use these kinds of figures to shock governments into action" (Bemme and D'souza, 2014, n.12; conference verbatim field notes by Bemme, 7 July 2012).

Chapter 8   Experts By Experience?

1 In this chapter, I have benefited greatly from advice from Diana Rose. Culpability for remaining mistakes, and for the argument presented here, remains with me.

2 A note on terminology is overdue. Each of these terms – lunatic, madman, mental patient, client, user of mental health services, survivor . . . is freighted with resonances; each comes into use at a particular time, in a particular practice, and each is hard to dislodge from its time and place. Some prefer the term 'mad', as did Michel Foucault in *Madness and Civilization*, and as does the contemporary 'mad studies' movement. Many activists in the 1990s onwards adopted the term 'user and survivor of psychiatry', and some, especially in the United States, added in the term 'consumer' – as if those who were recipients of psychiatry were consumers in any meaningful sense of the term. The UN's CRPD used the term 'people with psychosocial disabilities' to refer to those with impairments and restrictions on participation related to mental health conditions, and since its entry into force in 2008, many organizations, including psychiatric service user organizations, have adopted this language, though it is not clear whether those who are the subjects of the psychiatric or mental health system, or who experience mental distress, would recognize themselves in this terminology. In this chapter, as elsewhere in this book, I have tried where possible to use the language of those whose work I am describing, and to remain agnostic on the best, most accurate or least stigmatizing term.

3 Of course, some would argue that, given that family members are most often primary caregivers for those in mental distress, their voices should count most. But we cannot assume that the wishes of families are always compatible with those of the person who is, or has been, or could be, a subject of psychiatric attention. It is on those subjects that I focus in this chapter.

4 Many of the excerpts in the books cited in what follows, and much more material, can be found on the website created by the Survivor's History Group, at http://studymore.org.uk/mpu.htm.

5 For the residents of Kingsley Hall, set up by R. D. Laing, see http://www.dominicharris.co.uk/the_residents.html.

6 Some dispute the suggestion that the MPU was 'Marxist' – a term that meant many things at that time – although of course it was political. The MPU Demands, taken from the *Declaration of Intent* of April 1973, were:
   1. The abolition of compulsory treatment, i.e. we demand the effective right of patients to refuse any specific treatment.
   2. The abolition of the right of any authorities to treat patients in the face of opposition of relatives or closest friends unless it is clearly shown that the patient of his own volition desires the treatment.
   3. The abolition of irreversible psychiatric treatments (ECT, brain surgery, specific drugs).
   4. Higher standards in the testing of treatments before use on us.
   5. That patients be told what treatments they are receiving are experimental and should have the effective right to refuse to be experimented on.

6. That patients be told what treatments they are receiving and what the long-term effects are.

7. Also the abolition of isolation treatment (seclusion in locked side rooms, padded cells, etc.).

8. The right of any patient to inspect his case notes and the right to take legal action relating to the contents and consequences of them.

9. That the authorities should not discharge any patient against his will because they refuse treatment or any other reason.

10. That all patients should have the right to have any treatment which we believe will help them.

11. That local authorities should provide housing for patients wishing to leave hospital and that adequate security benefits should be provided. We will support any mental patients or ex-patients in their struggle to get these facilities and any person who is at risk of becoming a mental patient because of inadequate accommodation, financial support, social pressures, etc.

12. We call for the abolition of compulsory hospitalization.

13. An end to the indiscriminate use of the term 'mental subnormality'. We intend to fight the condemnation of people as 'mentally subnormal' in the absence of any real practical work to tackle the problem with active social understanding and help.

14. The abolition of the concept of 'psychopath' as a legal or medical category.

15. The right of patients to retain their personal clothing in hospitals and to secure their personal possessions without interference by hospital staff.

16. The abolition of compulsory work in hospitals and outside and the abolition of the right of the hospital to withhold and control patients' money.

17. The right of patients to join and participate fully in the trade union of their choice.

18. That trade union rates are paid to patients for any work done where such rates do not exist.

19. That patients should have recourse to a room where they can enjoy their own privacy or have privacy with others, of either sex, of their own choosing.

20. The abolition of censorship by hospital authorities of patients' communications with society outside the hospital and in particular the abolition of telephone and letter censorship.

21. We demand the abolition of any power to restrict patients' visiting rights by the hospital authorities.

22. The right of Mental Patients Union representatives to inspect all areas of hospitals or equivalent institutions.

23. We deny that there is any such thing as 'incurable' mental illness and demand the right to investigate the circumstances of any

mental hospital patient who believes he or she is being treated as incurable.

24. We demand that every mental patient or ex-patient should have the right to a free second opinion by a psychiatrist of the patient's or Mental Patients Union representative's choice, if he or she disagrees with the diagnosis and that every patient or ex-patient should have the right to an effective appeal machinery.

See https://pasttenseblog.wordpress.com/2016/03/21/today-in-londons-radical-history-mental-patients-union-founded-to-oppose-psychiatric-oppression-1973/.

7 http://studymore.org.uk/mpu.htm.
8 Jean Campbell (2005), who was the first service user researcher in the United States, provides a slightly different view from Chamberlin of the history up to 2005.
9 http://www.community-consortium.org/projects/chamberlin-judy.pdf.
10 While the civil rights movement, and the language of rights, was most salient in the United States in the early years, it did have its effects in many other regions, and later was to become a key theme for transforming the asylum-based mental health system in Eastern Europe. In 1989, The World Psychiatric Association adopted a charter on the rights of mental patients, bringing together "statements that the WPA's outgoing leadership has made public in the past six years, mainly on the occasion of our Association's interventions to the Working Group established by the Economic and Social Council (through the UN Commission on Human Rights) (on the question of persons detained on the grounds of mental ill health or suffering from mental disorder)"; see http://www.wpanet.org/detail.php?section_id=5&content_id=29. In 2017, under the presidency of Dinesh Bhugra, the WPA issued an updated bill of rights, in the context of the UN's CRPD, which concentrated on 'positive' rights as opposed to the 'negative' rights – that is to say legal protections – of the CRPD; see http://wpanet.org/WMMD16/BillofRights_Mentalillness_FINAL.pdf.
11 Surprisingly, Chamberlin seems unaware of the many problematic aspects of Szasz's work, his belief, for example, that *any* kind of treatment is legitimate so long as it is entered into by a contract, and his view that many of those who seek psychiatric help for 'mental illness' – something he considers to be a mythical condition – are malingerers who, rather than being supported in their dependency on others, should get a grip, accept their duties and responsibilities as citizens, and get on with their lives.
12 Chamberlin extends this criticism to so-called 'therapeutic communities', and to concept houses like R. D. Laing's Kingsley Hall, and others in the UK run by the Philadelphia Association, such as Arbours, and even to Soteria House in San Jose, California: she believes that despite their apparent informality, and their rejection of some aspects of the

disease model, they also fail to break down the strict role distinctions between doctors, nurses and patients, and are, in the end, controlled by psychiatric professionals.

13 http://studymore.org.uk/mpu.htm#EdaleCharter.

14 For a review of the Carter Administration's activities in mental health, see Grob, 2005.

15 Alex Mold has argued convincingly that "the patient-consumer was not conjured into being by the Conservative government alone, but was the product of an interaction between patient groups, the state, the medical profession, and the affluent society. Three interlinked themes were critical to the process: first, the collection, collation, and dissemination of information to patients; second, the development of patients' rights; and finally, the promotion of patient choice. Through their activities around information, rights, and choice, patient groups agitated for a greater role for individuals and the wider population in determining health policy and practice. In so doing, they created an identity that was collective as well as individual: patient groups were concerned with patient-consumers, as well as the patient-consumer" (2011: 511). This ambition to turn patients into consumers was set out in *Patients First*, a consultative paper published in 1979 (DHSS, 1979) and embodied in a restricted form in the NHS and Community Care Act 1990.

16 Although many of the rights extended to other patients were not extended to psychiatric patients and users of mental health services.

17 https://www.gov.uk/government/publications/quality-standards-for-mental-health-services.

18 For the South African experience, see the reflections of William Rowland (2001), the first chairperson of Disabled People South Africa.

19 The words 'revelational' and 'capsualized' are those used by Charlton.

20 This has been a constant topic of debate within patient activist movements themselves; thanks to Léonie Mol for alerting me to the debate on these issues in the Netherlands.

21 In England and Wales, the requirement for 'independent mental health advocates' was written into the Mental Health Act 2007 (amending the 1983 Mental Health Act).

22 For details of O'Hagan's work, see http://www.maryohagan.com/.

23 I discuss in chapter 1 the longstanding idea that some, if not all, of those who suffered from mental disorders differ from 'the rest of us' in that they were exceptionally liable to engage in troublesome, aggressive or violent behaviour.

24 These developments in the UK are to some extent mirrored in other European counties, as well as in Australia and New Zealand. There is also a growing user and survivor movement in many countries in the Global South, and although each has its own specific history, many are using rigorous research-based evidence to counter the ways in which psychiatry and mental health services often support, and rarely challenge,

the longstanding maltreatment of those diagnosed with mental disorders; see Robb, 2012; Davar, 2008.

25 For a review of some of the user-led services in the United States by that time, see Clay, 2005.

26 http://www.nshn.co.uk/; https://www.hearing-voices.org/.

27 Beresford (2002) cites an early paper by Rose (2001a) as one of his exemplars.

28 Jijian Voronka (2016) has also explored the limits of a mental health politics that relies on the idea of 'lived experience'.

29 Some have suggested that we need a new 'discipline' of mad studies. Lucy Costa defines this as "an area of education, scholarship, and analysis about the experiences, history, culture, political organising, narratives, writings and most importantly, the PEOPLE who identify as: Mad; psychiatric survivors; consumers; service users; mentally ill; patients, neuro-diverse; inmates; disabled – to name a few of the "identity labels" our community may choose to use. Mad Studies has grown out of the long history of consumer/survivor movements organised both locally and internationally. The methods, and approaches for research are drawn from other educational fields such as women's studies, queer studies, critical race studies, legal studies, ethnography, auto-ethnography (again, just to name a few) . . . Together, we can cultivate our own theories/ models/ concepts/ principles/ hypotheses/ and values about how we understand ourselves, or our experiences in relationship to mental health system(s), research and politics"; see https://madstudies2014.wordpress.com/2014/10/15/mad-studies-what-it-is-and-why-you-should-care-2/. See also LeFrançois et al., 2013; Menzies et al., 2013. I discuss this position briefly in my final chapter.

30 https://www.theguardian.com/society/2016/nov/16/ban-police-cells-mental-health-crisis.

31 https://www.cqc.org.uk/publications/major-report/state-care-mental-health-services-2014-2017. See also the report in the *Guardian* in July 2017: https://www.theguardian.com/society/2017/jul/20/thousands-of-mental-health-patients-spend-years-on-secure-wards-nhs.

32 The term 'intersectionality' is often used to refer to the ways in which some individuals or groups are positioned at the intersection of a number of distinct stigmatizing or exclusionary discourses and practices.

Chapter 9   Is Another Psychiatry Possible?

1 See also https://www.madinamerica.com/2017/06/antipsychiatry-say-what/; https://bizomadness.blogspot.fr/2014/07/on-antipsychiatry.html.

2 http://www.mindfreedom.org/. Unfortunately, these human rights-based arguments are often linked with the anti-psychiatry campaigns of the bizarre cult of Scientology, and their Citizens Commission on Human Rights (CCHR), set up in collaboration with Thomas Szasz. The

consequences of this are incredibly damaging to those who wish to make rational and evidence-based arguments for a radical reform of psychiatric theories and practices.

3 https://www.un.org/development/desa/disabilities/convention-on-the-rights-of-persons-with-disabilities.html; see especially Article 14.

4 This has been argued forcefully by Tina Minkowitz (2011), who represented the World Network of Users and Survivors of Psychiatry in the drafting and negotiation of the Convention on the Rights of Persons. For a thoughtful discussion, see Szmukler et al., 2014, and, more generally, McSherry and Freckelton, 2013; Szmukler, 2017. While I dispute the interpretation of the CRPD as forbidding any involuntary detention or treatment of those with 'psychosocial disabilities', there are many aspects of this Convention that do aim to 'resocialize' rather than 'individualize' and provide important support for the transformation in mental health practices that I argue for in this book.

5 Of course, all too often, the institutions in question do not provide safety, respite and care, and the administration of medication is excessive, prolonged and for the benefit of staff rather than patients.

6 Of course, involuntary or quasi-voluntary use of psychiatric drugs is widespread in psychiatric institutions, usually legitimated by mental health legislation, and it is here that the CRPD may bite. However, as I have argued elsewhere (Rose, 1985b), my own view is that the best way to reduce such use is by instilling best practice, rather than through legal measures that are often 'honoured in the breach' – that is to say, which may be on the books, but have limited effects in practice.

7 I made this argument many years ago, in the context of an earlier rights-based movement for reform of psychiatry and mental health, and have not substantially changed my criticisms: see Rose, 1985b.

8 The one explicit set of arguments from the service user perspective is focused specifically on problems with current mental health legislation as it relates to involuntary hospitalization and treatment, and is placed within a separate panel rather than being integrated into the overall report.

9 Quoted in the *Guardian* on 12 May 2013, at https://www.theguardian.com/society/2013/may/12/psychiatrists-under-fire-mental-health.

10 In 2018, the authors of the BPS statement restated their position at length, and with some fanfare, now terming it 'The Power Threat Meaning Framework: Towards the Identification of Patterns in Emotional Distress, Unusual Experiences and Troubled or Troubling Behaviour, as an Alternative to Functional Psychiatric Diagnosis' (Johnstone et al., 2018). Drawing on some of the criticisms of psychiatry that I have reviewed in this book, they argued that psychologists are best placed to understand the ways in which 'power' has operated in the lives of those with mental distress, the psychological processes by which the operation of 'power' has posed 'threats', the ways in which

people have made meanings of those threats, and the ways this has led to psychological 'threat responses' such as self-blame, self-harm, self-stigmatization and learned helplessness. They claim that this framework enables the establishment of patterns that can displace conventional psychiatric diagnoses. However, it is not at all clear what is gained by lumping together such a variety of structural, institutional and personal forces and experiences as 'power', or why they should then all be reconceptualized as 'threats' except to enable the deployment of some familiar psychological concepts of 'threat responses' as the major explanatory principle. At the same time, the 'power' of clinical psychology embedded in the claim of clinical psychologists to expertise in defining and managing 'pathologies' seems strangely exempt from critical analysis (cf. Rose, 1999a). No wonder, then, that many mental health service users have expressed scepticism as to whether psychologists are destined to be the antidote to the problems of psychiatry: see https://recoveryinthebin.org/2018/01/16/power-threat-meaning-threat-power-power-power-review-by-scheherazade/.

11 A conclusion also reached by Tim Kendall (2011), as discussed in an earlier chapter.

12 Many of the points I make here are also supported by the 2017 report by UN Special Rapporteur Dainius Pūras: *Report of the Special Rapporteur on the right of everyone to the enjoyment of the highest attainable standard of physical and mental health*, A/HRC/35/21. The report can be found at https://reliefweb.int/sites/reliefweb.int/files/resources/G1707604.pdf. For example, Pūras argues that: "the field of mental health continues to be over-medicalized and the reductionist biomedical model, with support from psychiatry and the pharmaceutical industry, dominates clinical practice, policy, research agendas, medical education and investment in mental health around the world. The majority of mental health investments in low-, middle- and high-income countries disproportionately fund services based on the biomedical model of psychiatry . . . There is also a bias towards first-line treatment with psychotropic medications, in spite of accumulating evidence that they are not as effective as previously thought, that they produce harmful side effects and, in the case of antidepressants, specifically for mild and moderate depression, the benefit experienced can be attributed to a placebo effect. . . Despite those risks, psychotropic medications are increasingly being used in high-, middle- and low-income countries across the world . . . We have been sold a myth that the best solutions for addressing mental health challenges are medications and other biomedical interventions" (*Report of the Special Rapporteur*, para. 19, references omitted).

13 The UN Special Rapporteur also makes this point in a different way: "While it is uncontroversial to note that millions of people around the world are grossly underserved, the current 'burden of disease' approach firmly roots the global mental health crisis within a biomedical model,

too narrow to be proactive and responsive in addressing mental health issues at the national and global level" (*Report of the Special Rapporteur*, para. 16).

14 As discussed in chapter 3.

15 For example, those targeted at cities such as Thrive NYC (https://thrivenyc.cityofnewyork.us/) and Thrive LDN (http://thriveldn.co.uk/) or those advocating for workplaces, such as the report by Farmer and Stevenson on *Thriving at Work*, at https://www.gov.uk/government/pub lications/thriving-at-work-a-review-of-mental-health-and-employers.

16 https://www.hearing-voices.org/. The aims of the network are to raise awareness of voice hearing, visions, tactile sensations and other sensory experiences; to give men women and children who have these experiences an opportunity to talk freely about this together; to support anyone with these experiences seeking to understand, learn and grow from them in their own way.

17 As I was thinking about these issues, I read Oliver Sacks's intriguing reflections on 'speed' in his posthumously published *River of Consciousness* (2017). Of course, the argument that there is no single sensory universe, and that not everyone inhabits the same one, has been central to the 'neurodiversity' movement in relation to autism, but applies much more widely. For one example, see the well-known but still compelling video by the 'autist' Amana Baggs, at https://www.youtube.com/watch?v=JnylM1hI2jc.

18 C. Pariante and N. Rose, 'There Are More Connections in the Human Brain Than There Are Stars in Our Milky Way Galaxy. . .', at http://www.huffingtonpost.co.uk/carmine-pariante/there-are-more-connec-tions_b_9980694.html.

19 "Physiologists and physicians must never forget that a living being is an organism with its own individuality. We really must learn, then, that if we break up a living organism by isolating its different parts, it is only for the sake of ease in experimental analysis and by no means in order to conceive them separately. Indeed, when we wish to ascribe to a physiological quality its value and true significance, we must always refer it to this whole and draw our final conclusion only in relation to its effects in the whole" (Bernard, 1957 [1878]).

20 For an overview of the way in which I use the term biopolitics, see Rabinow and Rose, 2006.

21 Intriguingly, my proposals have many elements in common with the four scenarios recently sketched out for the future of mental health care by a group of social psychiatrists writing in *Lancet Psychiatry* on the basis of a survey of 'professional stakeholders' and an 'international expert workshop'; see Giacco et al., 2017.

22 For pointers to how one might understand humans as organisms in their milieus, see Goldstein, 1995 [1939]; von Uexküll, 2010 [1934]. My position is a materialist vitalism: see Rose, 2008, a position broadly

shared by Osborne, 2016: on vitalism more generally, see Greco, 2005; Wolfe and Wong, 2014.

23 Des Fitzgerald and I discuss these issues in much more detail in our forthcoming book.

24 See also, for example, plans for 'forest cities': https://www.theguardian. com/cities/2017/feb/17/forest-cities-radical-plan-china-air-pollution-stefano-boeri.

25 Such endeavours have already begun, for example the Thrive initiatives that started in New York: https://thrivenyc.cityofnewyork.us/. And there is now an extensive literature on creating 'age-friendly' and 'dementia-friendly' cities; see, for example, Buffel et al., 2018.

26 My conception of passionate knowing is drawn from the soon to be published work of Sam McLean on addiction.

27 Many such free, online, facilities are already in existence, though undoubtedly at an early stage: for example, in the UK, Big White Wall: https://www.bigwhitewall.com/; many of them offer online programmes based on Cognitive Behaviour Therapy, such as Silver Clud: see https:// bhws.silvercloudhealth.com/.

28 In Brazil, many of those who worked for the mental health reform that took place in the 1990s were also inspired by Basaglia, but doubted that the strategies that worked in a small city like Trieste could work in a huge and heterogeneous country such as Brazil.

29 Despite the frequent references to Aristotle's eudemonia by those who advocate 'well-being' and 'happiness' as ideals, and who promote technologies to achieve these states, the deployment of these terms in the mental health field today is far too closely associated with the asocial individualism of 'positive psychology' in terms of positive emotions, personal autonomy, rewarding interpersonal relationships and self-realization: see Seligman, 2011; Slade et al., 2017. Indeed, some have argued that notions of 'recovery' and 'well-being' are 'culture-bound' and cannot be transferred to the Global South in any simple manner; see Bayetti et al., 2016; Kalathil et al., 2011. On the banality of 'happiness' as construed in recent positive psychology and associated writings, see Miller, 2008; Shaw and Taplin, 2007.

30 The historian and theorist of the life sciences Georges Canguilhem was fond of quoting this phrase from the French physiologist René Leriche.

31 There is, of course, a huge literature on the capabilities approaches advocated by Nussbaum and Amartya Sen, but this is not the place for an extensive discussion of the strengths and weaknesses of these positions. Some psychiatric service user-researchers are also exploring the potential of capabilities approaches; see Wallcraft and Hopper, 2015.

References

Abadie, R. (2010) *The Professional Guinea Pig: Big Pharma and the Risky World of Human Subjects.* Durham, NC: Duke University Press.

Abbing-Karahagopian, V., Huerta, C., Souverein, P., De Abajo, F., Leufkens, H., Slattery, J., Alvarez, Y., Miret, M., Gil, M. and Oliva, B. (2014) 'Antidepressant Prescribing in Five European Countries: Application of Common Definitions to Assess the Prevalence, Clinical Observations, and Methodological Implications', *European Journal of Clinical Pharmacology*, 70(7), pp. 849–857.

Abbott, A. (2016) 'US Mental Health Chief: Psychiatry Must Get Serious About Mathematics – An Interview with Joshua Gordon', *Nature*, 539(7627). At https://www.nature.com/news/us-mental-health-chief-psychiatry-must-get-serious-about-mathematics-1.20893.

Ahmed, S. (2010a) 'Killing Joy: Feminism and the History of Happiness', *Signs: Journal of Women in Culture and Society*, 35(3), pp. 571–594.

Ahmed, S. (2010b) *The Promise of Happiness.* Durham, NC: Duke University Press.

Ali, M. M. and Zurina, M. (2017) 'A Systematic Review of the Influence of Medical Representatives and Promotional Tools on Prescribing: A Comparison between Developed and Developing Countries', *International Journal of Pharmaceutical and Healthcare Marketing*, 11(4), pp. 361–394.

Almedom, A. M. (2005) 'Social Capital and Mental Health: An Interdisciplinary Review of Primary Evidence', *Social Science & Medicine*, 61(5), pp. 943–964.

Alonso, W. and Starr, P. (eds.) (1987) *The Politics of Numbers.* New York: Russell Sage Foundation.

Alpert, N. M., Badgaiyan, R. D., Livni, E. and Fischman, A. J. (2003) 'A Novel Method for Noninvasive Detection of Neuromodulatory Changes in Specific Neurotransmitter Systems', *Neuroimage*, 19(3), pp. 1049–1060.

American Medico-Psychological Association and National Committee for

Mental Hygiene (1918) *Statistical Manual for the Use of Institutions for the Insane*. New York: National Committee For Mental Hygiene.

Andersen, E. O. (2011) 'Hjernelidelser Er Dyre for Europa', *Politiken*, 2 October.

Andlin- Sobocki, P., Jönsson, B., Wittchen, H.-U. and Olesen, J. (2005) 'Costs of Disorders of the Brain in Europe', *European Journal of Neurology, Special Issue*, 12(Supplement 1), pp. i–vii; 1–90.

Angell, M. (2004) *The Truth About the Drug Companies: How They Deceive Us and What to Do About It*. New York: Random House.

Angell, M. (2011) 'The Epidemic of Mental Illness: Why?', *New York Review of Books*, 58(11), pp. 20–22.

Anthony, W. A. (1993) 'Recovery from Mental Illness: The Guiding Vision of the Mental Health Service System in the 1990s', *Psychosocial Rehabilitation Journal*, 16(4), p. 11.

APA (1952) *Diagnostic and Statistical Manual for Mental Disorders*. Washington, DC: American Psychiatric Association.

APA (1968) *Diagnostic and Statistical Manual of Mental Disorders: DSM-II*. Washington, DC: American Psychiatric Association.

APA (1980) *Diagnostic and Statistical Manual of Mental Disorders: DSM-III*. Washington, DC: American Psychiatric Association.

APA (1994) *Diagnostic and Statistical Manual of Mental Disorders: DSM-IV*. Washington, DC: American Psychiatric Association.

APA (2013) *Diagnostic and Statistical Manual of Mental Disorders: DSM-5*. Arlington, VA: American Psychiatric Association.

Araya, R., Dunstan, F., Playle, R., Thomas, H., Palmer, S. and Lews, G. (2006) 'Perceptions of Social Capital and the Built Environment and Mental Health', *Social Science & Medicine*, 62(12), pp. 3072–3083.

Austin, J. L. (1965) *How to Do Things with Words*. New York: Oxford University Press.

Awenat, F., Berger, B., Coles, S., Dooley, C., Foster, S., Hanna, J., Hemmingfield, J., Johnstone, L., Nadirshaw, Z. and Wainwright, T. (2013) 'Classification of Behaviour and Experience in Relation to Functional Psychiatric Diagnoses: Time for a Paradigm Shift', *Leicester: British Psychological Society*. At http://www.bps.org.uk/system/files/Public%20files/cat-1325.pdf.

Badgaiyan, R. (2013) 'Detection of Dopamine Neurotransmission in "Real Time"', *Frontiers in Neuroscience*, 7(125). At https://doi.org/10.3389/fnins.2013.00125.

Baistow, K. (1994) 'Liberation and Regulation? Some Paradoxes of Empowerment', *Critical Social Policy*, 14(42), pp. 34–46.

Ban, T. A. (2007) 'Fifty Years of Chlorpromazine: A Historical Perspective', *Neuropsychiatric Disease and Treatment*, 3(4), pp. 495–500.

Barker, P., Campbell, P. and Davidson, B. (1999) *From the Ashes of Experience: Reflections on Madness, Survival and Growth*. London: Wiley.

Barr, B., Kinderman, P. and Whitehead, M. (2015) 'Trends in Mental

Health Inequalities in England During a Period of Recession, Austerity and Welfare Reform 2004 to 2013', *Social Science & Medicine*, 147, pp. 324–331.

Baruch, G. and Treacher, A. (1978) *Psychiatry Observed*. London: Routledge & Kegan Paul.

Basaglia, F. (1968) *L'Istituzione Negata. (Rapporto Da Un Ospedale Psichiatrico.) a Cura Di Franco Basaglia. [by Various Contributors.]*. Torino: Baldini & Castoldi.

Basaglia, F., Scheper-Hughes, N. and Lovell, A. (1987) *Psychiatry Inside Out: Selected Writings of Franco Basaglia*. New York: Columbia University Press.

Bayer, R. (1981) *Homosexuality and American Psychiatry: The Politics of Diagnosis*. Princeton, NJ: Princeton University Press.

Bayer, R. and Spitzer, R. L. (1985) 'Neurosis, Psychodynamics, and DSM-III – a History of the Controversy', *Archives of General Psychiatry*, 42(2), pp. 187–196.

Bayetti, C., Jadhav, S. and Jain, S. (2016) 'The Re-Covering Self: A Critique of the Recovery-Based Approach in India's Mental Health Care', *Disability and the Global South*, 3(1), pp. 889–909.

Beaulieu, A. (2000a) 'The Brain at the End of the Rainbow: The Promise of Brain Scans in the Research Field and in the Media', in Marchessault, J. and Sawchuk, K. (eds.), *Wild Science: Reading Feminism, Medicine and the Media*. London: Routledge, pp. 39–54.

Beaulieu, A. (2000b) *The Space inside the Skull: Digital Representations, Brain Mapping and Cognitive Neuroscience in the Decade of the Brain*. PhD dissertation, University of Amsterdam.

Beaulieu, A. (2002) 'Images Are Not the (Only) Truth: Brain Mapping, Visual Knowledge and Iconoclasm', *Science, Technology and Human Values*, 27(1), pp. 53–86.

Beck, A. T. (1962) 'Reliability of Psychiatric Diagnoses: 1. A Critique of Systematic Studies', *American Journal of Psychiatry*, 119(3), pp. 210–216.

Becker, H. S. (1963) *Outsiders: Studies in the Sociology of Deviance*. New York: Free Press.

Beers, C. W. (1908) *A Mind that Found Itself. An Autobiography*. London: Longmans & Co.

Bemme, D. and D'souza, N. A. (2014) 'Global Mental Health and Its Discontents: An Inquiry into the Making of Global and Local Scale', *Transcultural Psychiatry*, 51(6), pp. 850–874.

Berardi, F. (2001) *La Fabbrica dell'Infelicità* [*'The Factory of Unhappiness'*]. Rome: Derive Approdi.

Berardi, F. (2009) *The Soul at Work: From Alienation to Autonomy*. Los Angeles, CA: Semiotext(e).

Beresford, P. (2000) 'Service Users' Knowledges and Social Work Theory: Conflict or Collaboration?', *The British Journal of Social Work*, 30(4), pp. 489–503.

Beresford, P. (2002) 'User Involvement in Research and Evaluation: Liberation or Regulation?', *Social Policy and Society*, 1(2), pp. 95–106.

Beresford, P. and Wallcraft, J. (1997) 'Psychiatric System Survivors and Emancipatory Research: Issues, Overlaps and Differences', in Barnes, C. and Mercer, G. (eds.), *Doing Disability Research*. Leeds: The Disability Press/University of Leeds, pp. 67–87.

Bernard, C. (1957 [1878]) *An Introduction to the Study of Experimental Medicine, with an Introduction by L. J. Henderson and a Foreword by I. B. Cohen*, trans. Greene, H. C. New York: Dover.

Bhugra, D., Tasman, A., Pathare, S., Priebe, S., Smith, S., Torous, J., Arbuckle, M. R., Langford, A., Alarcón, R. D. and Chiu, H. F. K. (2017) 'The WPA-Lancet Psychiatry Commission on the Future of Psychiatry', *The Lancet Psychiatry*, 4(10), pp. 775–818.

Bonnington, O. and Rose, D. (2014) 'Exploring Stigmatisation among People Diagnosed with either Bipolar Disorder or Borderline Personality Disorder: A Critical Realist Analysis', *Social Science & Medicine*, 123, pp. 7–17.

Bowker, G. C. and Star, S. L. (1999) *Sorting Things Out: Classification and Its Consequences. Inside Technology*. Cambridge, MA: MIT Press.

Bracken, P., Giller, J. and Summerfield, D. (2016) 'Primum Non Nocere. The Case for a Critical Approach to Global Mental Health', *Epidemiology and Psychiatric Sciences*, 25(6), pp. 506–510.

Bracken, P. and Thomas, P. (2001) 'Postpsychiatry: A New Direction for Mental Health', *British Medical Journal*, 322(7288), pp. 724–727.

Bracken, P., Thomas, P., Timimi, S., Asen, E., Behr, G., Beuster, C., Bhunnoo, S., Browne, I., Chhina, N. and Double, D. (2012) 'Psychiatry Beyond the Current Paradigm', *The British Journal of Psychiatry*, 201(6), pp. 430–434.

Brijnath, B. and Antoniades, J. (2016) '"I'm Running My Depression." Self-Management of Depression in Neoliberal Australia', *Social Science & Medicine*, 152, pp. 1–8.

Broberg, G. and Roll-Hansen, N. (1996) *Eugenics and the Welfare State: Sterilization Policy in Denmark, Sweden, Norway, and Finland*. East Lansing: Michigan State University Press.

Brown, B. J. and Baker, S. (2012) *Responsible Citizens: Individuals, Health, and Policy under Neoliberalism*. London: Anthem Press.

Brown, G. W. and Harris, T. (1978) *Social Origins of Depression: A Study of Psychiatric Disorder in Women*. London: Tavistock.

Buchanan, A. and Grounds, A. (2011) 'Forensic Psychiatry and Public Protection', *The British Journal of Psychiatry*, 198(6), pp. 420–423.

Bucknill, J. C. and Tuke, D. H. (1874) *A Manual of Psychological Medicine, by John Charles Bucknill and Daniel Tuke*. Third edition, revised . . . and much enlarged. London: X. J. & A. Churchill.

Buffel, T., Handler, S. and Phillipson, C. (2018) 'Age-Friendly Cities and

Communities: A Manifesto for Change', in Buffel, T., Handler, S. and Phillipson, C. (eds.), *Age-Friendly Communities: A Global Perspective*. Bristol: Policy Press.

Burki, T. (2017) 'China Faces Challenges to Fix Its Pharmaceutical System', *The Lancet*, 389(10067), pp. 353–354.

Burleigh, M. (1994) *Death and Deliverance: 'Euthanasia' in Germany c.1900–1945*. Cambridge: Cambridge University Press.

Burns, J. (2015) 'Poverty, Inequality and a Political Economy of Mental Health', *Epidemiology and Psychiatric Sciences*, 24(02), pp. 107–113.

Burri, R. and Dumit, J. (2007) 'Social Studies of Scientific Imaging and Visualization', in Hackett, E. J., Amsterdamska, O., Lynch, M. and Wajcman, J. (eds.), *Handbook of Science and Technology Studies*. Cambridge, MA: MIT Press, pp. 297–317.

Burstow, B. (2015) *Psychiatry and the Business of Madness: An Ethical and Epistemological Accounting*. New York: Palgrave.

Cacioppo, J. T. and Berntson, G. G. (1992) 'Social Psychological Contributions to the Decade of the Brain. Doctrine of Multilevel Analysis', *American Psychologist*, 47(8), pp. 1019–1028.

Cacioppo, J. T. and Patrick, W. (2008) *Loneliness: Human Nature and the Need for Social Connection*. New York: W. W. Norton.

Cacioppo, S., Capitanio, J. P. and Cacioppo, J. T. (2014) 'Toward a Neurology of Loneliness', *Psychological Bulletin*, 140(6), pp. 146–504.

Caldwell, A. E. (1970) *Origins of Psychopharmacology: From CPZ to LSD*. New York: Thomas.

Campbell, C. and Burgess, R. (2012) 'The Role of Communities in Advancing the Goals of the Movement for Global Mental Health', *Transcultural Psychiatry*, 49(3–4), pp. 379–395.

Campbell, J. (2005) 'The Historical and Philosophical Development of Peer-Run Support Programs', in Clay, S. (ed.), *On Our Own, Together: Peer Programs For People With Mental Illness*. Nashville, TN: Vanderbilt University Press, pp. 17–64.

Campbell, P. (1985) 'From Little Acorns. The Mental Health Service User Movement', in Sainsbury Centre for Mental Health (ed.), *Beyond the Water Towers. The Unfinished Revolution in Mental Health Services*. London: Sainsbury Centre for Mental Health.

Campbell, P. (1996) 'The History of the User Movement in the United Kingdom', in Gomm, R., Heller, T., Muston, R., Pattison, S., and Reynolds, J. (eds.), *Mental Health Matters: A Reader*. London: Palgrave, pp. 218–225.

Campbell, P. and Rose, D. (2010) 'Action for Change in the UK: Thirty Years of the User/Survivor Movement', *SAGE Handbook of Mental Health and Illness*, London: Sage, pp. 452.

Campion, J., Bhugra, D., Bailey, S. and Marmot, M. (2013) 'Inequality and Mental Disorders: Opportunities for Action', *The Lancet*, 382(9888), pp. 183–184.

Canguilhem, G. (1968) *Études d'Histoire et de Philosophie des Sciences. Problèmes et Controverses.* Paris: Vrin.

Canguilhem, G. (1978) *On the Normal and the Pathological,* trans. Fawcett, C. R. Dordrecht: Reidel.

Cannon, W. B. (1914) 'The Emergency Function of the Adrenal Medulla in Pain and the Major Emotions', *American Journal of Physiology,* 33(2), pp. 356–372.

Carlson, E. D. and Chamberlain, R. M. (2003) 'Social Capital, Health, and Health Disparities', *Journal of Nursing Scholarship,* 35(4), pp. 325–331.

Carlsson, A. (2001) 'A Paradigm Shift in Brain Research', *Science,* 294(5544), pp. 1021–1024.

Castel, F., Lovell, A. and Castel, R. (1979) *La Société Psychiatrique Avancée: Le Modèle Américain.* Paris: Bernard Grasset.

Chamberlin, J. (1978) *On Our Own: Patient-Controlled Alternatives to the Mental Health System.* New York: Hawthorn Books.

Chamberlin, J. (1990) 'The Ex-Patients' Movement: Where We've Been and Where We're Going', *The Journal of Mind and Behavior, Special Issue: Challenging the Therapeutic State: Critical Perspectives on Psychiatry and the Mental Health System,* 11(3/4), pp. 323–336.

Chamberlin, J. (2005) 'User/Consumer Involvement in Mental Health Service Delivery', *Epidemiology and Psychiatric Sciences,* 14(1), pp. 10–14.

Charlson, F. J., Baxter, A. J., Cheng, H. G., Shidhaye, R. and Whiteford, H. A. (2016) 'The Burden of Mental, Neurological, and Substance Use Disorders in China and India: A Systematic Analysis of Community Representative Epidemiological Studies', *The Lancet,* 388(10042), pp. 376–389.

Charlton, J. I. (1998) *Nothing About Us without Us: Disability Oppression and Empowerment.* Berkeley: University of California Press.

Chee, K. Y., Tripathi, A., Avasthi, A., Chong, M. Y., Sim, K., Yang, S. Y., Glover, S., Xiang, Y. T., Si, T. M. and Kanba, S. (2015) 'International Study on Antidepressant Prescription Pattern at 40 Major Psychiatric Institutions and Hospitals in Asia: A 10-Year Comparison Study', *Asia-Pacific Psychiatry,* 7(4), pp. 366–374.

Chesler, P. (1972) *Women and Madness.* Garden City, NY: Doubleday.

Cipriani, A., Furukawa, T. A., et al. (2018). 'Comparative Efficacy and Acceptability of 21 Antidepressant Drugs for the Acute Treatment of Adults with Major Depressive Disorder: A Systematic Review and Network Meta-Analysis.' *The Lancet,* 21 February. At http://www.thelan cet.com/journals/lancet/article/PIIS0140-6736(17)32802-7/fulltext.

Clare, A. W. (1976) *Psychiatry in Dissent: Controversial Issues in Thought and Practice.* London: Tavistock Publications.

Clay, S. (2005) *On Our Own, Together: Peer Programs for People with Mental Illness.* Nashville, TN: Vanderbilt University Press.

Cohen, A., Eaton, J., Radtke, B., De Menil, V., Chatterjee, S., Da Silva, M. and Patel, V. (2012a) *Case Study Methodology to Monitor & Evaluate*

Community Mental Health Programs in Low-Income Countries, London: London School of Hygiene and Tropical Medicine.

Cohen, A., Patel, V. and Minas, H. (2014) 'A Brief History of Global Mental Health', in Cohen, A., Patel, V., Minas, H. and Prince, M. J., *Global Mental Health: Principles and Practice*. Oxford: Oxford University Press, pp. 3–26.

Cohen, A., Raja, S., Underhill, C., Yaro, B. P., Dokurugu, A. Y., De Silva, M. and Patel, V. (2012b) 'Sitting with Others: Mental Health Self-Help Groups in Northern Ghana', *International Journal of Mental Health Systems*, 6(1), p. 1.

Cohen, C. I. and Timimi, S. (2008) *Liberatory Psychiatry: Philosophy, Politics and Mental Health*. Cambridge: Cambridge University Press.

Cohen, S. and Janicki-Deverts, D. (2012) 'Who's Stressed? Distributions of Psychological Stress in the United States in Probability Samples from 1983, 2006, and 2009', *Journal of Applied Social Psychology*, 42(6), pp. 1320–1334.

Cohn, S. (2008) 'Making Objective Facts from Intimate Relations: The Case of Neuroscience and Its Entanglements with Volunteers', *History of the Human Sciences*, 21(4), p. 86.

Coleman, J. S. (1988) 'Social Capital in the Creation of Human Capital', *American Journal of Sociology*, 94, pp. S95–S120.

Collins, P. Y., Patel, V., Joestl, S. S., March, D., Insel, T. R., Daar, A. S., Bordin, I. A., Costello, . . . and Walport, M. (2011) 'Grand Challenges in Global Mental Health', *Nature*, 475(7354), pp. 27–30.

Conrad, P. (2005) 'The Shifting Engines of Medicalization', *Journal of Health and Social Behavior*, 46(1), pp. 3–14.

Conrad, P. and Schneider, J. W. (1992) *Deviance and Medicalization: From Badness to Sickness: With a New Afterword by the Authors*. Philadelphia, PA: Temple University Press.

Cooper, R. (2004) 'What Is Wrong with the *DSM*?', *History of Psychiatry*, 15(57), pp. 5–25.

Craig, P., Dieppe, P., Macintyre, S., Michie, S., Nazareth, I. and Petticrew, M. (2008) 'Developing and Evaluating Complex Interventions: The New Medical Research Council Guidance', *British Medical Journal*, 337, p. a1655.

Crawley, J. N. (2007) *What's Wrong with My Mouse? Behavioral Phenotyping of Transgenic and Knockout Mice*. New York: Wiley.

Cruikshank, B. (1993) 'Revolutions Within: Self-Government and Self-Esteem', *Economy and Society*, 22(3), pp. 327–344.

Cruikshank, B. (1999) *The Will to Empower: Democratic Citizens and Other Subjects*. Ithaca, NY: Cornell University Press.

Cutting, G. (1987) 'Gaston Bachelard's Philosophy of Science', *International Studies in the Philosophy of Science*, 2(1), pp. 55–71.

Damasio, A. R. (1995) *Descartes' Error: Emotion, Reason, and the Human Brain*. New York: Avon Books.

Damiani, G., Federico, B., Silvestrini, G., Bianchi, C. B. N. A., Anselmi, A., Iodice, L., Ronconi, A., Navarra, P., Da Cas, R. and Raschetti, R. (2013) 'Impact of Regional Copayment Policy on Selective Serotonin Reuptake Inhibitor (SSRI) Consumption and Expenditure in Italy', *European Journal of Clinical Pharmacology*, 69(4), pp. 957–963.

Dannenberg, A. L., Jackson, R. J., Frumkin, H., Schieber, R. A., Pratt, M., Kochtitzky, C. and Tilson, H. H. (2003) 'The Impact of Community Design and Land-Use Choices on Public Health: A Scientific Research Agenda', *American Journal of Public Health*, 93(9), pp. 1500–1508.

Dantzer, R., O'Connor, J. C., Freund, G. G., Johnson, R. W. and Kelley, K. W. (2008) 'From Inflammation to Sickness and Depression: When the Immune System Subjugates the Brain', *Nature Reviews Neuroscience*, 9(1), pp. 46–56.

Davar, B. V. (2008) 'From Mental Illness to Disability', *Indian Journal of Gender Studies*, 15(2), pp. 261–290.

De Angelis, C., Drazen, J. M., Frizelle, F. A., Haug, C., Hoey, J., Horton, R., Kotzin, S., Laine, C., Marusic, A. and Overbeke, A. J. P. (2004). 'Clinical Trial Registration: A Statement from the International Committee of Medical Journal Editors', *New England Journal of Medicine*, 351, pp. 1250–1251.

De Silva, M. J., McKenzie, K., Harpham, T. and Huttly, S. R. (2005) 'Social Capital and Mental Illness: A Systematic Review', *Journal of Epidemiology and Community Health*, 59(8), pp. 619–627.

Deacon, A. (2003) '"Levelling the Playing Field, Activating the Players": New Labour and "the Cycle of Disadvantage"', *Policy & Politics*, 31(2), pp. 123–137.

Deegan, P. E. (1997) 'Recovery and Empowerment for People with Psychiatric Disabilities', *Social Work in Health Care*, 25(3), pp. 11–24.

Deleuze, G. (1992) 'Postscript on the Societies of Control', *October*, 59, pp. 3–7.

Desjarlais, R. R. (1995) *World Mental Health: Problems and Priorities in Low-Income Countries*. Oxford: Oxford University Press.

Deutsch, A. (1948) *The Shame of the States*. New York: Harcourt.

Devaney, J., Donarum, E., Brown, K., Meyer, J., Stöber, G., Lesch, K., Nestadt, G., Stephan, D. and Pulver, A. (2002) 'No Missense Mutation of WKL1 in a Subgroup of Probands with Schizophrenia', *Molecular Psychiatry*, 7(4), p. 419.

DHSS (1979) *Patients First: Consultative Paper on the Structure and Management of the National Health Service in England and Wales*. London: HMSO.

Didi-Huberman, G. and Charcot, J. M. (2003) *The Invention of Hysteria: Charcot and the Photographic Iconography of the Salpetriere*. Cambridge, MA: MIT Press.

Dikötter, F. (1998) *Imperfect Conceptions: Medical Knowledge, Birth Defects, and Eugenics in China*. New York: Columbia University Press.

Double, D. (2007) 'Adolf Meyer's Psychobiology and the Challenge for Biomedicine', *Philosophy, Psychiatry, & Psychology*, 14(4), pp. 331–339.

Dowbiggin, I. R. (1997) *Keeping America Sane: Psychiatry and Eugenics in the United States and Canada, 1880–1940*. Cornell Studies in the History of Psychiatry. Ithaca, NY: Cornell University Press.

Drain, P. K., Robine, M., Holmes, K. K. and Bassett, I. V. (2014) 'Trial Watch: Global Migration of Clinical Trials', *Nature Reviews Drug Discovery*, 13(3), pp. 166–167.

Dumit, J. (1999) 'Objective Brains, Prejudicial Images', *Science In Context*, 12(1), pp. 173–201.

Dumit, J. (2003) *Picturing Personhood: Brain Scans and Biomedical Identity*. Princeton, NJ: Princeton University Press.

Ecks, S. (2005) 'Pharmaceutical Citizenship: Antidepressant Marketing and the Promise of Demarginalization in India', *Anthropology & Medicine*, 12(3), pp. 239–254.

Ecks, S. (2013) *Eating Drugs: Psychopharmaceutical Pluralism in India*. New York: New York University Press.

Ecks, S. (2016) 'Commentary: Ethnographic Critiques of Global Mental Health', *Transcultural Psychiatry*, 53(6), pp. 804–808.

Ecks, S. and Basu, S. (2014) '"We Always Live in Fear": Antidepressant Prescriptions by Unlicensed Doctors in India', *Culture, Medicine, and Psychiatry*, 38(2), pp. 197–216.

Edwards, B., Foley, M. W. and Diani, M. (2001) *Beyond Tocqueville: Civil Society and the Social Capital Debate in Comparative Perspective*. Lebanon, NH: University Press of New England.

Ehsan, A. M. and De Silva, M. J. (2015) 'Social Capital and Common Mental Disorder: A Systematic Review', *Journal of Epidemiology and Community Health*, 69(10), pp. 1021–1028.

Elston, R. C. and Campbell, M. A. (1970) 'Schizophrenia: Evidence for the Major Gene Hypothesis', *Behavior Genetics*, 1(1), pp. 3–10.

Engel, G. L. (1977) 'The Need for a New Medical Model: A Challenge for Biomedicine', *Science*, 196(4286), pp. 129–136.

Epstein, S. (2008) 'Patient Groups and Health Movements', *The Handbook of Science and Technology Studies*, 3, pp. 499–539.

Epstein, S. (2011) 'Measuring Success Scientific, Institutional, and Cultural Effects of Patient Advocacy', in Hoffman, B., Tomes, N., Grob, R. and Schlesinger, R. (eds.), *Patients as Policy Actors*. New Brunswick, NJ: Rutgers University Press.

Esposito, L. and Perez, F. M. (2014) 'Neoliberalism and the Commodification of Mental Health', *Humanity & Society*, 38(4), pp. 414–442.

Esquirol, J. E. D. (1838) *Des Maladies Mentales, Considerées Sous les Rapports Médical, Hygiénique et Médico-Legal . . . Accompagnées de 27 Planches Gravées* (2 vols.). Paris: Baillière.

Evans-Lacko, S., Courtin, E., Fiorillo, A., Knapp, M., Luciano, M., Park,

A.-L., Brunn, M., Byford, S., Chevreul, K. and Forsman, A. (2014) 'The State of the Art in European Research on Reducing Social Exclusion and Stigma Related to Mental Health: A Systematic Mapping of the Literature', *European Psychiatry*, 29(6), pp. 381–389.

Faulkner, A. (2017a) 'Radical Change or Warm Sentiments', *Social Psychiatry and Psychiatric Epidemiology*, 52, pp. 777–779.

Faulkner, A. (2017b) 'Survivor Research and Mad Studies: The Role and Value of Experiential Knowledge in Mental Health Research', *Disability & Society*, 32(4), pp. 500–520.

Faulkner, A. and Layzell, S. (2000) *Strategies for Living: A Report of User-Led Research into People's Strategies for Living with Mental Distress.* London: Mental Health Foundation.

Faulkner, A. and Thomas, P. (2002) *User-Led Research and Evidence-Based Medicine.* London: Royal College of Psychiatry.

Feighner, J. P., Robins, E., Guze, S. B., Woodruff, R. A., Jr., Winokur, G. and Munoz, R. (1972) 'Diagnostic Criteria for Use in Psychiatric Research', *Archives of General Psychiatry*, 26(1), pp. 57–63.

Feinstein, A. R. (1967) *Clinical Judgment.* Baltimore, MD: Williams & Wilkins.

Fibiger, H. C. (2012) 'Psychiatry, the Pharmaceutical Industry, and the Road to Better Therapeutics', *Schizophrenia Bulletin*, 8(4), pp. 649–650.

Fisher, M. (2009) *Capitalist Realism: Is There No Alternative?* Ropley, UK: O Books.

Fleck, L. (1979 [1935]) *Genesis and Development of a Scientific Fact.* Chicago: Chicago University Press.

Flett, G. L. and Hewitt, P. L. (2014) 'A Proposed Framework for Preventing Perfectionism and Promoting Resilience and Mental Health among Vulnerable Children and Adolescents', *Psychology in the Schools*, 51(9), pp. 899–912.

Foucault, M. (1961) *Folie et Déraison. Histoire de la Folie à l'Âge Classique.* Paris: Plon.

Foucault, M. (1967) *Madness and Civilization: A History of Insanity in the Age of Reason.* London: Tavistock.

Frances, A. (2013) *Saving Normal: An Insider's Revolt against out-of-Control Psychiatric Diagnosis, DSM-5, Big Pharma, and the Medicalization of Ordinary Life.* New York: William Morrow.

Frances, A. and Cooper, A. M. (1981) 'Descriptive and Dynamic Psychiatry: A Perspective on DSM-III', *American Journal of Psychiatry*, 138(9), pp. 1198–1202.

Francis, E. (2016) 'Fanon, Photography, and the Limits of Social Marketing Campaigns', *Philosophy, Psychiatry, & Psychology*, 23(3), pp. 257–260.

Friedman, T. T., Rolfe, P. and Perry, S. E. (1960) 'Home Treatment of Psychiatric Patients', *American Journal of Psychiatry*, 116(9), pp. 807–809.

Frissen, A., Lieverse, R., Drukker, M., van Winkel, R., Delespaul, P. and Investigators, G. (2015) 'Childhood Trauma and Childhood Urbanicity in Relation to Psychotic Disorder', *Social Psychiatry and Psychiatric Epidemiology*, 50(10), pp. 1481–1488.

Fryers, T., Melzer, D. and Jenkins, R. (2003) 'Social Inequalities and the Common Mental Disorders', *Social Psychiatry and Psychiatric Epidemiology*, 38(5), pp. 229–237.

Fryers, T., Melzer, D., Jenkins, R. and Brugha, T. (2005) 'The Distribution of the Common Mental Disorders: Social Inequalities in Europe', *Clinical Practice and Epidemiology in Mental Health*, 1(1), p. 14.

Gaines, A. (1992) 'From DSM-I to III-R; Voices of Self, Mastery and the Other: A Cultural Constructivist Reading of US Psychiatric Classification', *Social Science & Medicine*, 35(1), pp. 3–24.

Galea, S. and Link, B. G. (2013) 'Six Paths for the Future of Social Epidemiology', *American Journal of Epidemiology*, 178(6), pp. 843–849.

Galton, F. (1904) 'Eugenics: Its Definition, Scope, and Aims', *American Journal of Sociology*, 10(1), pp. 1–25.

Gelder, M. G. (1996) *Oxford Textbook of Psychiatry*, 3rd edn. Oxford: Oxford University Press.

Gelman, S. (1999) *Medicating Schizophrenia: A History*. New Brunswick, NJ: Rutgers University Press.

Genovese, G., Fromer, M., Stahl, E. A., Ruderfer, D. M., Chambert, K., Landén, M., Moran, J. L., Purcell, S. M., Sklar, P. and Sullivan, P. F. (2016) 'Increased Burden of Ultra-Rare Protein-Altering Variants among 4,877 Individuals with Schizophrenia', *Nature Neuroscience*, 19(11), pp. 1433–1441.

Giacco, D., Amering, M., Bird, V., Craig, T., Ducci, G., Gallinat, J., Gillard, S. G., Greacen, T., Hadridge, P. and Johnson, S. (2017) 'Scenarios for the Future of Mental Health Care: A Social Perspective', *The Lancet Psychiatry*, 4(3), pp. 257–260.

Gilman, S. (1982) *Seeing the Insane*. New York: Wiley.

Goffman, E. (1959) 'The Moral Career of the Mental Patient', *Psychiatry*, 22(2), pp. 123–42.

Goffman, E. (1961) *Asylums: Essays on the Social Situation of Mental Patients and Other Inmates*. Garden City, NY: Anchor Books.

Goldacre, B. (2012) *Bad Pharma: How Medicine Is Broken, and How We Can Fix It*. London: HarperCollins UK.

Goldberg, D. and Huxley, P. (2003) *Mental Illness in the Community: The Pathway to Psychiatric Care*. Hove, UK: Psychology Press.

Goldstein, K. (1939) *The Organism*. New York: American Book Co.

Goldstein, K. (1995 [1939]) *The Organism: A Holistic Approach to Biology Derived from Pathological Data in Man*. London: MIT Press.

Gottesman, I. I. and Shields, J. (1972) 'A Polygenic Theory of Schizophrenia', *International Journal of Mental Health*, 1(1–2), pp. 107–115.

Granovetter, M. S. (1973) 'The Strength of Weak Ties', *American Journal of Sociology*, 78(6), pp. 1360–1380.

Gratten, J. (2016) 'Rare Variants Are Common in Schizophrenia', *Nature Neuroscience*, 19(11), pp. 1426–1428.

Greco, M. (2005) 'On the Vitality of Vitalism', *Theory, Culture & Society*, 22(1), pp. 15–27.

Greenhalgh, T. (1998) 'Getting Your Bearings (Deciding What the Paper Is About)', *Student British Medical Journal*, 6, pp. 21–24.

Grey, F. (2016) 'Benevolent Othering: Speaking Positively About Mental Health Service Users', *Philosophy, Psychiatry, & Psychology*, 23(3), pp. 241–251.

Griesinger, W., Robertson, C. A. L. and Rutherford, J. M. D. (1867) *Mental Pathology and Therapeutics Translated from the German . . . By C. L. Robertson . . . And J. Rutherford*. London.

Grob, G. N. (1991a) *From Asylum to Community: Mental Health Policy in Modern America*. Princeton, NJ: Princeton University Press.

Grob, G. N. (1991b) 'Origins of DSM I. A Study in Appearance and Reality', *American Journal of Psychiatry*, 148(4), pp. 421–431.

Grob, G. N. (2005) 'Public Policy and Mental Illnesses: Jimmy Carter's Presidential Commission on Mental Health', *The Milbank Quarterly*, 83(3), pp. 425–456.

Grotberg, E. H. (1995) *A Guide to Promoting Resilience in Children: Strengthening the Human Spirit*. The Hague: Bernard van Leer Foundation.

Gustavsson, A., Svensson, M., Jacobi, F., Allgulander, C., Alonso, J., Beghi, E., Dodel, R., Ekman, M., Faravelli, C. and Fratiglioni, L. (2011) 'Cost of Disorders of the Brain in Europe 2010', *European Neuropsychopharmacology*, 21(10), pp. 718–779.

Guyatt, G. H., Sackett, D. L., Sinclair, J. C., Hayward, R., Cook, D. J., Cook, R. J., Bass, E., Gerstein, H., Haynes, B. and Holbrook, A. (1995) 'Users' Guides to the Medical Literature: IX. A Method for Grading Health Care Recommendations', *Journal of the American Medical Association*, 274(22), pp. 1800–1804.

Haag, A. L. (2007) 'Biomarkers Trump Behavior in Mental Illness Diagnosis', *Nature Medicine*, 13(1), p. 3.

Hacking, I. (2004) 'Between Michel Foucault and Erving Goffman: Between Discourse in the Abstract and Face-to-Face Interaction', *Economy and Society*, 33(3), pp. 277–302.

Hacking, I. (2005) 'The Cartesian Vision Fulfilled: Analogue Bodies and Digital Minds', *Interdisciplinary Science Reviews*, 30(2), pp. 153–166.

Hacking, I. (2007) 'Our Neo-Cartesian Bodies in Parts', *Critical Inquiry*, 34(1), pp. 78–105.

Haddad, P. M. and Sharma, S. G. (2007) 'Adverse Effects of Atypical Antipsychotics', *CNS Drugs*, 21(11), pp. 911–936.

Harper, D. and Speed, E. (2012) 'Uncovering Recovery: The Resistible Rise of Recovery and Resilience', *Studies in Social Justice*, 6(1), pp. 9–25.

Healy, D. (1996) *The Psychopharmacologists: Interviews by David Healy.* London: Chapman and Hall.

Healy, D. (1998) 'Pioneers in Psychopharmacology', *International Journal of Neuropsychopharmacology*, 1(2), pp. 191–194.

Healy, D. (2000) 'Pioneers in Psychopharmacology II', *International Journal of Neuropsychopharmacology*, 3(4), pp. 351–354.

Healy, D. (2001) *The Creation of Psychopharmacology.* Cambridge, MA: Harvard University Press.

Healy, D. (2004) *Let Them Eat Prozac: The Unhealthy Relationship between the Pharmaceutical Industry and Depression. Medicine, Culture, and History.* New York: New York University Press.

Henderson, S. and Whiteford, H. (2003) 'Social Capital and Mental Health', *The Lancet*, 362(9383), pp. 505–506.

Hodgkin, D., Thomas, C. P., O'Brien, P. L., Levit, K., Richardson, J., Mark, T. L. and Malone, K. (2016) 'Projected Spending on Psychotropic Medications 2013–2020', *Administration and Policy in Mental Health and Mental Health Services Research*, 43(4), pp. 497–505.

Hoffman, L. (2011) 'Urban Modeling and Contemporary Technologies of City-Building in China', in Roy, A. and Ong, A. (eds.), *Worlding Cities: Asian Experiments and the Art of Being Global.* Chichester: Wiley, pp. 55–76.

Horton, R. (2007) 'Launching a New Movement for Mental Health', *The Lancet*, 370(9590), p. 806.

Horwitz, A. V. and Wakefield, J. C. (2007) *The Loss of Sadness: How Psychiatry Transformed Normal Sorrow into Depressive Disorder.* Oxford: Oxford University Press.

Houts, A. C. (2000) 'Fifty Years of Psychiatric Nomenclature: Reflections on the 1943 War Department Technical Bulletin, Medical 203', *Journal of Clinical Psychology*, 56(7), pp. 935–967.

Howell, A. and Voronka, J. (2012) 'The Politics of Resilience and Recovery in Mental Health Care', *Studies in Social Justice*, 6(1), pp. 1–7.

Hyman, S. E. (2003) 'Diagnosing Disorders', *Scientific American*, 289(3), pp. 96–103.

Hyman, S. E. (2008) 'A Glimmer of Light for Neuropsychiatric Disorders', *Nature*, 455(7215), pp. 890–893.

Hyman, S. E. (2010) 'The Diagnosis of Mental Disorders: The Problem of Reification', *Annual Review of Clinical Psychology*, 6, pp. 155–179.

Hyman, S. E. (2012) 'Revolution Stalled', *Science Translational Medicine*, 4(155), pp. 155cm11.

Ilyas, S. and Moncrieff, J. (2012) 'Trends in Prescriptions and Costs of Drugs for Mental Disorders in England, 1998–2010', *The British Journal of Psychiatry*, 200(5), pp. 393–398.

Ingleby, D. (1981) *Critical Psychiatry: The Politics of Mental Health.* Harmondsworth, UK: Penguin.

Ingleby, D. (2014) 'How 'Evidence-Based' is the Movement for Global Mental Health?', *Disability and the Global South*, 1(2), pp. 203–226.

Insel, T. (2012) 'The Top Ten Research Advances of 2012', *National Institute of Mental Health Director's Blog*. At https://www.nimh.nih.gov/about/directors/thomas-insel/blog/2012/the-top-ten-research-advances-of-2012.shtml.

Insel, T. R. (2014) 'The NIMH Research Domain Criteria (RDoC) Project: Precision Medicine for Psychiatry', *American Journal of Psychiatry*, 171(4), pp. 395–397.

Insel, T. R. and Quirion, R. (2005) 'Psychiatry as a Clinical Neuroscience Discipline', *Journal of the American Medical Association*, 294(17), pp. 2221–2224.

Jablensky, A. (2010) 'The Diagnostic Concept of Schizophrenia: Its History, Evolution, and Future Prospects', *Dialogues in Clinical Neuroscience*, 12(3), pp. 271–287.

Jackson, L. E. (2003) 'The Relationship of Urban Design to Human Health and Condition', *Landscape and Urban Planning*, 64(4), pp. 191–200.

Jackson, M. (2013) *The Age of Stress: Science and the Search for Stability.* Oxford: Oxford University Press.

Jacob, K. and Patel, V. (2014) 'Classification of Mental Disorders: A Global Mental Health Perspective', *The Lancet*, 383(9926), pp. 1433–1435.

Johnstone, L., Boyle, M., Cromby, J., Dillon, J., Harper, D., Kinderman, P., Longden, E., Pilgrim, D. and Read, J. (2018) *The Power Threat Meaning Framework: Towards the Identification of Patterns in Emotional Distress, Unusual Experiences and Troubled or Troubling Behaviour, as an Alternative to Functional Psychiatric Diagnosis.* Leicester: British Psychological Society.

Jones, K. (1972) *A History of the Mental Health Services.* London: Routledge & Kegan Paul.

Jutel, A. and Nettleton, S. (2011) 'Towards a Sociology of Diagnosis: Reflections and Opportunities', *Social Science & Medicine*, 73(6), pp. 793–800.

Kaddis, A. A. (2013) 'Trends in the 2013 Pharmaceutical Pipeline'. *American Health and Drug Benefits*, 6(3). At http://www.ahdbonline.com/issues/2013/april-2013-vol-6-no-3-payers-guide-to-new-fda-approvals/1387-article-1387.

Kaganovich, M., Peretz, A., Ritsner, M., Bening Abu-Shach, U., Attali, B. and Navon, R. (2004) 'Is the WKL1 Gene Associated with Schizophrenia?', *American Journal of Medical Genetics Part B: Neuropsychiatric Genetics*, 125(1), pp. 31–37.

Kalathil, J., Collier, B., Bhakta, R., Daniel, O., Joseph, D. and Trivedi, P. (2011) *Recovery and Resilience: African, African-Caribbean and South Asian Women's Narratives of Recovering from Mental Distress.* London: Mental Health Foundation.

Kallmann, F. J. (1938) *The Genetics of Schizophrenia.* Oxford: Augustin.

Kallmann, F. J. (1946) 'The Genetic Theory of Schizophrenia: An Analysis of 691 Schizophrenic Twin Index Families', *American Journal of Psychiatry*, 103(3), pp. 309–322.

Kamat, V. R. (2014) 'Fast, Cheap, and Out of Control? Speculations and Ethical Concerns in the Conduct of Outsourced Clinical Trials in India', *Social Science & Medicine*, 104, pp. 48–55.

Kawachi, I. and Berkman, L. F. (2001) 'Social Ties and Mental Health', *Journal of Urban Health*, 78(3), pp. 458–467.

Kawachi, I., Kennedy, B. P. and Glass, R. (1999) 'Social Capital and Self-Rated Health: A Contextual Analysis', *American Journal of Public Health*, 89(8), pp. 1187–1193.

Kay, L. E. (1993) *The Molecular Vision of Life: Caltech, the Rockefeller Foundation, and the Rise of the New Biology.* New York: Oxford University Press.

Kelleher, C. (2003) 'Mental Health and "the Troubles" in Northern Ireland: Implications of Civil Unrest for Health and Wellbeing', *Journal of Epidemiology and Community Health*, 57(7), pp. 474–475.

Kendall, T. (2011) 'The Rise and Fall of the Atypical Antipsychotics', *The British Journal of Psychiatry*, 199, pp. 266–8.

Kendell, R. E. (1975) *The Role of Diagnosis in Psychiatry.* Oxford: Blackwell.

Kendler, K. S., Munoz, R. A. and Murphy, G. (2010) 'The Development of the Feighner Criteria: A Historical Perspective', *American Journal of Psychiatry*, 167(2), pp. 134–142.

Kessler, R. C., Chiu, W. T., Demler, O. and Walters, E. E. (2005) 'Prevalence, Severity, and Comorbidity of 12-Month DSM-IV Disorders in the National Comorbidity Survey Replication', *Archives of General Psychiatry*, 62(6), pp. 617–627.

Kessler, R. C., McGonagle, K. A., Zhao, S. Y., Nelson, C. B., Hughes, M., Eshleman, S., Wittchen, H.-U. and Kendler, K. S. (1994) 'Lifetime and 12-Month Prevalence of DSM-III-R Psychiatric Disorders in the United States. Results from the National Comorbidity Survey', *Archives of General Psychiatry*, 51, pp. 8–19.

Keyes, K. M. and Galea, S. (2017) 'Commentary: The Limits of Risk Factors Revisited: Is It Time for a Causal Architecture Approach?', *Epidemiology*, 28(1), pp. 1–5.

Kiely, R. (2007) 'Poverty Reduction through Liberalisation? Neoliberalism and the Myth of Global Convergence', *Review of International Studies*, 33(3), pp. 415–434.

Kinderman, P., Read, J., Moncrieff, J. and Bentall, R. P. (2013) 'Drop the Language of Disorder', *Evidence Based Mental Health*, 16(1), pp. 2–3.

Kirmayer, L. (2001) 'Cultural Variations in the Clinical Presentation of Depression and Anxiety: Implications for Diagnosis and Treatment', *The Journal of Clinical Psychiatry*, 62(Supplement 13), pp. 22–28.

Kirmayer, L. J. (2012) 'Cultural Competence and Evidence-Based Practice in Mental Health: Epistemic Communities and the Politics of Pluralism', *Social Science & Medicine*, 75(2), pp. 249–256.

Kirmayer, L. J. and Crafa, D. (2014) 'What Kind of Science for Psychiatry?', *Frontiers in Human Neuroscience*, 8. At https://doi.org/10.3389/fnhu m.2014.00435.

Kirmayer, L. J. and Gold, I. (2012) 'Critical Neuroscience and the Limits of Reductionism', Choudhury, S. and Slaby, J. (eds.), *Critical Neuroscience: A Handbook of the Social and Cultural Contexts of Neuroscience*. Malden, MA: Wiley Blackwell, pp. 307–330.

Kirmayer, L. J. and Pedersen, D. (2014) 'Toward a New Architecture for Global Mental Health', *Transcultural Psychiatry*, 51(6), pp. 759–776.

Kirmayer, L. J. and Swartz, L. (2013) 'Culture and Global Mental Health', in Patel , V., Minas, H., Cohen, A. and Prince, M. (eds.), *Global Mental Health: Principles and Practice*. Oxford: Oxford University Press, pp. 41–62.

Kirsch, I. (2009) *The Emperor's New Drugs: Exploding the Antidepressant Myth*. London: Bodley Head.

Kleinman, A. (2012) 'Rebalancing Academic Psychiatry: Why It Needs to Happen and Soon', *The British Journal of Psychiatry*, 201(6), pp. 421–422.

Klerman, G. L. and Weissman, M. M. (1989) 'Increasing Rates of Depression', *Journal of the American Medical Association*, 261(15), pp. 2229–2235.

Knorr Cetina, K. (1999) *Epistemic Cultures: How the Sciences Make Knowledge*. Boston, MA: Harvard University Press.

Kohn, R., Saxena, S., Levav, I. and Saraceno, B. (2004) 'The Treatment Gap in Mental Health Care', *Bulletin of the World Health Organization*, 82(11), pp. 858–866.

Kramer, M. (1983) 'The Increasing Prevalence of Mental Disorders: A Pandemic Threat', *Psychiatric Quarterly*, 55(2), pp. 115–143.

Kramer, P. D. (1992) *Listening to Prozac*. New York: Viking.

Krishna, A. (2002) *Active Social Capital: Tracing the Roots of Development and Democracy*. New York: Columbia University Press.

Krishnan, K. R. R. (2012) 'Structural Imaging in Psychiatric Disorders', in Schlepfer, T. E. and Nemeroff, C. B. (eds.), *Handbook of Clinical Neurology*. New York: Elsevier.

Kuhn, T. S. (1962) *The Structure of Scientific Revolutions*. Chicago: University of Chicago Press.

Kyziridis, T. C. (2005) 'Notes on the History of Schizophrenia', *German Journal of Psychiatry*, 8(3), pp. 42–48.

Laine, C., Horton, R., DeAngelis, C. D., Drazen, J. M., Frizelle, F. A., Godlee, F., Haug, C., Hébert, P. C., Kotzin, S. and Marusic, A. (2007). 'Clinical Trial Registration: Looking Back and Moving Ahead', *New England Journal of Medicine*, 356, pp. 2734–2736.

Lamb, S. D. (2014) *Pathologist of the Mind: Adolf Meyer and the Origins of American Psychiatry*. Baltimore, MD: Johns Hopkins University Press.

Lane, C. (2007) *Shyness: How Normal Behavior Became a Sickness*. New Haven, CT; London: Yale University Press.

Langer, K. G. (2009) 'Babinski's Anosognosia for Hemiplegia in Early Twentieth-Century French Neurology', *Journal of the History of the Neurosciences*, 18(4), pp. 387–405.

Latour, B. (1987) *Science in Action: How to Follow Scientists and Engineers through Society*. Cambridge, MA: Harvard University Press.

Law, J. (1992) 'Notes on the Theory of the Actor-Network: Ordering, Strategy, and Heterogeneity', *Systems Practice*, 5(4), pp. 379–393.

Lee, S. (2011) 'Depression Coming of Age in China', in Kleinman, A. (ed.), *Deep China: The Moral Life of the Person*. Berkeley: University of California Press, pp. 177.

Lee, S., Tsang, A., Huang, Y.-Q., He, Y.-L., Liu, Z., Zhang, M.-Y., Shen, Y.-C. and Kessler, R. C. (2009) 'The Epidemiology of Depression in Metropolitan China', *Psychological Medicine*, 39(5), pp. 735–747.

LeFrançois, B. A., Menzies, R. and Reaume, G. (2013) *Mad Matters: A Critical Reader in Canadian Mad Studies*. Toronto, ON: Canadian Scholars' Press.

Leucht, S., Corves, C., Arbter, D., Engel, R. R., Li, C. and Davis, J. M. (2009) 'Second-Generation Versus First-Generation Antipsychotic Drugs for Schizophrenia: A Meta-Analysis', *The Lancet*, 373(9657), pp. 31–41.

Lewer, D., O'Reilly, C., Mojtabai, R. and Evans-Lacko, S. (2015) 'Antidepressant Use in 27 European Countries: Associations with Sociodemographic, Cultural and Economic Factors', *The British Journal of Psychiatry*, 207(3), pp. 221–226.

Lewis, A. J. S. (1967 [1953]) 'Health as a Social Concept', in *The State of Psychiatry*. London: Routledge & Kegan Paul, pp. 179–194.

Lidbetter, E. J. (1932) 'The Social Problem Group: As Illustrated by a Series of East London Pedigrees', *The Eugenics Review*, 24(1), pp. 7.

Link, B. G., Cullen, F. T., Struening, E., Shrout, P. E. and Dohrenwend, B. P. (1989) 'A Modified Labeling Theory Approach to Mental Disorders: An Empirical Assessment', *American Sociological Review*, 54(3), pp. 400–423.

Little, J. C. (1961) 'The Care and Treatment of the Psychiatric Patient in the Home', *Journal of the College of General Practice*, 4(3), pp. 394–404.

Littlewood, R. and Lipsedge, M. (1997) *Aliens and Alienists: Ethnic Minorities and Psychiatry*. 3rd edn. London: Routledge.

Logothetis, N. K. (2008) 'What We Can Do and What We Cannot Do with FMRI', *Nature*, 453(7197), pp. 869–878.

López-Muñoz, F. and Alamo, C. (2009) 'Monoaminergic Neurotransmission: The History of the Discovery of Antidepressants from 1950s until Today', *Current Pharmaceutical Design*, 15(14), pp. 1563–1586.

Lund, C. (2014) 'Poverty and Mental Health: Towards a Research Agenda for Low and Middle-Income Countries', *Social Science & Medicine*, 111, pp. 134–136.

Lund, C., Breen, A., Flisher, A. J., Kakuma, R., Corrigall, J., Joska, J. A.,

Swartz, L. and Patel, V. (2010) 'Poverty and Common Mental Disorders in Low and Middle Income Countries: A Systematic Review', *Social Science & Medicine*, 71(3), pp. 517–528.

Manning, N. (2001) 'Psychiatric Diagnosis under Conditions of Uncertainty: Personality Disorder, Science, and Professional Legitimacy', in Busfield, J. (ed.), *Rethinking the Sociology of Mental Health*. Oxford: Blackwell, pp. 76–94.

Marazzi, C. (2010) *The Violence of Financial Capitalism*. Los Angeles: Semiotext(e).

Marmot, M. (2015) *The Health Gap: The Challenge of an Unequal World*. London: Bloomsbury.

Marmot, M. and Bell, R. (2012) 'Fair Society, Healthy Lives', *Public Health*, 126, pp. S4–S10.

Martin, E. (2006) 'The Pharmaceutical Person', *BioSocieties*, 1(3), pp. 273–287.

Mason, J. W. (1975) 'A Historical View of the Stress Field. Part One', *Journal of Human Stress*, 1(1), pp. 6–12.

Masten, A. S. (2015) *Ordinary Magic: Resilience in Development*. New York: Guilford Press.

McCarroll, S. A., Feng, G. and Hyman, S. E. (2014) 'Genome-Scale Neurogenetics: Methodology and Meaning', *Nature Neuroscience*, 17(6), pp. 756–763.

McCoy, M. S., Carniol, M., Chockley, K., Urwin, J. W., Emanuel, E. J. and Schmidt, H. (2017) 'Conflicts of Interest for Patient-Advocacy Organizations', *New England Journal of Medicine*, 376(9), pp. 880–885.

McEwen, B. S. (2012) 'Brain on Stress: How the Social Environment Gets under the Skin', *Proceedings of the National Academy of Sciences*, 109(Supplement 2), pp. 17180–17185.

McEwen, B. S. (2013) 'The Brain on Stress toward an Integrative Approach to Brain, Body, and Behavior', *Perspectives on Psychological Science*, 8(6), pp. 673–675.

McEwen, B. S. and Lasley, E. N. (2002) *The End of Stress as We Know It*. New York: DANA Press.

McEwen, B. S. and Stellar, E. (1993) 'Stress and the Individual: Mechanisms Leading to Disease', *Archives of Internal Medicine*, 153(18), pp. 2093–2101.

McEwen, C. A. and McEwen, B. S. (2017) 'Social Structure, Adversity, Toxic Stress, and Intergenerational Poverty: An Early Childhood Model', *Annual Review of Sociology*, 43. pp. 445–472.

McGann, P. (2011) *Sociology of Diagnosis*. Bingley: Emerald Group Publishing.

McGrath, J., McLaughlin, K., Saha, S., Aguilar-Gaxiola, S., Al-Hamzawi, A., Alonso, J., Bruffaerts, R., de Girolamo, G., de Jonge, P. and Esan, O. (2017) 'The Association between Childhood Adversities and Subsequent First Onset of Psychotic Experiences: A Cross-National Analysis of

23998 Respondents from 17 Countries', *Psychological Medicine*, 47(7), pp. 1230–1245.

McGuffin, P., Owen, M. and Farmer, A. (1995) 'Genetic Basis of Schizophrenia', *The Lancet*, 346(8976), pp. 678–682.

McKenzie, K., Whitley, R. and Weich, S. 2002. 'Social Capital and Mental Health', *The British Journal of Psychiatry*, 181(4), pp. 280–283.

McManus, S., Bebbington, P., Jenkins, R. and Brugha, T. (eds.) (2016) *Adult Psychiatric Morbidity Survey: Survey of Mental Health and Wellbeing, England, 2014.* Leeds: NHS Digital.

McSherry, B. and Freckelton, I. (2013) *Coercive Care: Rights, Law and Policy.* London: Routledge.

Menninger, K. A. (1965) *The Vital Balance. The Life Process in Mental Health and Illness. [by] Karl Menninger . . . With Martin Mayman . . . And Paul Pruyser, Etc.* New York: Viking Press.

Menninger, W. C. (1947) 'The Role of Psychiatry in the World Today', *American Journal of Psychiatry*, 104(3), pp. 155–163.

Menzies, R., LeFrançois, B. A. and Reaume, G. (2013) 'Introducing Mad Studies', in Menzies, R., LeFrançois, B. A. and Reaume, G. (eds.), *Mad Matters: A Critical Reader in Canadian Mad Studies.* Toronto, ON: Gazelle.

Metzl, J. (2003) *Prozac on the Couch: Prescribing Gender in the Era of Wonder Drugs.* Durham, NC: Duke University Press.

Metzl, J. M. (2010) *The Protest Psychosis: How Schizophrenia Became a Black Disease.* New York: Beacon Press.

Meyer, A. (1928) 'The Complaint as the Center of Genetic-Dynamic and Nosologigal Teaching in Psychiatry', *New England Journal of Medicine*, 199(8), pp. 360–370.

Meyer, J., Huberth, A., Ortega, G., Syagailo, Y., Jatzke, S., Mössner, R., Strom, T., Ulzheimer-Teuber, I., Stöber, G. and Schmitt, A. (2001) 'A Missense Mutation in a Novel Gene Encoding a Putative Cation Channel is Associated with Catatonic Schizophrenia in a Large Pedigree', *Molecular Psychiatry*, 6(3), pp. 302.

Mezzina, R. (2014) 'Community Mental Health Care in Trieste and Beyond: An "Open Door–No Restraint" System of Care for Recovery and Citizenship', *The Journal of Nervous and Mental Disease*, 202(6), pp. 440–445.

Miller, A. (2008) 'A Critique of Positive Psychology – or "the New Science of Happiness"', *Journal of Philosophy of Education*, 42(3–4), pp. 591–608.

Miller, G. (2010) 'Is Pharma Running Out of Brainy Ideas?', *Science*, 329(5991), pp. 502–504.

Miller, P. and Rose, N. (1988) 'The Tavistock Programme: The Government of Subjectivity and Social Life', *Sociology*, 22(2), pp. 171–192.

Miller, P. B. and Rose, N. (1986) *The Power of Psychiatry.* Cambridge: Polity.

Minkowitz, T. (2011) 'Prohibition of Compulsory Mental Health Treatment and Detention under the CRPD'. At https://ssrn.com/abstract=1876132.

Mold, A. (2011) 'Making the Patient-Consumer in Margaret Thatcher's Britain', *The Historical Journal*, 54(2), pp. 509–528.

Monbiot, G. (2016) 'Neoliberalism Is Creating Loneliness', *Guardian*, 12 October. At https://www.theguardian.com/commentisfree/2016/oct/12/neoliberalism-creating-loneliness-wrenching-society-apart.

Moncrieff, J. (2006) 'Psychiatric Drug Promotion and the Politics of Neoliberalism', *The British Journal of Psychiatry*, 188(4), pp. 301–302.

Moncrieff, J. (2008a) *The Myth of the Chemical Cure: A Critique of Psychiatric Drug Treatment*. Basingstoke, UK: Palgrave Macmillan.

Moncrieff, J. (2008b) 'Neoliberalism and Biopsychiatry: A Marriage of Convenience', in Cohen, C. I. and Timimi, S. (eds.), *Liberatory Psychiatry: Philosophy, Politics, and Mental Health*. Cambridge: Cambridge University Press, pp. 235–255.

Moore, S. and Kawachi, I. (2017) 'Twenty Years of Social Capital and Health Research: A Glossary', *Journal of Epidemiology and Community Health*, 71(5), pp. 513–517.

Morgan, C., Burns, T., Fitzpatrick, R., Pinfold, V. and Priebe, S. (2007) 'Social Exclusion and Mental Health', *The British Journal of Psychiatry*, 191(6), pp. 477–483.

Moynihan, R. (2008) 'Key Opinion Leaders: Independent Experts or Drug Representatives in Disguise?', *British Medical Journal*, 336(7658), pp. 1402–1403.

Moynihan, R. and Cassels, A. (2005) *Selling Sickness: How the World's Biggest Pharmaceutical Companies Are Turning Us All into Patients*. New York: Nation Books.

Muntaner, C. (2004) 'Commentary: Social Capital, Social Class, and the Slow Progress of Psychosocial Epidemiology', *International Journal of Epidemiology*, 33(4), pp. 674–680.

Muntaner, C., Lynch, J. and Smith, G. D. (2000) 'Social Capital and the Third Way in Public Health', *Critical Public Health*, 10(2), pp. 107–124.

Muntaner, C., Lynch, J. and Smith, G. D. (2001) 'Social Capital, Disorganized Communities, and the Third Way: Understanding the Retreat from Structural Inequalities in Epidemiology and Public Health', *International Journal of Health Services*, 31(2), pp. 213–237.

Murray, C. J. L., Lopez, A. D., Harvard School of Public Health, World Health Organization, and World Bank. (1996) *The Global Burden of Disease: A Comprehensive Assessment of Mortality and Disability from Diseases, Injuries, and Risk Factors in 1990 and Projected to 2020*. Global Burden of Disease and Injury Series. Cambridge, MA: Published by the Harvard School of Public Health on behalf of the WHO and the World Bank; distributed by Harvard University Press.

Murray, R. M. (2016) 'Mistakes I Have Made in My Research Career', *Schizophrenia Bulletin*, 43(2), pp. 253–256.

Murray, R. M., Quattrone, D., Natesan, S., van Os, J., Nordentoft, M., Howes, O., Di Forti, M. and Taylor, D. (2016) 'Should Psychiatrists

Be More Cautious About the Long-Term Prophylactic Use of Antipsychotics?', *The British Journal of Psychiatry*, 209(5), pp. 361–365.

Nature Neuroscience (1999) 'Celebrating a Decade of Progress', *Nature Neuroscience* 2, p. 487. doi: 10.1038/9131.

Nussbaum, M. C. (2011) *Creating Capabilities*. Cambridge, MA: Harvard University Press.

O'Brien, P. L., Thomas, C. P., Hodgkin, D., Levit, K. R. and Mark, T. L. (2014) 'The Diminished Pipeline for Medications to Treat Mental Health and Substance Use Disorders', *Psychiatric Services*, 65(12), pp. 1433–1438.

O'Hagan, M. (2004) 'Guest Editorial', *Australian e-Journal for the Advancement of Mental Health*, 3(1), pp. 5–7.

Oakley, A., Strange, V., Bonell, C., Allen, E., Stephenson, J. and Team, R. S. (2006) 'Health Services Research: Process Evaluation in Randomised Controlled Trials of Complex Interventions', *British Medical Journal*, 332(7538), p. 413.

OECD (2013) *Health at a Glance 2013: OECD Indicators*, Organisation for Economic Co-operation and Development Publishing. At http://dx.doi.org/10.1787/health_glance-2013-en.

Office of Public Health and Human Services Department (2015) *Health, United States, 2013, with Special Feature on Prescription Drugs*. Washington, DC: Government Printing Office.

Olfson, M., Druss, B. G. and Marcus, S. C. (2015) 'Trends in Mental Health Care among Children and Adolescents', *New England Journal of Medicine*, 372(21), pp. 2029–2038.

Olfson, M., Gameroff, M. J., Marcus, S. C. and Jensen, P. S. (2003) 'National Trends in the Treatment of Attention Deficit Hyperactivity Disorder', *American Journal of Psychiatry*, 160(6), pp. 1071–1077.

Olfson, M. and Marcus, S. C. (2009) 'National Patterns in Antidepressant Medication Treatment', *Archives of General Psychiatry*, 66(8), pp. 848.

Orr, J. (2006) *Panic Diaries: A Genealogy of Panic Disorder*. Durham, NC: Duke University Press.

Osborne, T. (2016) 'Vitalism as Pathos', *Biosemiotics*, 9(2), pp. 185–205.

Pariante, C. M. and Lightman, S. L. (2008) 'The HPA Axis in Major Depression: Classical Theories and New Developments', *Trends in Neurosciences*, 31(9), pp. 464–468.

Parsons, T. (1951) 'Illness and the Role of the Physician: A Sociological Perspective', *American Journal of Orthopsychiatry*, 21(3), pp. 452–460.

Patel, M. X. and David, A. S. (2004) 'Medication Adherence: Predictive Factors and Enhancement Strategies', *Psychiatry*, 3(10), pp. 41–44.

Patel, V. (2012) 'Global Mental Health: From Science to Action', *Harvard Review of Psychiatry*, 20(1), pp. 6–12.

Patel, V. (2014a) 'Rethinking Mental Health Care: Bridging the Credibility Gap', *Intervention*, 12, pp. 15–20.

Patel, V. (2014b) 'Why Mental Health Matters to Global Health', *Transcultural Psychiatry*, 51(6), pp. 777–789.

Patel, V., Boyce, N., Collins, P. Y., Saxena, S. and Horton, R. (2011) 'A Renewed Agenda for Global Mental Health', *The Lancet*, 378(9801), pp. 1441–1442.

Patel, V., Garrison, P., de Jesus Mari, J., Minas, H., Prince, M. and Saxena, S. (2008) 'The Lancet's Series on Global Mental Health: 1 Year On', *The Lancet*, 372(9646), pp. 1354–1357.

Patel, V. and Kleinman, A. (2003) 'Poverty and Common Mental Disorders in Developing Countries', *Bulletin of the World Health Organization*, 81(8), pp. 609–615.

Patel, V., Lund, C., Hatherill, S., Plagerson, S., Corrigall, J., Funk, M. and Flisher, A. (2010) 'Mental Disorders: Equity and Social Determinants', in Blas, E. and Kurup, A.S. (eds.), *Equity, Social Determinants and Public Health Programmes*. Geneva: World Health Organization.

Patel, V., Minas, H., Cohen, A. and Prince, M. (eds.) (2014) *Global Mental Health: Principles and Practice*. New York: Oxford University Press.

Patel, V. and Prince, M. (2010) 'Global Mental Health: A New Global Health Field Comes of Age', *Journal of the American Medical Association*, 303(19), pp. 1976–1977.

Pearce, N. and Davey Smith, G. (2003) 'Is Social Capital the Key to Inequalities in Health?', *American Journal of Public Health*, 93(1), pp. 122–129.

Peedicayil, J. (2017) 'The Role of Epigenetics in Social Psychiatry', *International Journal of Social Psychiatry*, 63(1), pp. 14–20.

Perkins, R. and Repper, J. (2003) *Social Inclusion and Recovery: A Model for Mental Health Practice*. London: Baillière Tindall.

Peterson, D. (1982) *A Mad People's History of Madness*. Pittsburgh, PA: University of Pittsburgh Press.

Pick, D. (1989) *Faces of Degeneration: A European Disorder c.1848–c.1918. Ideas in Context*. Cambridge: Cambridge University Press.

Porter, R. (1985) 'The Patient's View', *Theory and Society*, 14(2), pp. 175–198.

Porter, R. (1987) *A Social History of Madness: Stories of the Insane*. London: Weidenfeld and Nicolson.

Porter, R. (1991) *The Faber Book of Madness*. London: Faber and Faber.

Porto, P. R., Oliveira, L., Mari, J., Volchan, E., Figueira, I. and Ventura, P. (2009) 'Does Cognitive Behavioral Therapy Change the Brain? A Systematic Review of Neuroimaging in Anxiety Disorders', *The Journal of Neuropsychiatry and Clinical Neurosciences*, 21(2), pp. 114–125.

Pratt, L. A., Brody, D. J. and Gu, Q. (2011): *Antidepressant Use in Persons Aged 12 and Over: United States, 2005–2008. NCHS Data Brief, No 76.* Hyattsville, MD: National Center for Health Statistics.

Priebe, S., Frottier, P., Gaddini, A., Kilian, R., Lauber, C., Martínez-Leal,

R., Munk-Jørgensen, P., Walsh, D., Wiersma, D. and Wright, D. (2008) 'Mental Health Care Institutions in Nine European Countries, 2002 to 2006', *Psychiatric Services*, 59(5), pp. 570–573.

Prince, M., Patel, V., Saxena, S., Maj, M., Maselko, J., Phillips, M. R. and Rahman, A. (2007) 'Global Mental Health 1. No Health without Mental Health', *The Lancet*, 370, pp. 859–877.

Proctor, R. (1988) *Racial Hygiene: Medicine under the Nazis.* Cambridge, MA: Harvard University Press.

Purves, D. (2010) *Brains: How They Seem to Work.* Upper Saddle River, NJ: Financial Times/Prentice Hall.

Putnam, R. D. (1995) 'Bowling Alone: America's Declining Social Capital', *Journal of Democracy*, 6(1), pp. 65–78.

Rabinow, P. and Rose, N. (2006) 'Biopower Today', *BioSocieties*, 1(2), pp. 195–218.

Rack, P. (1982) *Race, Culture, and Mental Disorder.* London: Tavistock.

Rapoport, A. (1978) 'Culture and the Subjective Effects of Stress', *Urban Ecology*, 3(3), pp. 241–261.

Rapport, R. L. (2005) *Nerve Endings: The Discovery of the Synapse.* New York: W. W. Norton.

Read, J., Fosse, R., Moskowitz, A. and Perry, B. (2014) 'The Traumagenic Neurodevelopmental Model of Psychosis Revisited', *Neuropsychiatry*, 4(1), pp. 65–79.

Rebello, T. J., Marques, A., Gureje, O. and Pike, K. M. (2014) 'Innovative Strategies for Closing the Mental Health Treatment Gap Globally', *Current Opinion in Psychiatry*, 27(4), pp. 308–314.

Reddy, M. S. (2010) 'Depression: The Disorder and the Burden', *Indian Journal of Psychological Medicine*, 32(1), pp. 1–2.

Rees, E., O'Donovan, M. C. and Owen, M. J. (2015) 'Genetics of Schizophrenia', *Current Opinion in Behavioral Sciences*, 2, pp. 8–14.

Regier, D. A., Goldberg, I. D. and Taube, C. A. (1978) 'The De Facto US Mental Health Services System: A Public Health Perspective', *Archives of General Psychiatry*, 35(6), pp. 685–693.

Regier, D. A., Narrow, W. E., Kuhl, E. A. and Kupfer, D. J. (2009) 'The Conceptual Development of DSM-V', *American Journal of Psychiatry*, 166(6), pp. 645–50.

Relman, A. S. and Angell, M. (2002) 'Americas' Other Drug Problem', *New Republic*, 227(25), pp. 27–41.

Robb, A. (2012) *Towards Strengthening the Rights of Persons with Psychosocial Disabilities in Africa.* Cape Town: Pan African Network of People with Psychosocial Disabilities (PANUSP).

Robertson, I. T., Cooper, C. L., Sarkar, M. and Curran, T. (2015) 'Resilience Training in the Workplace from 2003 to 2014: A Systematic Review', *Journal of Occupational and Organizational Psychology*, 88(3), pp. 533–562.

Robins, E. and Guze, S. B. (1970) 'Establishment of Diagnostic Validity in

Psychiatric Illness: Its Application to Schizophrenia', *American Journal of Psychiatry*, 126(7), pp. 983–987.

Rogers, A. (2017) 'Star Neuroscientist Tom Insel Leaves the Google-Spawned Verily For . . . A Startup?', *Wired*. At https://www.wired.com/2017/05/star-neuroscientist-tom-insel-leaves-google-spawned-verily-startup/.

Rose, D. (2001a) 'Some Reflections on Epistemology in Relation to User-Led Research', paper presented to *Survivors Research Network*, Mental Health Foundation, February.

Rose, D. (2001b) *Users' Voices: The Perspectives of Mental Health Service Users*. London: Sainsbury Centre for Mental Health.

Rose, D. (2014) 'The Mainstreaming of Recovery', *Journal of Mental Health*, 23(5), pp. 217–218.

Rose, D. (in press) 'Navigating an Insider/Outsider Identity in Exclusive Academic Spaces: How Far Can Boundaries Be Pushed?' *Journal of Ethics in Mental Health*.

Rose, D., Ford, R., Lindley, P. and Gawith, L. (1998) *In Our Experience: User-Focused Monitoring of Mental Health Services in Kensington & Chelsea and Westminster Health Authority*. London: Sainsbury Centre for Mental Health.

Rose, N. (1985a) *The Psychological Complex: Psychology, Politics and Society in England, 1869–1939*. London: Routledge & Kegan Paul.

Rose, N. (1985b) 'Unreasonable Rights: Mental Illness and the Limits of the Law', *Journal of Law and Society*, 12(2), pp. 199–218.

Rose, N. (1986) 'Psychiatry: The Discipline of Mental Health', in Miller, P. and Rose, N. (eds.), *The Power of Psychiatry*. Cambridge: Polity, pp. 43–84.

Rose, N. (1991) 'Governing by Numbers', *Accounting Organizations and Society*, 16(7), pp. 673–692.

Rose, N. (1996a) 'The Death of the Social? Re-Figuring the Territory of Government', *Economy and Society*, 25(3), pp. 327–356.

Rose, N. (1996b) 'Governing "Advanced" Liberal Democracies', in Rose, N., Osborne, T. and Barry, A. (eds.), *Foucault and Political Reason: Liberalism, Neo-Liberalism and Rationalities of Government*. London: Routledge, pp. 37–64.

Rose, N. (1996c) 'Psychiatry as a Political Science: Advanced Liberalism and the Administration of Risk', *History of the Human Sciences*, 9(2), pp. 1–23.

Rose, N. (1999a) *Governing the Soul: The Shaping of the Private Self*. London: Free Association Press.

Rose, N. (1999b) *Powers of Freedom: Reframing Political Thought*. Cambridge: Cambridge University Press.

Rose, N. (2000) 'Biological Psychiatry as a Style of Thought.' Unpublished Manuscript.

Rose, N. (2002) 'Society, Madness and Control', in Buchanan, A. (ed.),

Care of the Mentally Disordered Offender in the Community. Oxford: Oxford University Press, pp. 3–25.

Rose, N. (2003a) 'The Neurochemical Self and Its Anomalies', in Ericson, R. V. and Doyle, A. (eds.), *Risk and Morality*. Toronto, ON: University of Toronto Press, pp. 407–437.

Rose, N. (2003b) 'Neurochemical Selves', *Society*, 41(1), pp. 46–59.

Rose, N. (2004) 'Becoming Neurochemical Selves', in Stehr, N. (ed.), *Biotechnology, Commerce and Civil Society*. New York: Transaction Press, pp. 89–128.

Rose, N. (2006a) 'Disorders without Borders? The Expanding Scope of Psychiatric Practice', *BioSocieties*, 1(4), pp. 465–484.

Rose, N. (2006b) 'Psychopharmaceuticals in Europe', in McDaid, D., Knapp, M. and Thornicroft, G. (eds.), *Mental Health Policy and Practice in Europe*. Milton Keynes: Open University Press.

Rose, N. (2007a) 'Beyond Medicalisation', *The Lancet*, 369(9562), pp. 700–702.

Rose, N. (2007b) *The Politics of Life Itself: Biomedicine, Power, and Subjectivity in the Twenty–First Century*. Princeton, NJ: Princeton University Press.

Rose, N. (2008) '"Was Ist Leben? – Versuch Einer Wiederbelebung" (What Is Life – Revitalized, in German Translation)', in Weiss, M. (ed.), *Die Menschliche Natur Im Zeitalter Ihrer Technischen Reproduzierbarkeit* [*Human Nature in the Age of Biotechnology*]. Berlin: Suhrkamp.

Rose, N. (2010) '"Screen and Intervene": Governing Risky Brains', *History of the Human Sciences*, 23(1), pp. 79–105.

Rose, N. (2016) 'Society, Madness and Control', in Buchanan, A. (ed.), *Care of the Mentally Disordered Offender in the Community*, 2nd edn. Oxford: Oxford University Press.

Rose, N. and Abi-Rached, J. M. (2013) *Neuro: The New Brain Sciences and the Management of the Mind*. Princeton, NJ: Princeton University Press.

Rose, N. and Lentzos, F. (2017) 'Making Us Resilient: Responsible Citizens for Uncertain Times', in Trnka, S. and Trundle, C. (eds.), *Competing Responsibilities*. Durham, NC: Duke University Press, pp. 27–48.

Rosen, G. (1974) *From Medical Police to Social Medicine: Essays on the History of Health Care*. New York: Science History Publications, Neale Watson Academic Publications.

Rosenberg, C. E. (1975) 'The Crisis in Psychiatric Legitimacy: Reflections on Psychiatry, Medicine, and Public Policy', in Kriegman, G., Gardner, R. D. and Abse, D. W. (eds.), *American Psychiatry: Past, Present, and Future*. Charlottesville: University Press of Virginia, pp. 135–148.

Rosenberg, C. E. (2002) 'The Tyranny of Diagnosis: Specific Entities and Individual Experience', *The Milbank Quarterly*, 80(2), pp. 237–260.

Rosenberg, C. E. (2006) 'Contested Boundaries – Psychiatry, Disease, and Diagnosis', *Perspectives in Biology and Medicine*, 49(3), pp. 407–424.

Rosenberg, C. E. (2009) 'Managed Fear', *The Lancet*, 373(9666), pp. 802–803.

Rosenhan, D. L. (1973) 'On Being Sane in Insane Places', *Science*, 179, pp. 250–258.

Rowland, W. (2001) 'Nothing About Us without Us; Some Historical Reflections on Disability Movement in South Africa', *Disability World*, 11.

Rudra, N. and Tobin, J. (2017) 'When Does Globalization Help the Poor?', *Annual Review of Political Science*, 20, pp. 287–307.

Rutter, M. and Madge, N. (1976) *Cycles of Disadvantage: A Review of Research*. London: Heinemann Educational Books.

Sacks, O. (2017) *The River of Consciousness*. New York: Picador.

Saegert, S. and Evans, G. W. (2003) 'Poverty, Housing Niches, and Health in the United States', *Journal of Social Issues*, 59(3), pp. 569–589.

Sandi, C. and Haller, J. (2015) 'Stress and the Social Brain: Behavioural Effects and Neurobiological Mechanisms', *Nature Reviews Neuroscience*, 16(5), pp. 290–304.

Sartorius, N. (2002) 'Iatrogenic Stigma of Mental Illness: Begins with Behaviour and Attitudes of Medical Professionals, Especially Psychiatrists', *British Medical Journal*, 324(7352), pp. 1470.

Sartorius, N. (2003) 'Social Capital and Mental Health', *Current Opinion in Psychiatry*, 16, pp. S101–S105.

Satcher, D. (2001) 'Global Mental Health: Its Time Has Come', *Journal of the American Medical Association*, 285(13), pp. 1697–1697.

Scheff, T. J. (1966) *Being Mentally Ill: A Sociological Theory*. Observations. London: Weidenfeld & Nicolson.

Scheper-Hughes, N. and Lovell, A. (eds.), (1987) *Psychiatry Inside Out: Selected Writings of Franco Basaglia*. New York: Columbia University Press.

Schildkraut, J. J. (1965) 'The Catecholamine Hypothesis of Affective Disorders: A Review of Supporting Evidence', *American Journal of Psychiatry*, 122, pp. 509–522.

Schizophrenia Working Group of the Psychiatric Genomics Consortium (2014) 'Biological Insights from 108 Schizophrenia-Associated Genetic Loci', *Nature*, 511(7510), pp. 421–427.

Schneider, K. 1950. *Klinische Psychopathologie*. Stuttgart: Thieme.

Scott, J. W. (1991) 'The Evidence of Experience', *Critical Inquiry*, 17(4), pp. 773–797.

Scull, A. (1989) *Social Order/Mental Disorder: Anglo-American Psychiatry in Historical Perspective*. London: Routledge.

Seligman, M. 2011. *Flourish: A New Understanding of Happiness and Wellbeing and How to Achieve Them*. London: Nicholas Brealey Publishing.

Selye, H. (1936) 'A Syndrome Produced by Diverse Nocuous Agents', *Nature*, 138(3479), p. 32.

Selye, H. (1956) *The Stress of Life*. New York: McGraw-Hill.

Shapin, S. and Schaffer, S. (1985) *Leviathan and the Air-Pump: Hobbes, Boyle, and the Experimental Life*. Princeton, NJ: Princeton University Press.

Shaw, I. and Taplin, S. (2007) 'Happiness and Mental Health Policy: A Sociological Critique', *Journal of Mental Health*, 16(3), pp. 359–373.

Shepherd, M. and Cooper, B. (1964) 'Epidemiology and Mental Disorder: A Review', *Journal of Neurology, Neurosurgery & Psychiatry*, 27(4), pp. 277–290.

Shern, D. L., Blanch, A. K. and Steverman, S. M. (2016) 'Toxic Stress, Behavioral Health, and the Next Major Era in Public Health', *American Journal of Orthopsychiatry*, 86(2), pp. 109–123.

Shonkoff, J. P., Garner, A. S., Siegel, B. S., Dobbins, M. I., Earls, M. F., McGuinn, L., Pascoe, J., Wood, D. L. (2012) 'The Lifelong Effects of Early Childhood Adversity and Toxic Stress', *Pediatrics*, 129(1), pp. e232–e246.

Slade, M. (2009) *Personal Recovery and Mental Illness: A Guide for Mental Health Professionals*. Cambridge: Cambridge University Press.

Slade, M., Amering, M., Farkas, M., Hamilton, B., O'Hagan, M., Panther, G., Perkins, R., Shepherd, G., Tse, S. and Whitley, R. (2014) 'Uses and Abuses of Recovery: Implementing Recovery-Oriented Practices in Mental Health Systems', *World Psychiatry*, 13(1), pp. 12–20.

Slade, M., Oades, L. and Jarden, A. (2017) *Wellbeing, Recovery and Mental Health*. Cambridge: Cambridge University Press.

Slater, E. (1958) 'The Monogenic Theory of Schizophrenia', *Human Heredity*, 8(1), pp. 50–56.

Smith, D. (1978) 'K Is Mentally Ill: The Anatomy of a Factual Account', *Sociology*, 12, pp. 23–53.

Smith, M. C. (1991) *A Social History of the Minor Tranquilizers: The Quest for Small Comfort in the Age of Anxiety*. New York: Pharmaceutical Products Press.

Social Exclusion Unit (2004) *Mental Health and Social Exclusion*. London: Office of the Deputy Prime Minister.

Soja, E. (2009) 'The City and Spatial Justice', *Justice Spatiale/Spatial Justice*, 1, pp. 1–5.

Spitzer, R. L. and Wilson, P. T. (1968) 'A Guide to the American Psychiatric Association's New Diagnostic Nomenclature', *American Journal of Psychiatry*, 124(12), pp. 1619–1629.

Sprooten, E., Rasgon, A., Goodman, M., Carlin, A., Leibu, E., Lee, W. H. and Frangou, S. (2017) 'Addressing Reverse Inference in Psychiatric Neuroimaging: Meta-Analyses of Task-Related Brain Activation in Common Mental Disorders', *Human Brain Mapping*, 38(4), pp. 1846–1864.

Srole, L., Langner, T. S., Michael, S. T., Opler, M. K. and Rennie, T. A. (1962) *Mental Health in the Metropolis: The Midtown Manhattan Study*. New York; McGraw-Hill.

Stahl, S. M. (1996) *Essential Psychopharmacology: Neuroscientific Basis and Practical Applications*. Cambridge: Cambridge University Press.

Starr, P. (1987) 'The Sociology of Official Statistics', in Alonso, W. and Starr, P. (eds.), *The Politics of Numbers*. New York: Russell Sage, pp. 7–58.

Stein, D. J., He, Y., Phillips, A., Sahakian, B. J., Williams, J. and Patel, V. (2015) 'Global Mental Health and Neuroscience: Potential Synergies', *The Lancet Psychiatry*, 2(2), pp. 178–185.

Stepan, N. (1991) *'The Hour of Eugenics': Race, Gender and Nation in Latin America*. Ithaca, NY: Cornell University Press.

Stoudemire, A., Frank, R., Hedemark, N., Kamlet, M. and Blazer, D. (1986) 'The Economic Burden of Depression', *General Hospital Psychiatry*, 8(6), pp. 387–394.

Stovall, S. (2011) 'R&D Cuts Curb Brain-Drug Pipeline', *Wall Street Journal*, 27 March. At https://www.wsj.com/articles/SB10001424052748 70447480457622463927753954.

Sullivan, P. F., Daly, M. J. and O'Donovan, M. (2012) 'Genetic Architectures of Psychiatric Disorders: The Emerging Picture and Its Implications', *Nature Reviews Genetics*, 13(8), pp. 537–551.

Summerfield, D. (2008) 'How Scientifically Valid Is the Knowledge Base of Global Mental Health?', *British Medical Journal*, 336, pp. 992–994.

Summerfield, D. (2012) 'Afterword: Against "Global Mental Health"', *Transcultural Psychiatry*, 49(3–4), p. 519.

Summerfield, D. (2013) '"Global Mental Health" Is an Oxymoron and Medical Imperialism', *British Medical Journal*, 346, f3509.

Szasz, T. (1962) *The Myth of Mental Illness*. London: Secker and Warburg.

Szasz, T. (1989) *The Myth of the Rights of Mental Patients*. New York: Liberty.

Szmukler, G. (2017) *Men in White Coats: Treatment under Coercion*. Oxford: Oxford University Press.

Szmukler, G., Daw, R. and Callard, F. (2014) 'Mental Health Law and the UN Convention on the Rights of Persons with Disabilities', *International Journal of Law and Psychiatry*, 37(3), pp. 245–252.

Szmukler, G. and Rose, N. (2013) 'Risk Assessment in Mental Health Care: Values and Costs', *Behavioral Sciences & the Law*, 31(1), pp. 125–140.

Szumilas, M. (2010) 'Explaining Odds Ratios', *Journal of the Canadian Academy of Child and Adolescent Psychiatry*, 19(3), pp. 227–229.

Teghtsoonian, K. (2009) 'Depression and Mental Health in Neoliberal Times: A Critical Analysis of Policy and Discourse', *Social Science & Medicine*, 69(1), pp. 28–35.

Thomas, P. (2016) 'Psycho Politics, Neoliberal Governmentality and Austerity', *Self & Society*, 44(4), pp. 382–393.

Tomasi di Lampedusa, G. (1960) *The Leopard*. London: Harvill.

Tone, A. (2009) *The Age of Anxiety: A History of America's Turbulent Affair with Tranquilizers*. New York: Basic Books.

Trimble, M. R. (1987) *Biological Psychiatry*. Chichester: Wiley.

Trimble, M. R. and George, M. S. (2010) *Biological Psychiatry*, 3rd edn. Oxford: Wiley Blackwell.

Twenge, J. M. (2015) 'Time Period and Birth Cohort Differences in

Depressive Symptoms in the Us, 1982–2013', *Social Indicators Research*, 121(2), pp. 437–454.

Twenge, J. M., Gentile, B., DeWall, C. N., Ma, D., Lacefield, K. and Schurtz, D. R. (2010) 'Birth Cohort Increases in Psychopathology among Young Americans, 1938–2007: A Cross-Temporal Meta-Analysis of the MMPI', *Clinical Psychology Review*, 30(2), pp. 145–154.

Tyrer, P., Duggan, C., Cooper, S., Crawford, M., Seivewright, H., Rutter, D., Maden, T., Byford, S. and Barrett, B. (2010) 'The Successes and Failures of the DSPD Experiment: The Assessment and Management of Severe Personality Disorder', *Medicine, Science and the Law*, 50(2), pp. 95–99.

Tyrer, P. and Kendall, T. (2009) 'The Spurious Advance of Antipsychotic Drug Therapy', *The Lancet*, 373(9657), pp. 4–5.

US Department of Heath and Human Services (1999) *Mental Health: A Report of the Surgeon General* (2 vols). Rockville, MD: Department of Health and Human Services.

US Government (1978) *The President's Commission on Mental Health. Report to the President*, vol. 1. Washington, DC: President's Commission on Mental Health.

Valenstein, E. S. (1986) *Great and Desperate Cures: The Rise and Decline of Psychosurgery and Other Radical Treatments for Mental Illness*. New York: Basic Books.

Valenstein, E. S. (2005) *The War of the Soups and the Sparks: The Discovery of Neurotransmitters and the Dispute over How Nerves Communicate*. New York: Columbia University Press.

van der Geest, S., Reynolds Whyte, S. and Hardon, A. (1996) 'The Anthropology of Pharmaceuticals: A Biographical Approach', *Annual Review of Anthropology*, 25(1), pp. 153–178.

van der Kooij, M. A., Fantin, M., Rejmak, E., Grosse, J., Zanoletti, O., Fournier, C., Ganguly, K., Kalita, K., Kaczmarek, L. and Sandi, C. (2014) 'Role for MMP-9 in Stress-Induced Downregulation of Nectin-3 in Hippocampal CA1 and Associated Behavioural Alterations', *Nature Communications*, 5, p. 4995.

van Os, J. (2016) '"Schizophrenia" Does Not Exist', *British Medical Journal (Online)*. At http://www.bmj.com/content/352/bmj.i375.

van Voren, R. (2009) 'Political Abuse of Psychiatry: An Historical Overview', *Schizophrenia Bulletin*, 36(1), pp. 33–35.

Varese, F., Smeets, F., Drukker, M., Lieverse, R., Lataster, T., Viechtbauer, W., Read, J., van Os, J. and Bentall, R. P. (2012) 'Childhood Adversities Increase the Risk of Psychosis: A Meta-Analysis of Patient-Control, Prospective and Cross-Sectional Cohort Studies', *Schizophrenia Bulletin*, 38(4), pp. 661–671.

Ventriglio, A., Gupta, S. and Bhugra, D. (2016) 'Why Do We Need a Social Psychiatry?' *The British Journal of Psychiatry*, 209(1), pp. 1–2.

Venugopal, R. (2015) 'Neoliberalism as Concept', *Economy and Society*, 44(2), pp. 165–187.

Verdoux, H., Tournier, M. and Bégaud, B. (2010) 'Antipsychotic Prescribing Trends: A Review of Pharmaco-Epidemiological Studies', *Acta Psychiatrica Scandinavica*, 121(1), pp. 4–10.

Vigo, D., Thornicroft, G. and Atun, R. (2016) 'Estimating the True Global Burden of Mental Illness', *The Lancet Psychiatry*, 3(2), pp. 171–178.

von Uexküll, J. (2010 [1934]) *A Foray into the Worlds of Animals and Humans*. Minneapolis: University of Minnesota Press.

Voronka, J. (2016) 'The Politics of 'People with Lived Experience: Experiential Authority and the Risks of Strategic Essentialism', *Philosophy, Psychiatry, & Psychology*, 23(3), pp. 189–201.

Voronka, J. (2017) 'Turning Mad Knowledge into Affective Labor: The Case of the Peer Support Worker', *American Quarterly*, 69(2), pp. 333–338.

Wagenfeld, M. O. (1983) 'Primary Prevention and Public Mental Health Policy', *Journal of Public Health Policy*, pp. 168–180.

Wahlberg, A. (2008) 'Above and Beyond Superstition. Western Herbal Medicine and the Decriminalizing of Placebo', *History of the Human Sciences*, 21(1), pp. 77–101.

Wahlberg, A. and Rose, N. (2015) 'The Governmentalization of Living: Calculating Global Health', *Economy and Society*, 44(1), pp. 60–90.

Wallcraft, J. and Hopper, K. (2015) 'The Capabilties Approach and the Social Model of Mental Health', in Spandler, H., Anderson, J. and Sapey, B. (eds.), *Madness, Distress and the Politics of Disablement*. Bristol: Policy Press.

Wallcraft, J., Read, J. and Sweeney, A. (2003) *On Our Own Terms*. London: Sainsbury Centre for Mental Health.

Wang, P. S., Simon, G. and Kessler, R. C. (2003) 'The Economic Burden of Depression and the Cost-Effectiveness of Treatment', *International Journal of Methods in Psychiatric Research*, 12(1), pp. 22–33.

Wang, W.-J. (2016) 'Neurasthenia and the Rise of Psy Disciplines in Republican China', *East Asian Science, Technology and Society*, 10(2), pp. 141–160.

Watters, E. (2010) *Crazy Like Us: The Globalization of the American Psyche*. New York: Simon and Schuster.

Wedge, P. and Prosser, H. (1973) *Born to Fail? The National Children's Bureau Reports on Striking Differences in the Lives of British Children*. London: Arrow

Welshman, J. (2007) *From Transmitted Deprivation to Social Exclusion: Policy, Poverty and Parenting*. Bristol: Policy Press.

Werner, E. E. (1993) 'Risk, Resilience, and Recovery: Perspectives from the Kauai Longitudinal Study', *Development and Psychopathology*, 5, pp. 503–515.

Whitaker, R. (2010) *Anatomy of an Epidemic: Magic Bullets, Psychiatric Drugs, and the Astonishing Rise of Mental Illness in America*. New York: Crown Publishers.

White, P., Rickards, H. and Zeman, A. (2012) 'Time to End the Distinction between Mental and Neurological Illnesses', *British Medical Journal*, 344(e3), p. 4540.

Whittington, C. J., Kendall, T., Fonagy, P., Cottrell, D., Cotgrove, A. and Boddington, E. (2004) 'Selective Serotonin Reuptake Inhibitors in Childhood Depression: Systematic Review of Published Versus Unpublished Data', *The Lancet*, 363(9418), pp. 1341–1345.

WHO (1993) *The ICD-10 Classification of Mental and Behavioural Disorders: Diagnostic Criteria for Research*. Geneva: World Health Organization.

WHO (2001) *Mental Health: New Understanding, New Hope*. Geneva: World Health Organization.

WHO (2003) *Investing in Mental Health*. Geneva: World Health Organization.

WHO (2008a) *The Global Burden of Disease: 2004 Update*. Geneva: World Health Organization.

WHO (2008b) *mhGAP: Mental Health Gap Action Programme: Scaling up Care for Mental, Neurological and Substance Use Disorders*. Geneva: World Health Organization.

WHO (2013) *Mental Health Action Plan 2013–2020. Sixty-Sixth World Health Assembly. Resolution WHA66/8*. Geneva: World Health Organization.

WHO (2014) *Social Determinants of Mental Health*. World Health Organization.

WHO (2017) *mhGAP Training Manuals for the mhGAP Intervention Guide for Mental, Neurological and Substance Use Disorders in Non-Specialized Health Settings-Version 2.0 (for Field Testing)*. Geneva: World Health Organization.

Wilby, K. J., Herrmann, N. and Mamdani, M. M. (2013) 'Cross-National Comparison of Antidepressant Utilization in North America and Europe', *Journal of Clinical Psychopharmacology*, 33(4), pp. 585–587.

Wilkinson, R. G. (1996) *Unhealthy Societies: From Inequality to Well-Being*. London: Routledge.

Wilson, E. A. (2004) 'The Brain in the Gut', in Wilson, E. A. (ed.), *Psychosomatic*. Durham, NC: Duke University Press, pp. 31–48.

Wittchen, H.-U. and Jacobi, F. (2005) 'Size and Burden of Mental Disorders in Europe: A Critical Review and Appraisal of 27 Studies', *European Neuropsychopharmacology*, 15(4), pp. 357–376.

Wittchen, H.-U., Jacobi, F., Rehm, J., Gustavsson, A., Svensson, M., Jönsson, B., Olesen, J., . . . and Steinhausen, H. C. (2011) 'The Size and Burden of Mental Disorders and Other Disorders of the Brain in Europe 2010', *European Neuropsychopharmacology*, 21(9), pp. 655–679.

Wittchen, H.-U., Knauper, B. and Kessler, R. C. (1994) 'Lifetime Risk of Depression', *The British Journal of Psychiatry*, 165, pp. 16–22.

Wittkampf, L. C., Smeets, H. M., Knol, M. J., Geerlings, M. I., Braam, A. W. and De Wit, N. J. (2010) 'Differences in Psychotropic Drug Prescriptions among Ethnic Groups in the Netherlands', *Social Psychiatry and Psychiatric Epidemiology*, 45(8), pp. 819–826.

Wolfe, C. T. and Wong, A. (2014) 'The Return of Vitalism: Canguilhem,

Bergson and the Project of Biophilosophy', in Beistegui, M., Bianco, G. and Gracieuse, M. (eds.), *The Care of Life: Transdisciplinary Perspectives in Bioethics and Biopolitics*. New York: Rowman and Littlefield, pp. 63–75.

Wolff, N. (2001) 'Randomised Trials of Socially Complex Interventions: Promise or Peril?', *Journal of Health Services Research & Policy*, 6(2), pp. 123–126.

Woodhead, M. (2016) '80% of China's Clinical Trial Data Are Fraudulent, Investigation Finds', *British Medical Journal*, 355, p. i5396.

World Bank (1993) *Investing in Health*. New York: Oxford University Press.

Wright, N. and Stickley, T. (2013) 'Concepts of Social Inclusion, Exclusion and Mental Health: A Review of the International Literature', *Journal of Psychiatric and Mental Health Nursing*, 20(1), pp. 71–81.

Young, M. D. and Willmott, P. (1957) *Family and Kinship in East London*. London: Routledge & Kegan Paul.

Index